OAKWOOD LIBRARY OF RAILWAY HISTORY OL125

The Freshwater, Yarmouth & Newport Railway

by
R.J. Maycock and R. Silsbury

THE OAKWOOD PRESS

© Oakwood Press, R.J. Maycock & R. Silsbury 2003
Reprinted 2017 with addendum of new information.

British Library Cataloguing in Publication Data
A Record for this book is available from the British Library
ISBN 0 85361 226 1

Typeset by Oakwood Graphics.
Repro by Ford Graphics, Ringwood, Hants.
Printed by
Blissetts, Unit 1 Shield Drive, West Cross Industrial Park, Brentford, TW8 9EX

All rights reserved. No part of this book may be reproduced or transmitted in any form or by any means, electronic or mechanical, including photocopying, recording or by any information storage and retrieval system, without permission from the Publisher in writing.

Published by The Oakwood Press, 54-58 Mill Square, Catrine, KA5 6RD.
E-mail: sales@stenlake.co.uk   01290 551122
Website: www.stenlake.co.uk

Contents

	Abbreviations	4
	Foreword	4
	Acknowledgements	5
	Introduction	7
Chapter One	Developments in West Wight	9
Chapter Two	The Freshwater Railway Company is Formed	21
Chapter Three	Construction and Opening	29
Chapter Four	A Descent into Bankruptcy	41
Chapter Five	The Railway in use, 1883 to 1893	48
Chapter Six	The Board of Trade step in	55
Chapter Seven	A Change of Owners, 1893 to 1905	61
Chapter Eight	1906 to 1911	75
Chapter Nine	The Break with the Central	87
Chapter Ten	An Independent Railway, 1913 to 1923	95
Chapter Eleven	The Line Described	113
Chapter Twelve	Locomotives and Rolling Stock	139
Chapter Thirteen	A Solent Tunnel	159
Chapter Fourteen	Life under the Southern Railway and its successor	164
Appendix One	Directors and Chief Officers	166
Appendix Two	Relevant Acts of Parliament	167
Appendix Three	Signal Diagrams	169
Appendix Four	Summaries of Locomotives and Rolling Stock	172
Appendix Five	Vessels plying between Lymington and Yarmouth prior to 1923	174
	Bibliography	175
	Addendum	176
	Index	180

Abbreviations

The following abbreviations have been used in this book:

BHIR	Brading Harbour Improvement & Railway
CNR	Cowes & Newport Railway
FYN	Freshwater, Yarmouth & Newport Railway
GCR	Great Central Railway
IWC	Isle of Wight Central Railway
IWNJ	Isle of Wight (Newport Junction) Railway
IWR	Isle of Wight Railway
LBSCR	London, Brighton & South Coast Railway
LSWR	London & South Western Railway
MSJ&A	Manchester South Junction & Altrincham Railway
MSWJ	Midland & South Western Jn Railway
NGStL	Newport, Godshill & St Lawrence Railway
RNR	Ryde & Newport Railway
RPC	Ryde Pier Company
SR	Southern Railway

Foreword

This is the third book in our series of histories of the railways of the Isle of Wight. Railways were late in coming to West Wight as it was not until 1880 that the Freshwater company was formed and another nine years before its railway opened to passenger traffic. By then the company's finances were in a parlous state, thoughts of extensions were given up and it was only a matter of time before a receiver was appointed. The poor state of the railway matched the company's finances and the Board of Trade had to intervene before improvements were made. Soon afterwards the promoters of the abortive Solent Tunnel scheme purchased the undertaking. Relations with the Isle of Wight Central Railway, which worked the Freshwater line, were never good and there was constant friction between the two companies. The well-publicised break took place in 1913 when the Freshwater company took over the operation of its railway albeit in the hands of a Receiver for a second time. In this form the railway survived until its purchase by the Southern Railway in 1923.

The other two books by the same authors, and published by The Oakwood Press, are *The Isle of Wight Railway* (OL109 - 1999) and *The Isle of Wight Central Railway* (OL115 - 2001).

Acknowledgements

The Minute books and other records of the Freshwater, Yarmouth & Newport Railway, Isle of Wight Central, other Island companies and of the London & South Western and London, Brighton & South Coast railways held by the Public Record Office have formed the basis of this book. They are supplemented by Parliamentary records, newspaper extracts and numerous other official and unofficial documents including an invaluable bundle of Freshwater company correspondence lodged in the archives of the Isle of Wight Steam Railway.

Our thanks for help in writing this book go to numerous individuals and organisations. We should particularly mention Tim Cooper, Roy and Mark Brinton, Paddy Jardine and Norman Thearle (archivists to the Isle of Wight Steam Railway) together with staff at the Public Record Office and House of Lords Record Office.

Wherever possible the quotations and wording in Minute books, Bills, Acts of Parliament and press reports are exactly as written. Many of the plans and drawings are to scale but they are for illustrative purposes and should not be relied upon as accurate in all respects.

No attempt has been made to update imperial measurements or pre-decimal currency. A number of the drawings are reproduced with permission of Railtrack Plc and remain their copyright. The illustrations have been selected for their historical interest and as a result a few photographs may not be to the standard we would wish.

Dates of opening and closure of railways and tramway for passenger traffic in the Isle of Wight

Railway/tramway	*Owning company*	*Distance miles*	*Date opened*	*Date closed*
Cowes to Newport	CNR	4¼	16th June, 1862	21st February, 1966
Ryde St Johns Road to Shanklin	IWR	7¼	23rd August, 1864	
Ryde Pier Gates to Pier Head*	RPC	½	29th August, 1864	26th January, 1969
Shanklin to Ventnor	IWR	4	10th September, 1866	18th April, 1966
Ryde Pier Gates to the Castle*	RPC	¼	28th January, 1870	5th April, 1880
The Castle to St Johns Road*	RPC	½	7th August, 1871	5th April, 1880
Sandown to Shide	IWNJ	8¼	1st February, 1875	6th February, 1956
Shide to Pan Lane (Newport)	IWNJ	½	6th October, 1875	6th February, 1956
Ryde St Johns Road to Newport	RNR	7¾	20th December, 1875	21st February, 1966
Pan Lane to Newport	IWNJ	½	1st June, 1879	6th February, 1956
Ryde St Johns Road to Ryde Esplanade	LSWR & LBSCR	¾	5th April, 1880	
Ryde Esplanade to Ryde Pier Head	LSWR & LBSCR	½	12th July, 1880	
Brading to Bembridge	BHIR	2¾	27th May, 1882	21st September, 1953
Newport to Freshwater	FYN	12	20th July, 1889	21st September, 1953
Merstone to St Lawrence	NGStL	5½	20th July, 1897	15th September, 1952
St Lawrence to Ventnor Town	NGStL	1¼	1st June, 1900	15th September, 1952

* a tramway, all other lines in the Isle of Wight were railways.

Total railway mileage	
IWR	14
IWC	28
FYN	12
LSWR/LBSCR Joint	1 ¼
Total	55 ¼

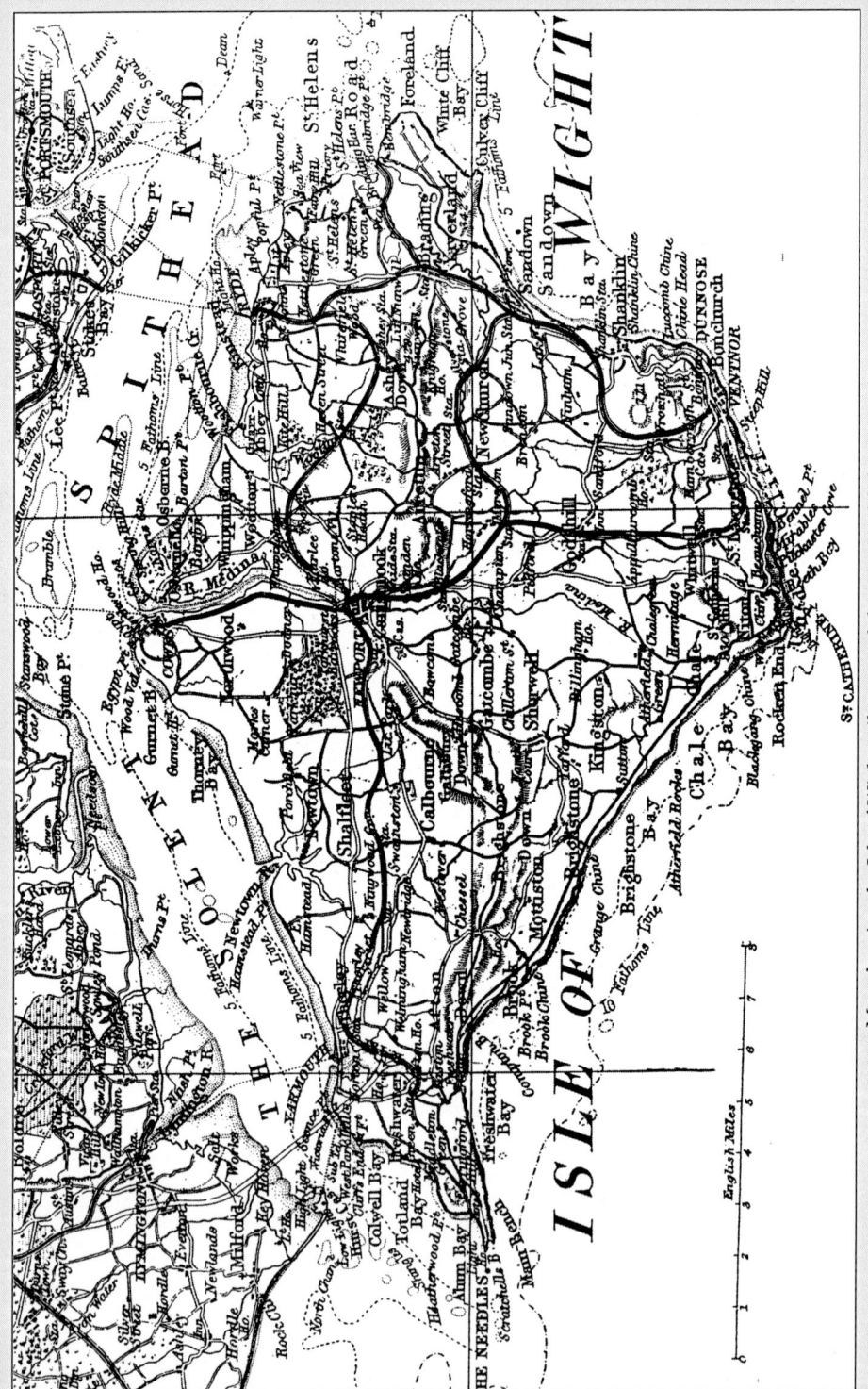

Map showing the Isle of Wight railways and the proposed Solent tunnel.

Introduction

The first railway in the Isle of Wight between Cowes and Newport gained its Act of Incorporation in 1859 but by the time it opened for traffic in 1862 the Isle of Wight (Eastern Section) Railway, later renamed the Isle of Wight Railway, was already building its line from Ryde to Ventnor. It opened to Shanklin in 1864 and to Ventnor in 1866. Also in 1864 the Ryde Pier Company (RPC) began carrying passengers along its pier on a horse tramway which was extended through the town to the railway terminus in 1871. In 1880 the London & South Western (LSWR) and London, Brighton & South Coast (LBSCR) railway companies opened a replacement railway; the mainland companies worked no trains within the Island, the Isle of Wight and Isle of Wight Central companies operating all services.

It was 1879 before the Isle of Wight (Newport Junction) Railway completed its railway from Sandown to Newport by which time the Ryde & Newport Railway had opened its line and formed a joint committee with the Cowes & Newport to work their lines. The three companies amalgamated in 1887 to form the Isle of Wight Central Railway. The Freshwater, Yarmouth & Newport Railway opened to passengers in 1889 and the Newport, Godshill & St Lawrence Railway opened throughout from Merstone on the Sandown to Newport line to its own terminus at Ventnor in 1900; these two railways were worked by the Central company. In 1913 the Freshwater company broke away and operated its own trains until all three railway companies became part of the Southern Railway (SR) in 1923; a year later the company purchased the Ryde Pier Company's pier.

The SR greatly improved stations and transferred new locomotives and rolling stock. The railways were nationalised in 1948 but decline set in and the first section of railway, that between Merstone and Ventnor, closed in 1952. A year later it was the turn of the Bembridge and Freshwater to Newport lines, followed in 1956 by that from Sandown to Newport. The lines from Shanklin to Ventnor and Ryde to Newport and Cowes closed in 1966; the Ryde pier tramway went in 1969. The remaining 8½ mile section between Ryde and Shanklin was electrified and has since been worked by former London Underground tube stock. Some steam locomotives and rolling stock survive on the Isle of Wight Steam Railway which operates a line from Wootton to Havenstreet and Smallbrook.

SOLENT STEAM-PACKET COMPANY.

SUMMER ARRANGEMENTS.

On and after Tuesday, May 1st, 1866,

THE COMPANY'S STEAM-PACKETS, "MAY FLOWER," "SOLENT," OR "RED LION,"

WEATHER PERMITTING, WILL RUN DAILY, (SUNDAYS EXCEPTED) UNTIL FURTHER NOTICE,

BETWEEN LYMINGTON AND YARMOUTH AS FOLLOWS:—

From Lymington to Yarmouth at 8·30 a.m., 11·40 a.m., 3·0 p.m., and 6·35 p.m.
From Yarmouth to Lymington at 9·15 a.m., 12·30 p.m., 4·35 p.m., and 7·15 p.m.

Between LYMINGTON, YARMOUTH, COWES, RYDE, & PORTSMOUTH, as follows:—

From Lymington to Yarmouth .... 9 15 a.m.
" Yarmouth to Cowes .... 10 0 "
" Cowes to Ryde and Portsmouth .... 11 0 "

From Portsmouth (Royal Albert Pier) to Ryde 3 30 p.m.
Calling at Victoria and Southsea Piers.
" Ryde to Cowes .... 4 10 "
" Cowes to Yarmouth .... 5 10 "
" Yarmouth to Lymington .... 6 10 "

FARES.

	Quarter-deck.	Forecastle.
Lymington to Yarmouth	1s. 6d.	1s. 0d.
Day Tickets	2s. 0d.	1s. 6d.
Lymington to Cowes	2s. 6d.	1s. 6d.
Day Tickets	3s. 6d.	2s. 6d.
Lymington to Ryde or Portsmouth	3s. 6d.	2s. 6d.
Day Tickets	5s. 0d.	4s. 0d.

	Quarter-deck.	Forecastle.
Yarmouth to Cowes	2s. 0d.	1s. 6d.
Day Tickets	3s. 0d.	2s. 0d.
Yarmouth to Ryde or Portsmouth	3s. 0d.	2s. 0d.
Day Tickets	4s. 0d.	3s. 0d.

Return Tickets from Yarmouth to Portsmouth (available from Saturday till Monday)—5s. 0d. and 4s. 0d. Return Tickets from Yarmouth to Cowes (available from Saturday till Monday)—3s. 0d. and 2s. 0d. Airing Tickets, Lymington to Yarmouth, 1s. each; persons taking these Tickets are not to land at Yarmouth. Children above 3 and under 12, half-price. The Proprietors of the Steamer contract to pay all Pier Dues at Lymington, Yarmouth, and Cowes, for Passengers and their Personal Luggage.

Commodious TOW-BOATS, for the conveyance of Carriages, Horses, and Cattle, between Lymington and Yarmouth at Low Rates.

Receiving Houses for Parcels: Wheat-Sheaf Inn, Gosport Street, Lymington. Places of Call: Mr. Grunsell's Office, Lymington; Railway Office and the George Inn, Yarmouth; Fountain Hotel, Cowes; Pier Hotel, Ryde; The Royal Albert Pier Gate, Portsea; Victoria Pier, Portsmouth; and Southsea Pier. Where Particulars may always be obtained.

William Grunsell, Coal Merchant, Manager.

An advert for the Solent Steam Packet Company 1866.

Chapter One

Developments in West Wight

The western half of the Isle of Wight shows the Garden Isle at its best. The rolling hills and glimpses of the sea give the impression of a landscape miles from any habitation - at one time the majority of the Island was like that. The Western Yar which separates Freshwater Isle from the rest of the Isle of Wight, rises in marshes close to Freshwater Bay and flows north to enter the sea at Yarmouth. Freshwater Isle was a peaceful place with unspoilt bays at Alum, Totland and Colwell. Between Yarmouth and Newport the clay lands are laid out to farmland; to the south lies a chalk ridge that runs along much of the length of the Island and beyond is the 'Back of the Wight', a stretch of farmland and scattered communities notable for never having seen a railway.

In the 18th century the only building at Freshwater Bay was a small inn providing accommodation for the few travellers that ventured there; little more than the undoubted beauty of the countryside existed to attract them. The only town of any size was Yarmouth, an ancient borough and long established landing place. Its situation at the mouth of the river backed by Thorley Brook made the town easy to defend but greatly restricted expansion. By 1851 572 people lived in Yarmouth and 1,400 in the whole of Freshwater Isle out of a total Island population of 50,324 - it was said there were more rabbits than humans.

The population worked on the land apart from residents of the coastal villages who earned a living from the sea; they had few reasons to go to the Island's capital, Newport, let alone to the mainland and given the propensity for smuggling would have been more familiar with the coasts of France and the Channel Islands than their own country! In 1790 one writer claimed that 52 gates had to be negotiated when using the road between Yarmouth and Newport. Most visitors to this part of the Isle of Wight came by sea from Lymington to Yarmouth. A steam vessel began a service on 5th April, 1830 but it initially ran only during summer months; tow boats for the carriage of vehicles and livestock were introduced in May 1836 and a second passenger vessel arrived in 1841 when the Solent Sea Company was formed. Its steamers also operated to Cowes, Ryde and Portsmouth along with other vessels that plied the south coast; excursions began to Totland Bay in April 1842 and soon afterwards to the Needles and Alum Bay. The London & South Western Railway opened from London to Brockenhurst on 1st June, 1847 and to Lymington on 12th July, 1858. At Yarmouth a breakwater to the Harbour was built between 1843 and 1847; the town quay was the principal landing place but could not be used at low tide until dredged several years later. Of the town, it was said:

> Though it skirts the shore and has the advantage of a small river flowing on its western side, it has on account of some local circumstances, failed to rise into the list of fashionable resorts. There is a packet daily to Lymington, but the want of a stagecoach from this place to the capital of the Island, very much checks its growth and its commerce.

VENTNOR, FRESHWATER, ALUM BAY, AND THE NEEDLES.

ON AND AFTER SATURDAY, MARCH 27th, 1875, the Old-Established and Well-Appointed

FOUR-HORSE COACH, "THE ROCKET"

WILL RUN EVERY DAY (Sunday Excepted) between the above places, starting from the RAILWAY STATION, Ventnor, on the arrival of the train from Ryde which reaches Ventnor at 10.15 a.m., leaving the Marine Hotel, Ventnor, at 10.30, passing SANDROCK, BLACKGANG, CHALE, SHORWELL, BRIXTON and BROOKE, and arrive at Lambert's Hotel. Freshwater, about 1.30, where a fresh conveyance will be in readiness to convey passengers to ALUM BAY, and return in time for the coach to Ventnor, which will leave Freshwater at 3.45, arriving at Ventnor for the 7.10 train for Ryde.

The trip by this Coach affords unrivalled advantages for viewing the magnificent scenery of the Undercliff, and the picturesque villages on the Southern Coast of the Island. Regularity is ensured by the fact that

THREE TEAMS OF HORSES

are employed on this journey, horses being changed at Chale & Brixton.

FARES :—

SINGLE—FRESHWATER 5s. 0d. ;   ALUM BAY 5s. 6d.
RETURN,   DITTO   8s. 6d. ;   DITTO   9s. 6d.

No difference is made between the Inside and Outside Fare ; but persons wishing to secure any particular seat can do so by booking beforehand, and paying 6d. extra. The hours given above will be strictly kept, but the proprietors cannot hold themselves for unavoidable delays.

W. BUSH AND Co., Proprietors.

An advert for the stage coach *The Rocket* from the *Isle of Wight Express*, 15th May, 1875.

The emergence of West Wight from obscurity was prompted by fears of an invasion. The naval port of Portsmouth depended on fortifications around the coastline of the Isle of Wight for its defence against sea attack. The first dated from the reign of Henry VIII but Britain's poor relations with France in the 1850s led to expenditure in the years 1852-1856 on fortifications including Fort Victoria on Sconce Point, nearby Fort Albert and Freshwater Redoubt overlooking Freshwater Bay. For friendly vessels a new lighthouse was built at the Needles in 1858. This was followed by more work for the military which saw completion of the Needles Battery in 1863 and Golden Hill Fort near Freshwater in 1867. This attracted workmen from all over the South of England, including men who had worked on railways on the mainland and some would go on to build the Island railways. They had to be housed and their other needs catered for, roads were built and when the forts were completed their garrisons had money to spend - in this way the isolation of the area came to an end.

There was a person whose presence also had a profound effect. It is not hard to see why the poet Alfred Tennyson was attracted to the charms of the Isle of Wight. Farringford, the house near Freshwater that he and his family rented in 1853, was as distant as any location - such was its remote character that the domestic staff, being used to London, were close to tears when they first arrived. Three years later Tennyson needed no encouragement to buy the property but he could not have perceived how the neighbourhood would change before his eyes. Tennyson became a national personality and his presence acted as a magnet not just to Britain's intellectuals but all and sundry. Within 10 years this shy man's privacy at Farringford had gone. When visiting the family in October 1864 Edward Lear commented that he '. . . found all that quiet part of the Island fast spoiling, and how they can stay I can't imagine'. There was already a big hotel, 300 new houses and plans for a railway. It was all too much and Tennyson had a new house built at Blackdown near Haslemere in the late 1860s '. . . whither we can escape when the cockneys are running over my lawns at Freshwater'. He continued to visit Farringford during the quieter months of the year until his death in 1892.

In 1858 the *Rocket* coach began a twice-daily service between Yarmouth and Freshwater connecting with the ferry and two years later to Newport, albeit only on market days. The road service between Yarmouth and Freshwater Isle was greatly improved after the Yar Bridge Company, formed by an Act of Parliament in 1858, completed a road toll bridge and embankments across the River Yar two years later. There were a few who liked to travel by road and during 1860, in an obvious reference to the spread of railways, it was said 'The treat of a ride on the top of a well-appointed four-horse coach, on a fine day, through beautiful country, is one peculiar to the Isle of Wight'. In 1864 the coach *Emerald* began operating from Yarmouth to Freshwater Bay and in 1866 newspapers reported that an omnibus ran three days a week all the year round between Newport, Yarmouth and Freshwater. The *Rocket* operated a summer service from the newly opened terminus of the Isle of Wight Railway at Ventnor to Brighstone, Freshwater and Yarmouth - it was still being advertised in 1875.

The first proposals for a railway in the area appeared in November 1858 when Parliamentary Agents McLachlen & Cole announced they were preparing a Prospectus for the promoters of the Isle of Wight West Coast Railway from Yarmouth to West Cowes. At Cowes a tramway from the railway terminus would have connected with Fountain Quay from where the mainland steamers operated. Other tramways at Yarmouth crossed Yar Bridge and followed the road to Freshwater, Colwell, Totland and Alum Bay. The promoters supposedly had connections with the Lymington Railway, but were more likely inspired by the LSWR which was engaged in a territorial squabble with the LBSCR that year. No Prospectus was issued and the proposal faded away before any Bill or plans reached Parliament.

Whilst the next proposal for a railway in West Wight did not reach Parliament until late 1864 it had origins at the same time as the West Coast Railway. The Isle of Wight (Eastern Section) Railway obtained an Act of Parliament in 1860 for a railway between Ryde and Ventnor - it opened throughout to Ventnor in 1866. In 1863 the company gained powers for a change of name to the Isle of Wight Railway (IWR) and for 'Central Lines' extensions from Ryde to Newport and then to Wroxall; there was also a branch to the other railway in the Island, the Cowes & Newport Railway (CNR). In 1865 more proposals appeared for the 'Western Lines' from Newport to Yarmouth and Freshwater. Although it is not clear who were behind the Western Lines (the IWR agreed to fund Parliamentary and initial costs but expected others to raise the capital), 'friends' of Thomas Webster and Thomas Willis Fleming, gentlemen who dabbled in numerous railway and ferry schemes within the Island, favoured a railway to Alum Bay where they planned to build a pier and hotel. However, one Island resident commented that prospects for the Western Lines were hopeless, there being 'hardly a house' (of substance) in that part of the Island. The railways did not on their own present the expectation of any great level of profits, but it was expected that development would follow their opening just as was occurring at Sandown, Shanklin and Ventnor. Most of the population was too poor to afford the fares but the railways might bring visitors who could.

The Western Lines (railway No. 1) branched from the Central Lines railway to Wroxall just south of Newport with a junction facing Ryde. It then followed a generally straight route towards Yarmouth; passing south of the town, railway No. 2 followed the east bank of the river before heading due south to a terminus at Freshwater Bay. By the time Parliament considered the Bill the railway had been cut back to end near Hooke Hill, School Green; this was in response to objections from Alfred Tennyson and other expressions of public opinion.

In the same Parliamentary session there appeared a scheme in direct opposition to the IWR extensions. The Brading, Newport and Yarmouth Railway proposed to raise £170,000 in shares and loans of £56,000 for a railway that branched from the IWR just south of Brading before meandering across the Island to the southern edge of Newport, where there would have been a station at the junction of Elm Grove and South Mall Terrace (now St Johns Road). One line then looped around Newport to connect with the CNR whilst a second headed for Yarmouth. Immediately to the east of Yarmouth the railway tunnelled under the turnpike road to reach the shore and a 300 yard pier north of Bank Street roughly where the present pier is located; the facility for the direct transfer of passengers between railway and ferry was seen as a distinct advantage over the facilities then existing at Ryde and Cowes. Sir Francis Fox, the Engineer and promoter, contended that it could be built more cheaply than the IWR lines and the maximum gradient at 1 in 100 would make it easier to operate.

A committee of the House of Lords heard evidence for and against the Bills on 8th and 9th May, 1865. The Brading Bill was opposed by a number of wealthy Yarmouth residents who objected to the manner in which the railway would have obstructed views of the Solent from their properties and destroyed the only public walk in the town. Supporters for the IWR contended that the line should be built by an established company but this prompted some banter about the IWR's financial position and its ability to finance the extensions, interest rates having recently risen to 10 per cent. Even so, the Brading Bill was thrown out in favour of the Western Lines Bill - it became law on 5th July, 1865.

The Central and Western lines were seen as the best chance for a comprehensive network of railways within the Island. That opportunity was lost when the IWR slipped into financial difficulties and during 1868 the extensions were abandoned. This opened the field to other promoters who had to go through the Parliamentary process all over again.

It was clearly in the minds of some speculators that the arrangements at Yarmouth were unsatisfactory and a proper pier was needed at which passengers and goods could be landed at all states of the tide and connected to the Island railways. The opposition to railways in the town prompted consideration of an unpromising spot at Bouldnor, to the east of Yarmouth. The site was a jumble of unstable clays with a shifting coastline quite unsuited to large scale development; certain individuals thought otherwise. On 21st November, 1868 the *Isle of Wight Herald* reported that surveyors were taking levels with a view to getting a Bill into Parliament in the 1869 session. When the Parliamentary notices appeared the following month they announced an intention to:

> . . . construct a pier commencing in the parish of Shalfleet at a point above high water mark, northwards of, and nearly opposite the brickworks on the Bouldnor Estate, for about 400 yards into the sea; and a railway commencing at the southern end of the said pier, and passing through Yarmouth, Thorley and Freshwater to a terminus near the Needles Hotel.

The Bouldnor, Yarmouth & Freshwater Railway & Pier Company proposed to raise £50,000 in £10 shares and £16,600 in loans for a five mile railway between Bouldnor and Alum Bay. It would have commenced at a pier at Bouldnor and curved around the back of the town of Yarmouth before following the east bank of the river. About half a mile from Freshwater it crossed to the opposite bank, passed through Freshwater village and turned to the west to terminate at Alum Bay. The promoters, who were not local men, were named as Edward K. Bulman, Christopher Nugent Nixon and John William Williamson. They had formed the Bouldnor Land Company Ltd and purchased 220 acres of land forming the Bouldnor estate. Their plans for development anticipated an esplanade, church, ornamental gardens and

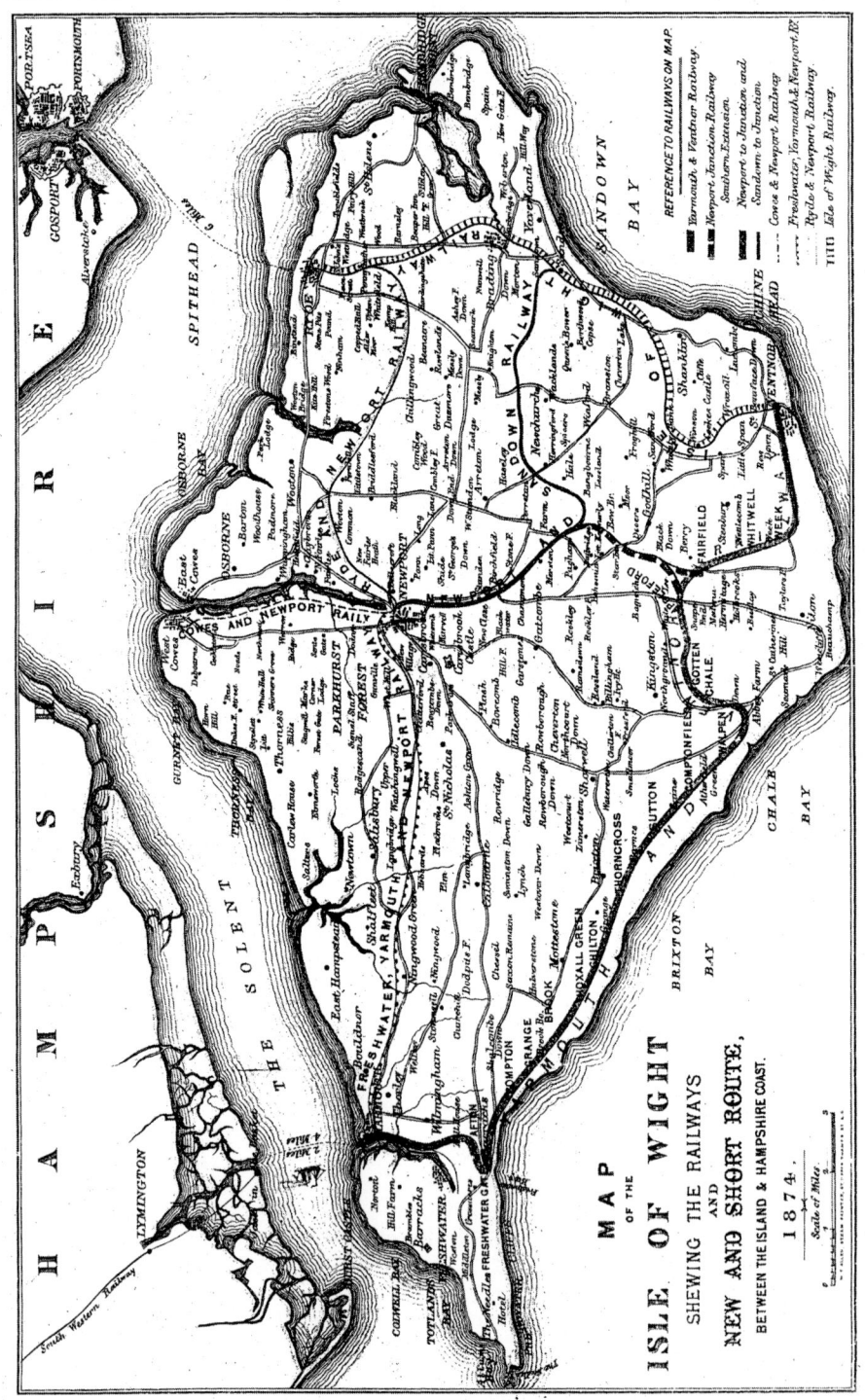

Map showing the 1873 Freshwater and Yarmouth & Ventnor railways.

residential roads serving 52 building plots. There was already a brickworks on the site linked by a tramway to a short pier - possibly it supplied bricks for use in the forts in the vicinity. Remains of the tramway and stone jetty survived for many years afterwards. The promoters envisaged further development at Alum Bay where a large hotel had been built in 1860 on the cliffs overlooking the bay.

Apart from the pier and a bridge across the river, the railway would have presented the Engineer, Mr Tolmie, with no great engineering problems. Lord Heytesbury, the principal landowner, saw things differently. His solicitors complained that four important roads would be crossed on the level and it was a grossly under-capitalised speculative venture that was of no use to the public.

Although the Bill had its second reading before the House of Lords during March 1869 Lord Heytesbury petitioned Parliament in opposition and the promoters made it known in April that they were not proceeding with the Bill.

Activities at Alum Bay did not end with the withdrawal of the railway Bill. On 5th May, 1869 construction began of a pier by a contractor J. White of Cowes and the Board of Trade authorised the Alum Bay Pier Company to charge tolls for its use. A new company of the same name was formed in 1887 to demolish the wooden structure and build an iron replacement. The nearby Royal Needles Hotel passed through a number of owners but is best remembered as the base from which Guglielmo Marconi broadcast the first long-distance wireless transmission on 23rd January, 1901 - there is a memorial to this event on the cliff top.

At Bouldnor it was 1873 before Christopher Nixon obtained powers for the construction of a pier about '. . . 1,000 ft or thereabouts along the foreshore eastward of the remains of the Old Pier at Bouldnor' and a tramway along its length. Just one year later the Mayor and Chief Burgesses of the borough of Yarmouth took powers for a 700 ft-long pier closer to the town; work began in June 1875 and it opened the next year. Time limits for the completion of the Bouldnor pier were renewed in 1880 for five years, possibly in the hope that it would tempt railway promoters, but to no avail.

The Bouldnor and Alum Bay speculators were not alone. In 1871 a Bill was placed before Parliament for the creation of the Yarmouth & Ventnor Railway, Tramway & Pier Company with a share capital of £135,000 in £10 shares and loans of £45,000. The 19 mile railway would have begun at a pier on the shore near the Turnpike gate, about halfway between Yarmouth and Little Bouldnor, before looping around the town to a station from where a tramway ran north of Yarmouth Mill and along the town quay. Leaving Yarmouth, the railway followed the east bank of the river and then south to Freshwater Bay. At that point the road had to be diverted as the line took a sharp left curve to join the old Military Road which it followed doggedly with gradients of 1 in 40 over the chalk ridge overlooking Freshwater Bay. The railway accompanied the road past Brook, over Chilton Chine on a 30 ft bridge and Grange Chine on a 297 ft viaduct. Beyond Atherfield the railway curved sharply inland before beginning a gentler curve to the right past Chale Green and Southford Mill to Whitwell and along the high road to Ventnor where there would have been a fall at 1 in 60 through a tunnel or covered way to an end-on junction with the IWR at its Ventnor station. The cost was estimated at £133,579 15s. 9d. for the railway, tramway and pier or jetty.

JACKMAN'S
FAVORITE ISLE OF WIGHT
EXCURSIONS.

AT AND AFTER EASTER
TWO CHARS-A-BANC,
will run on these delightful Summer Excursions as follows.

CARISBROOKE ROUTE.
From VENTNOR to NITON, BLACKGANG, CARISBROOKE, NEWPORT, ARRETON, and WROXALL, EVERY DAY (Sunday Excepted).

Leaving the Ventnor Railway Station on the arrival of the 10.20 train, calling at the Freemasons' Tavern, the Prince of Wales Hotel, the Globe Inn, the Commercial, the Crab and Lobster, the Marine, and the Royal Hotels, leaving Jackman's Excursion Booking Office at 10.45; arriving at Blackgang at 12.0, allowing time to visit the Chine, arriving at Carisbrooke at the Red Lion Hotel, at 2.30, allowing two hours to visit the Castle and the Roman Villa.

Leaving Carisbrooke for Ventnor, at 4.30, calling at the Bugle Hotel and the Wheatsheaf Inn, Newport; returning through Arreton, allowing time to see the Church and the Dairyman's Daughter's Grave, arriving at Wroxall and Ventnor in time for the 6.10 train to Ryde. FARE 5s. for the whole Route.

THE ALUM BAY ROUTE.
From VENTNOR to FRESHWATER, ALUM BAY, and THE NEEDLES, Every MONDAY, WEDNESDAY, and FRIDAY.

Leaving the Ventnor Railway Station on the arrival of the 8.46 train, calling at the same Hotels in Ventnor, leaving Jackman's Excursion Booking Office at 9.30, giving three hours to inspect The Needles, and other attractions in this far-famed locality; Returning from Alum Bay at 3.30, and Freshwater at 4.0, arriving in Ventnor in time for 7.10 train to Ryde. FARE 9s. the whole Route.

FOR HIRE,
BY THE DAY, HOUR, MILE, OR JOB,
THE WELL-SELECTED
SADDLE HACKS AND HUNTERS.
ALSO
CARRIAGES OF EVERY DESCRIPTION.

FOUR-IN-HAND AND TANDEM TEAM WITH A PERFECT LEADER.
A RIDE AND DRIVE WITH A PAIR OR SINGLE.
LESSONS GIVEN IN RIDING AND DRIVING FREE OF CHARGE.

GEORGE JACKMAN, Proprietor.
RIDING-MASTER, 6, MILL STREET, VENTNOR.

An advert for 'chars-a-banc' excursions from the *Isle of Wight Express*, 15th May, 1875.

Opposition was surprisingly muted, perhaps it was apathy. Lord Heytesbury had been placated by a lengthy agreement that promised several crossings and bridges to connect parcels of his land. The only complaint was in a letter from Mr Estcourt on behalf of the Island Road Commissioners stating that they considered the Military Road to be a public as opposed to a private road. However, they reckoned without the opinions of the War Office which supported the construction of the railway along the Military Road so that it could transport troops quickly to key points - the threat of invasion by the French was still very real. At a hearing before a House of Lords Select Committee on 23rd March, 1871 it was reported that opposition had been withdrawn, the Bill was allowed to proceed and it became law. Twelve months later, a second Act authorised a diversion at Yarmouth to Yar bridge, with a tramway along the quay to a new pier - the railway around the town and pier on its eastern side were abandoned. An additional £45,000 in capital was authorised. The Directors were named in the original Act as George Wythes, Ulysses De Lunge and John Atkinson Longridge; none had connections with existing railways in the Island. Powers were obtained by the Isle of Wight (Newport Junction) Railway (IWNJ) during 1872 for a branch connecting its line at Merstone with the Yarmouth & Ventnor Railway near Southford Mill.

Meanwhile promoters of another proposed railway in West Wight had been active. In 1872 the Freshwater, Bouldnor & Newport Railway proposed a Bill to raise £90,000 in shares and borrow £30,000 for a 11 mile 27¼ chain railway from Freshwater to Newport. Between Freshwater and Yarmouth the route would have followed that of the Yarmouth & Ventnor Railway; it then curved around the back of Yarmouth and then east towards Newport. The railway passed well to the north of Carisbrooke and Hunnyhill to join the CNR near Hurstake, north of Newport with a junction facing Cowes. The Bill was withdrawn in August 1872 but a fresh attempt was made in the next session under the title Freshwater, Yarmouth & Newport Railway. Christopher Nugent Nixon, John William Williamson, Moritz Maurice and Stanislas Joseph Paris were the promoters (two had been involved in the 1869 attempt) and the Engineer was William Hunt; the Bill became law in July 1873.

The Freshwater company's Act authorised a 1 mile 77 chain railway (No. 1) from the foot of Hooke Hill, Freshwater along the east bank of the River Yar to Yarmouth where it ended at the proposed terminus of the Yarmouth and Ventnor Railway. Railway No. 2 also began with a junction facing Yarmouth (unlike the 1872 Bill, there was no direct line between Freshwater and Newport), looped around the town and then headed east criss-crossing the Newport turnpike. Curving to the north of Hunnyhill, it made a south-facing junction with the CNR a few hundred yards from its Newport terminus; its length was 9 miles 39 chains and the maximum gradient was 1 in 66. The share capital was less than that for the IWR Western Lines and reflected the cheaper land and construction costs at the Newport end. The Freshwater company was authorised to raise £130,000 in £10 shares and borrow £43,000 for railways estimated to cost a total of £119,288 9s. 1d. The Yarmouth & Ventnor Railway was given until 24th June, 1874 to buy the land from Freshwater to Yarmouth Mill and until 30th June, 1876 to complete the railway from Yarmouth to

ISSUE OF £180,000 OF SIX PER CENT. SHARES GUARANTEED FOR TEN YEARS BY INVESTMENT IN CONSOLS. IN

The Yarmouth and Ventnor Railway, Tramway, and Pier Company.

(Incorporated by Acts of Parliament, 34 and 35 Vic. cap. 56—35 and 36 Vic. cap. 28.)

Capital £180,000 in 18,000 shares of £10 each. Payable £1 on application and £2 on allotment. The balance by calls, not exceeding £2 each, at intervals of not less than three months.

PRICE OF ISSUE, PAR.

Interest at the rate of 6 per cent. per annum, payable half-yearly, guaranteed for ten years, the due and punctual payment of which will be secured by the deposit in the hands of Trustees, to be appointed by the Company, of £70,000 in consols, affording to the Shareholders an ample guarantee of satisfactory interest, not only during construction, but extending over a period sufficient to secure the full development of the traffic.

Allotment will be made strictly in the order of priority of application.

The Directors are now prepared to receive subscriptions for the 18,000 shares of £10 each, capital authorised to be created by acts of Parliament.

The line is nineteen miles in length, and traverses the most picturesque and attractive portions of the Isle of Wight, which, though well known and frequented, are at this moment entirely without any railway accommodation.

The prospects of paying traffic are most encouraging and are much enhanced by the fact that the Newport Junction railway will, within the present year, be completed and opened, and the southern extension of the Newport Junction Railway, which forms a junction with this Company's line, and connects it with the Cowes and Newport and Newport Junction systems, will shortly be constructed, and thus a direct line of communication will be established through the very heart of the island, from Cowes in the north to Ventnor in the south.

This conjunction of lines will constitute the main artery of traffic in the Island, and will be fed from the lines from Cowes to Newport (already completed and working), from Newport to the southern extension, and from Sandown to the southern extension, both now approaching completion, also by the Ryde and Newport Railway expected to be completed this year, and by the authorised line from Freshwater and Yarmouth to Newport.

The traffic will also be greatly contributed to by the Isle of Wight Railway, which has been completed and working for ten years, so that, as may be seen by the plan accompanying this Prospectus, the traffic of the Yarmouth and Ventnor Railway will be fed by all the Railways of the Island; and the Directors have every confidence in inviting subscriptions to this undertaking.

It will be appropriate to state that the Isle of Wight Railway, eleven and a half miles in length, carried in the year 1873 450,529 passengers, and the gross earnings amounted to £24,842, giving a return of over £2,000 per mile, and it is fair to assume that the bulk of this traffic will pass over the line for which this capital is required. Taking, then, the traffic under all these conditions to amount to not more than £50,000 for the first year, and the working of the line at 60 per cent. of the earnings, the result would give an available net revenue for the capital invested of £12,000.

A Contract has been entered into for the construction forthwith of the Yarmouth and Ventnor Railway. the shares of which are now offered for subscription, and the Contractors have agreed to deposit in the hands of Trustees to be appointed by the Company, £70,000 in Consols, to secure to the Shareholders the guaranteed interest for 10 years.

The Directors have considered it advisable to enter into an agreement with the Contractors for the construction, under which, during the period of their guarantee, they will work the railway when completed on satisfactory terms, affording thereby an identity of interest between the guarantee and the prospects of the traffic.

The interest will be payable half-yearly, on the 30th of June and 31st December in each year, and the first payment will be made on the 31st December, 1874.

Applications for shares may be made to the Bankers, Brokers, and Solicitors of the Company, or the Directors, at either of the offices of the Company, on the form annexed, accompanied by a deposit of £1 per share.

The Acts of Parliament, and the plans and sections of the line, &c., may be seen at the offices of Messrs. Saunders, Hawksford, and Bennett, 36, Carey-street, Lincoln's Inn, and at the offices of the Company.

DIRECTORS.

WILLIAM HAMILTON, Esq., 8, James-street, Westbourne-terrace, W., Chairman.
C. Crawford, Esq., 1, Wilton-place, Belgrave-square.
J. B. Cumming, Esq., 32, Great St. Helens, E.C.
The Hon. Fredk. Walpole, M.P., 4, Dean-street, Park-lane, and Rainthorpe Hall, Norfolk.
Lt.-Col. C. H. T. B. De Ruvignes, 17, Whitehall-place, S.W.

Bankers.—London and County Bank, 21, Lombard-street, and branches.

Consulting Engineer.
W. H. Barlow, Esq., 2, Old Palace-yard, Westminster.

Engineer.
C. M. Holland, Esq., 19, Great George-st., Westminster.

Brokers.—Messrs. Holderness, Nott, and Co., 1, St. Michael's-house, St. Michael's-alley, Cornhill.

Agent in Southampton.
John J. Burnett, Esq., 2, High-street, Southampton.

Solicitors—Messrs. Saunders, Hawksford, and Bennett, 36, Carey-street, Lincoln's-Inn; Messrs. Ashurst, Morris, and Co., 6, Old Jewry, E.C., and 22, Abingdon-street, Westminster.

Auditors.
Messrs. C. F. Kemp, Ford, and Co., 8, Walbrook, E.C.
Secretary.—T. Abercromby Hedley, Esq., C.E.
Offices.—19, Great George-street, Westminster, and 3, Abchurch-lane, Lombard-street, E.O.

A Prospectus for the Yarmouth & Ventnor Railway.

Freshwater Gate (the dates laid down in the Yarmouth company's Act); if that happened the Freshwater company agreed not to proceed with its railway No. 1.

In May 1874 the Yarmouth & Ventnor company issued a Prospectus inviting subscriptions for £180,000 in £10 shares paying a guaranteed 6 per cent per annum for 10 years. The payments were guaranteed by the deposit of £70,000 in securities by unnamed contractors with whom the company was said to have reached an agreement. The Prospectus was accompanied by the usual optimistic forecasts; much was made of the existing traffic on the IWR, how the IWNJ branch would create a Cowes to Ventnor link and earning in its first year '. . . not more than £50,000'. Nothing was said about the spectacular scenery traversed by the railway nor its failure to serve any centres of population *en route*; in fact it seems to have avoided even the smallest of hamlets! The Board of Directors had completely changed and were named as William Hamilton, C. Crawford, J.B. Cumming, Hon. Frederick Walpole MP, and Lt Col C.H.T.B. De Ruvignes. William H. Barlow remained the Engineer (Mr Barlow is better known for designing the second Tay railway bridge). The *Isle of Wight Times* for 21st May, 1874 claimed that plans for the pier at Yarmouth had been completed and it was hoped that construction would begin shortly. Despite this optimism, the company failed to raise the necessary capital, the five year time limits for completion expired and nothing more was heard of the Yarmouth & Ventnor Railway.

The failure of the Yarmouth & Ventnor Railway was matched in equal measure by the Freshwater company. In April 1876 the *Isle of Wight Times* reported that the Freshwater company had itself been reformed with Vice-Admiral Ommaney as Chairman. In May it was said that a contract had been let for construction and the line was expected to be completed in 15 months - there were also thoughts of an extension from Freshwater to Alum Bay.

At this point control of the Freshwater company seems to have changed again. In 1875, the Ryde & Newport Railway (RNR) opened its railway; income proved less than expected and in November 1876 the RNR Board discussed the construction of a branch from Newport to Carisbrooke. A few months later plans were deposited with Parliament for a 2 mile 30½ chain deviation of the Freshwater company's railway to take it closer to Carisbrooke. The Engineers were named as Henry Martin, Engineer of the CNR and Joseph Bourne, Manager and Engineer of the IWR, IWNJ, RPC and a Director of the CNR. Mr Bourne tried to canvass the support of the LSWR and LBSCR but without success. There is no doubt that they were acting on behalf of George Young, the RNR Chairman, as in May 1878 surveys by Messrs Stratton and Perross were paid by the RNR on his behalf. Despite this activity, when a Bill appeared before Parliament in the 1877 session it sought to abandon the railway. In May 1877 the LSWR Board received a letter from Messrs Ramwest (a firm of solicitors) stating that '. . . the promoter is prepared to withdraw on terms to be agreed with this Company' - the LSWR Board refused to become involved and the Bill to abandon the railway became law.

In 1877 there was a Bill proposing the formation of the Newport, Chale, Freshwater and Yarmouth Railway. The promoters hoped to raise £165,000 for an 18 mile three foot gauge railway from the station at Newport to Blackwater (alongside the IWNJ), and then to Chale where it followed the Military Road to Freshwater with a final section to a terminus near Yar bridge at Yarmouth. The Bill passed through the House of Lords but was withdrawn apparently because of the abandonment of the Freshwater company's railway. The promoters then announced proposals for a 28 mile Ventnor, Yarmouth, Freshwater and Newport Railway. It resurrected the Freshwater company's railway from Newport to Yarmouth but added a completely new line to Ventnor that began with a junction at Ningwood, passed through a gap in the downs at Chessell, ran inland of Hulverstone, Mottistone and Brighstone before describing some wild loops near Little Atherfield and Chale to reach Whitwell and Ventnor to make an end-on junction with the IWR. The scheme was abandoned before it reached Parliament.

At Newport, proposals for tramways within and outside the borough included in 1878 from the railway station to The Mall (now Carisbrooke Road). In 1888 a 3 ft gauge electric tramway to Carisbrooke was proposed. Assurances were made that the rails would not protrude above the surface of the roads and tramcars be no more than 5 ft 6 in. wide. The promoters were James W. Haynes and Henry D. Poole of 81 Gracechurch St, London. Members of Newport Corporation voted against it at a meeting on 7th August, 1888 but, following a second meeting on 30th August when the scheme received the support of local residents, they reversed their decision. Much encouraged, the promoters (who were by then quoted as J.W. & J.E. Haynes) proposed a second tramway from St James's Square to the gates of Parkhurst Prison and applied to the Board of Trade for a provisional Tramway Order authorising them to construct the two tramways. They would have been 2 miles 24 chains in length with an additional 11 chains of double line at crossing points, worked by horse, electric or any mechanical power; fares were not to exceed 1d. a mile with a minimum charge of 2d. The Board of Trade refused permission for the use of electricity on the Carisbrooke tramway whilst the local authority insisted on the use of accumulators in the tramcars as a means of propulsion, a system that would have been impractical up Hunnyhill. Although a Tramway Order was granted in respect of the Newport & Parkhurst tramway, the council delayed a start by claiming that a sewage scheme through Lower St James Street and Hunnyhill had to be carried out beforehand. Repeated extensions of time were obtained until 1892 when the sewage scheme was abandoned. Although there was again talk of a tramway to Carisbrooke, the local authority voiced its opposition to the idea and the time limits lapsed.

In December 1889 the same promoters proposed a narrow gauge railway from Newport to Chale with a branch to Shorwell and Brighstone. In June 1890 the *Isle of Wight County Press* wrote: 'There can be no doubt the line will open up districts which are not likely to be reached by an ordinary railway, and many local people are firmly convinced of the merits of the scheme'. Despite this accolade nothing more was heard of the idea. Attempts to build a railway from Shanklin to Chale and along the back of the Island to Freshwater were mentioned in our book on the Isle of Wight Central Railway.

Chapter Two

The Freshwater Railway Company is Formed

A fresh attempt to construct a railway from Freshwater and Yarmouth to Newport followed the formation of the Totland Bay Pier & Hotel Company in 1878. The first three Directors were Edwin Fox, William Charles Harvey, a barrister, and Alfred Bayliffe, a solicitor, all with London addresses. Other subscribers included Samuel H. Yockney, an engineer and John Norton, an architect. They applied to the Board of Trade for permission to build a pier 550 ft in length at Totland below 'the Coastguard Watch House' about 624 ft north-east of an existing wooden pier and to charge tolls for its use; a proposed tramway was also mentioned. On 18th March, 1880 the *Isle of Wight Times* optimistically wrote:

> The new pier which is under construction at Totland Bay is fast approaching completion, and the tenth span has now been finished. The old wooden one is in a ruinous condition. When opened, the new one will form a capital promenade, and with the projected railway in full swing, Totland may look forward to a prosperous future.

Totland did indeed have a future. A hotel built on the cliff tops overlooking the bay proved so popular with the wealthy that it was significantly enlarged a few years later. A service by LSWR steamers from Lymington began using the 450 ft-long iron pier in summer months and together the pier and hotel prospered.

In December 1879 *Herapath's Railway Journal* reported the holding of a public meeting at Freshwater Bay concerning proposals for a Freshwater, Yarmouth and Newport Railway. As a first step in raising capital a subscription list was opened so that potential investors could pay a deposit to secure shares when they became available. The meeting followed the presentation of a Bill in Parliament to create a company and construct a 13 mile 20 chains railway from a proposed western terminus from Freshwater Gate* adjacent to the road leading to Calbourne at Black Bridge. The railway headed in a north-westerly direction north of School Green before looping in a wide semi-circle around Freshwater Isle before crossing the Western Yar south of the toll bridge on a bridge with one 30 ft arch just 4 ft above high water mark. The railway passed between the town and Yarmouth Mill, curved around the southern edge of Yarmouth until reaching the Newport turnpike near Bouldnor where it turned eastwards across open country in the general direction of Newport. Approaching Carisbrooke the railway looped close to the castle before sweeping to the north of Hunnyhill and through a tunnel to join the CNR at a junction facing Newport. The maximum gradient was said to be 1 in 50. The estimated £100,000 cost included £12,000 for the purchase of land, £3,000 for the river bridge and £5,610 for the tunnel. The Bill was not opposed and became law on 26th August, 1880.

The Act authorised the creation of the Freshwater, Yarmouth & Newport Railway (FYN) and the raising of £100,000 by the issue of £10 shares and

---

* The small creek Freshwater Gate rises close to the source of the Western Yar and runs south to Freshwater Bay.

borrowings of £33,300. It contained the usual rules governing the management of the company including the provision of Directors that could be between three and six, a quorum at meetings would be three, or two if only three Directors were appointed; shareholders had to hold a minimum of 50 shares in order to qualify for a seat on the Board. The first Directors were named as Lt Col John Walker, Edwin Fox, William Charles Harvey, John Norton and George Gordon Leicester Macpherson. A meeting of shareholders had to take place within two months at Yarmouth Town Hall '. . . or some other convenient place'. (The meeting did not take place until the first shares were issued several years later.) Messrs Fox and Harvey were already Directors of Totland Bay Pier & Hotel Company. Other Directors are thought to have had connections with the Yar Bridge Company or owned land on the route of the railway.

Powers to compulsorily purchase land lapsed after two years and the time limit for completion was five years. The railway was permitted to reclaim marshland abutting the River Yar subject to the consent of the owner and Board of Trade. Running powers were granted over the CNR, RNR and IWNJ in order to reach the station at Newport. Traffic arrangements were authorised also with the IWR, LSWR, LBSCR and a working agreement was proposed with the Yar Bridge Company that could require the railway company to buy its undertaking; a similar arrangement in respect of the pier at Yarmouth was removed from the Bill before it became law.

The first meeting of the Board took place on 25th October, 1880 in the offices of the solicitors Booty and Bayliffe at 1 Raymund Buildings, Grays Inn, London. Three Directors were present: Col Walker (as Chairman), William Harvey and Edwin Fox. Mr Fox was appointed General Manager at a salary of £500 per annum although it is doubtful whether the FYN ever possessed the cash to pay him. In reality he replaced Col Walker as Chairman, an appropriate position for a person who was the prime mover in the undertaking. After the appointment of solicitors to the company and Messrs Yockney & Son as Engineers, the meeting came to an end. Apart from an undated entry no further meetings were minuted until 1886.

Activity then shifted to the LSWR. The LSWR had for many years pursued a policy of non-involvement in the Isle of Wight railways, a consequence of an 1859 agreement with the LBSCR to share the railway traffic at Portsmouth. Instead the LSWR had acquired smaller companies within its sphere of influence; in 1879 the Lymington Railway Company was purchased sparking off speculation that the LSWR had eyes on the Island railways. Correspondence began before the Freshwater company's Act became law. At a meeting of the LSWR Board on 22nd January, 1880 a letter was read from Mr Fox enclosing a resolution from a public meeting at Freshwater strongly supporting the construction of a railway and improved ferry links. At the next LSWR Board meeting on 5th February, 1880 a deputation from Freshwater attended and '. . . explained their views and suggestions for improving the communication with the Western Side of the Isle of Wight via Yarmouth and Lymington'. This had little immediate result and powers to lease the FYN to the LSWR or LBSCR were struck out of the company's Bill during its passage through Parliament. Mr Fox then wrote proposing an agreement with the LSWR or jointly with the LBSCR '. . . for guarantee of interest on the capital . . . with option to purchase at any time' - the LSWR Board declined the request. In May Col Walker warned that the LSWR ought to come to an accommodation with the FYN '. . . rather than allow it to get into the hands of other parties', e.g. the Midland & South Western Junction Railway then seeking an extension to Southampton and the operation of ferries to the Isle of Wight.

The intrigue surrounding the affair then became caught up in LSWR and LBSCR negotiations with other Island companies for the lease or purchase of their railways. As a first step on 16th February, 1882 the LSWR Board sanctioned a proposal to work the FYN for 50 per cent of gross receipts. Encouraged by positive noises emanating from across the Solent the LSWR Board then decided on 9th November to include clauses in a Bill pending before Parliament for powers to buy or lease the Island railways. Unfortunately the Island companies thought they were worth rather more than the mainland companies were willing to pay, negotiations were broken off and early in 1883 the clauses were taken out of the Bill. Meanwhile there had been further letters from the FYN Directors who, sensing a willing partner, explained that they were experiencing difficulties in raising the necessary capital and asking for a guaranteed rent of 4½ per cent - the LSWR refused. The LBSCR refused to join the LSWR in a working agreement with the FYN after discussions with the other Island companies did not bear fruit, forcing the LSWR to have doubts about its commitment to the FYN. This was despite having spent considerable sums in extending the Lymington railway to a new pier, opened on 1st May, 1884, and the purchase of the Solent Sea Company on 1st July. On 1st May the LSWR Board resolved 'That the Brighton Company having declined to enter into a Joint Agreement with this Company for working the Freshwater Railway, the offer of 22nd March, 1882 is considered as no longer in force.' Having wasted much time in corresponding with the LSWR the FYN Directors were no further forward with their railway.

Nothing had been achieved in raising capital for construction of the railway. It is not hard to see why City investors were wary of investing in the FYN. The capital was significantly less than that in earlier Acts and the railway was longer:

	Proposed capital	*Length of line*
IWR Western Lines Act 1865	£180,000	11 miles
Freshwater railway Act 1873	£130,000	11 miles
FYN Act 1880	£100,000	13 miles

The compulsory purchase powers had expired so the company was forced to return to Parliament for an extension of the time limits for completion of the line. The Bill applied for an increase in capital by £72,000 in shares and loans of £24,000 for a 55 chain branch to Totland Bay. The branch would have been a remarkable feat of engineering had it been built. It left the main line just south of Brambles Farm with a junction facing Newport, looped to the west before turning south and descended through an eight chain tunnel on a gradient of 1 in 52½ to emerge just above high water mark at a terminus north of Totland Bay pier. Sir John Hawkshaw, Son & Hayter of 33 Great George Street, Westminster prepared the plans and estimated the cost at £29,977 12s. 11d. including £7,000 for the tunnel. The difficult route and high costs evidently led to second thoughts and the Totland Bay branch was abandoned. When the Bill became law in August 1883 it authorised an increase in capital of £42,000 in ordinary or preference shares and borrowings of £14,000. Time to exercise compulsory purchase powers was extended to 26th August, 1886 but the railway had to be completed by 26th August, 1888. The remainder of the Act was given over to an agreement to buy the Totland Bay Pier and Hotel Company. The FYN undertook to pay £31,500 for the pier, hotel and land or, if the sellers agreed, the pier and adjacent land could be bought for £7,500.

Between 1883 and 1885 the route of the railway was surveyed and trial borings carried out to ascertain the soil conditions. The company lacked ready cash so a contractor had to be found who could be persuaded to accept shares in payment. This meant he had to possess financial backers who would advance the necessary money to pay wages, etc. The *Isle of Wight County Press* reflected growing frustration at the lack of activity in an article published on 31st October, 1885:

> Doubtless Yarmouth ought to have a railway. That interesting and ancient town, and slumberous withal, wants waking up. It is behind the age. It has an unreformed corporation. It closes its sewer ventilators before providing an efficient substitute. It lies like a stranded craft on its sleepy shore! Yes, Yarmouth wants rousing, and there is nothing like the screech of a railway whistle to do the work. Nearly six years ago there was a public meeting at Newport, presided over by the Mayor, at which resolutions in favour of a Freshwater-Yarmouth-Newport railway were passed with wonderful unanimity. And what has come of it all? Good resolutions may serve a purpose as a pavement for a place which shall be nameless here, but is not easy to construct a railway out of them. And so here we are, and where is Yarmouth? 'As it was in the beginning.' I forebear to quote further, for I have faith in the future.

On 10th March, 1886 the FYN Board met at 17 Great George Street, Westminster when they resolved to accept an offer from William Jackson '. . . to finance and carry out the necessary works for the construction and completion of the Railway, he taking the share capital and Debentures in payment'. A contract was promptly sealed as was a working agreement with the Cowes & Newport and Ryde & Newport Railway companies.

At Mr Jackson's suggestion the Board agreed to some changes in the route of the railway ostensibly '. . . to improve gradients and meet the wishes of landowners' but actually to save money. The Board of Trade could authorise changes once certain formalities had been gone through so on 4th November, 1886 the solicitors Booty & Baycliffe wrote a letter that began the process. Instead of an expensively engineered line around Freshwater Isle, a completely new route was adopted following the east bank of the river between Yarmouth and a terminus facing Totland near Hooke Hill, Freshwater. To avoid large earthworks there were minor deviations between Yarmouth and Ningwood and near Watchingwell to follow the contours of the land but resulting in a succession of rising and falling gradients and sharp curves. Approaching Newport the original route through an expensive tunnel north of Hunnyhill was replaced by a new line to a junction that trailed into the CNR just north of Newport station but facing Cowes.

Public notice of the changed route resulted in a letter of objection from Mr Pittis. He said the railway near Newport laid down in the Act '. . . touches my Estate in a very outlying portion of it, but I wholly object to the proposed deviation which would cut up the Estate and prejudicially affect the Mansion House called Newport House in which I have resided for the last 28 years as to totally destroy its value as to residential property'; Mr Pittis indicated he would not sell willingly. The railway would also have swept through the remains of a 12th century priory at St Cross presumably because it was no longer of any great merit in the eyes of the local population. The Board of Trade authorised the changes to the route but a letter from the company's solicitors indicated that a Bill would shortly be promoted in Parliament. This was probably because of the compulsory purchase powers that an Act would contain - Mr Pittis was clearly a reason for this. The Freshwater, Yarmouth & Newport Railway (Deviations) Act became law in 1887 giving two years for the exercise of compulsory purchase powers on land affected by the new route and three years for completion of the deviations. Despite murmurings that Mr Jackson should pay for the Act, the FYN ended up paying for it.

In June 1887 the Engineer was asked to supply plans for an extension from Freshwater to Totland Bay but nothing more transpired until November 1888 when the company announced it would have to promote a further Bill in Parliament. The Bill proposed to raise £54,000 in shares and loans of £18,000 to fund the extension and reaffirmed the intention to buy the Totland Bay company. The cost of the 1 mile 28.1 chain line was estimated at £29,142 18s. 0d. including £1,300 for a lift from the pier. Powers to take the railway in the opposite direction towards Freshwater Bay had long since lapsed.

The company also proposed to obtain powers for a branch at Yarmouth. There would be a triangular junction east of the town leading to a new pier; the 41½ chain branch would have cost £22,907 7s. 9d. including £1,200 for a sea wall and £1,300 for the 200 yard pier. Evidently the cost was too high as there was a change of heart. William Lidstone, the Engineer, submitted plans for a cheaper westerly route branching from a realigned siding at Yarmouth station leading past the gas works and mill to end on the town quay. The local authority made its objections abundantly clear and the Yarmouth branches were given up before the Bill appeared in the 1889 Parliamentary session.

The company's proposals for an extension to Totland met with more opposition. On 29th December, 1888 the *Isle of Wight County Press* reprinted a letter from Alfred Lord Tennyson to *The Times*:

> The company which has just completed the railway from Newport to Freshwater now proposes to extend the line to Totland Bay. Against this proposal, allow me, through you, to make an emphatic protest. By such an extension, no end would be served which could by any degree compensate for the loss of what remains to us of quiet beauty in this, our narrow peninsula.

The poet laureate had friends in Parliament and on 23rd May, 1889, when the Bill was brought before the House of Commons for a second reading, Mr Chamberlain moved an amendment:

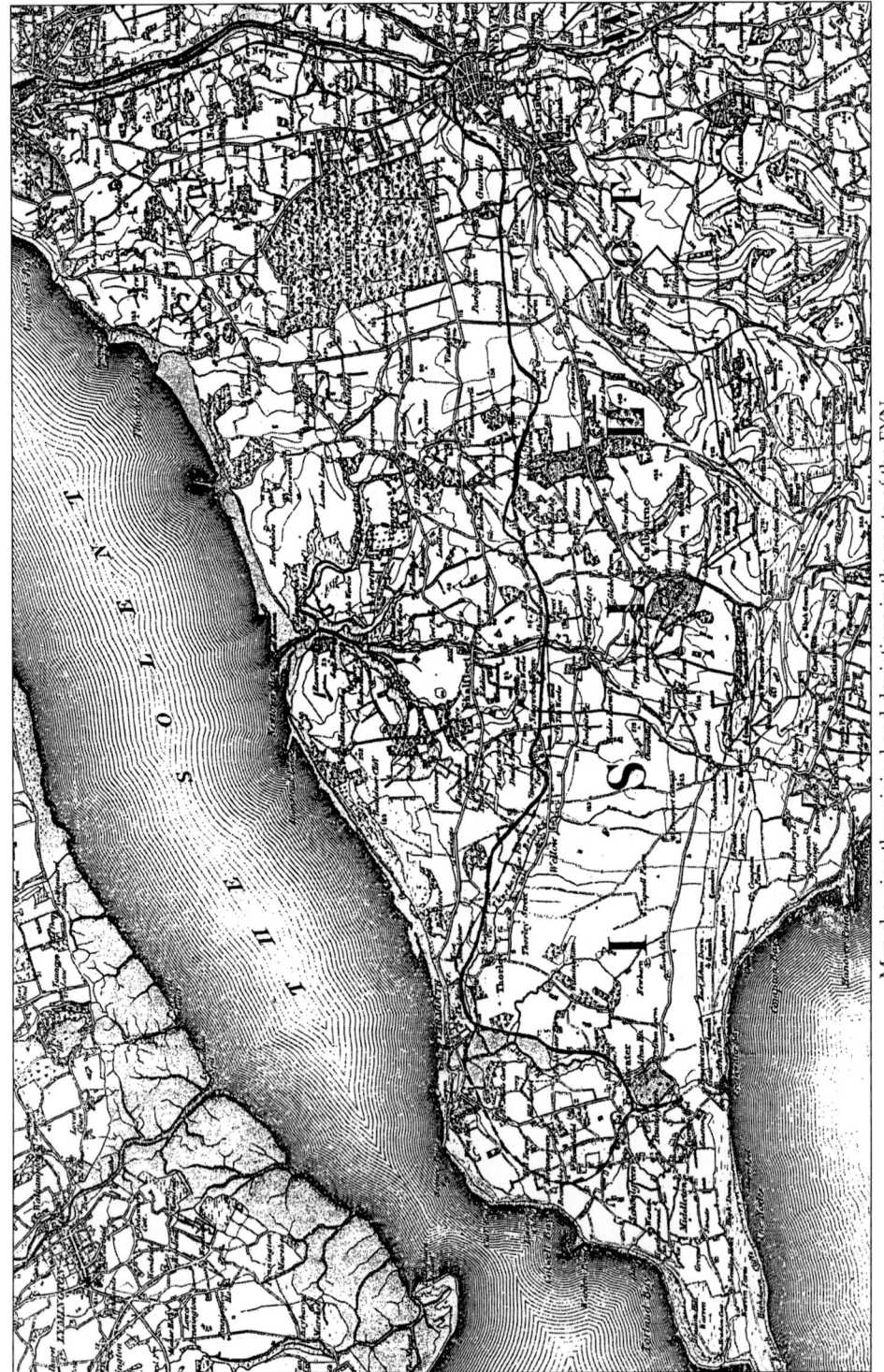

Map showing the original and deviations in the route of the FYN.

That, having regard for the character of the south-western corner of the Isle of Wight and the railway accommodation at present authorised, it is undesirable to give any further powers to a company which is only now opening for passenger traffic a line the construction of which was authorised in 1880.

Mr Chamberlain added that there was neither need nor demand for the railway which would spoil the scenery and divide the peninsula. This was not the first time that he had spoken out in opposition to an Isle of Wight railways' Bill as in 1886 he and other members of the House succeeded in throwing out a proposal for a Shanklin & Chale Railway extension from Chale to Freshwater. This time he lacked support, the amendment was lost and the Bill continued on its way to become law.

The company's 1889 Act authorised an extension leaving the railway a few yards east of the Freshwater station and headed west across three roads to reach a terminus on the cliffs overlooking Totland Bay. Four years was given for its completion and compulsory purchase powers lapsed after two years. Subject to the sanction of shareholders, the company could issue an additional £36,000 in ordinary or preference shares and £12,000 in loans. There were discussions with the Engineer and Henry Jackson about the extension but no construction work began.

The Act required purchase of the Totland Bay company on or before 1st January, 1891; if only part of the undertaking was purchased a further £7,500 of capital could be raised or if the whole was taken that figure increased to £19,000 in shares and £9,000 in loans.

From this capital £2,000 was to be spent on a pier shelter, refreshment rooms, lifts, etc. and £4,000 on an additional wing or separate building to the hotel. There would be a special class of debenture stock secured on the assets of the pier and hotel. On 12th November, 1890 the Board authorised the preparation of legal documents for the purchase of the hotel, etc. and the design of the debenture certificates. The Board then discovered that it was unlikely to gain the assent of three-quarters of preference and debenture stockholders to the issue of the necessary capital, as required by the Act, because of the level of the company's existing debt - consequently the stock in the 1889 Act was never issued.

On 28th April, 1891 the Totland Bay company wrote demanding that the railway fulfil its agreement. The FYN Board agreed to give the hotel £1,000 in debenture stock provided the Totland Bay company extended the time limits to January 1892. It was not recorded whether the Totland Bay company took up the offer but the purchase did not go through. Nothing more was recorded until 21st October, 1896 when the FYN Board decided to write off £500 loaned to the Totland Bay company. A decision to wind up the Totland Bay Pier & Hotel Company had been taken in 1895 because it '. . . cannot, by reason of its liabilities, continue its business'. The hotel and pier were sold in 1897 to a new company set up by Frank G. Aman, a gentleman we shall hear more about.

Thoughts of a branch to the town quay at Yarmouth still occupied the minds of the Directors. The Minutes for 6th August, 1891 contained a letter:

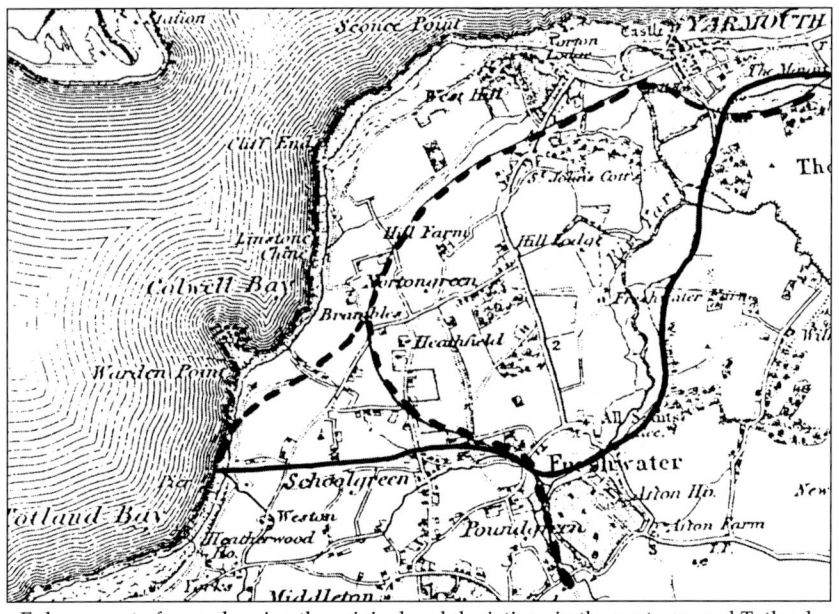

Enlargement of map showing the original and deviations in the route around Totland.

Yarmouth
July 4th 1891

Gentlemen,

In consideration of your allowing me to level the Bank and have a Frontage to Station Road and make Footpath I will hold the piece of Land which you wish to purchase for three years and will sell to you any time during that term for Five hundred and Fifty pounds (£550) you paying five per cent Interest on the purchase money from date hereof up to time of completion of purchase, should you not complete the purchase no Interest to be paid. I will also throw into your Road the corner situate near the Gateway shown on plan. The land which I intend to hold for the said three years runs parallel with present Railway Siding and marked on Plan Y. N. & F. Ry. Kindly let me have your reply accepting same.

I am Gentlemen
Yours truly
(Signed) Harry Lee

To the Directors of the Freshwater &c Railway

The Secretary was instructed to accept the offer but nothing more was heard about the branch.

The extension to Totland took somewhat longer to die. During 1892 and 1893 numerous discussions took place with individuals in the hope they could be persuaded to fund it; even the LSWR was asked to take it on! At a meeting of the IWC* Board on 21st November, 1894 a circular issued by a shareholder Mr Cotterill was read concerning a fresh application to Parliament for an extension to Totland Bay. The *coup de grâce* to the extension followed the decision of the LSWR to extend its Lymington-Yarmouth steamer service to the pier at Totland Bay; visitors to the hotel greatly preferred to use the LSWR's vessels in preference to a journey by rail from Cowes or Ryde.

A lack of money was the principal reason why none of the FYN extension railways were built - we shall see precisely why in a later chapter.

---

* Formed in 1887 by amalgamation of the CNR, RNR and IWNJ.

Chapter Three

Construction and Opening

In a contract signed on 10th March, 1886 between William Jackson and the company, he undertook to purchase the necessary land, construct and maintain the railway for 12 months after opening. It specified that the line from Freshwater to Yarmouth should be completed by 31st July, 1886 and the remaining section to Newport by 30th June, 1887.

The next meeting of the Board did not take place until 30th July, 1886 when the Directors read a letter from the contractor explaining that he had been unable to complete the line from School Green to Yarmouth because Lord Heytesbury's agent refused to release the necessary land until construction had commenced beyond Yarmouth. Jackson intimated that his financial friends required an extension of time for completion of the railway to which the Directors agreed but not beyond 30th September, 1887. The Board ordered the issue of compulsory purchase notices to landowners and tenants. A month later Mr Jackson claimed he had expended £7,000 on work, including land purchases.

According to correspondence in the Isle of Wight County Records Office, construction had begun by October 1886 when R.J.C. Barbenson was belatedly appointed Engineer to the company; he was paid £260 per annum. In the absence of a wealthy benefactor the company forwent a ceremony to cut the first sod.

Although William Jackson based himself at an office in Freshwater most activity took place near Mill Lane, Yarmouth where materials were brought in; there was also a temporary siding to the foreshore at Wilmington. In January 1887 the *Isle of Wight County Press* reported that over 400 tons of rails had been delivered in the screw steamer *Mascott*. The line between Freshwater and Yarmouth had been 'practically formed' and considerable progress had been made with the section from Yarmouth to Newport. Mr Barbenson wrote to a meeting of shareholders in London on 4th April:

> I have much pleasure in reporting to you that considering the bad weather we have had during the past winter the works have progressed favourably.
> Practically speaking five miles of the line are formed and ready for the permanent way, three miles of which have been delivered and a portion laid.
> All the Bridges for the first five miles of the line are built, with the exception of one, and the culverts put in.
> The land for six miles of the railway has been purchased and negociations [sic] for the remainder are in hand.

Construction was carried out in the time honoured fashion by labourers assisted by horse and cart. The locomotive *Freshwater* arrived on 14th June, 1887 and was employed hauling materials forward to the railhead as it crept closer to Newport. On 26th June, 1887 the *Isle of Wight County Press* reported:

The celebrations of the Jubilee of Queen Victoria at Yarmouth and Freshwater were notable for the running of the first train between Yarmouth and Freshwater, on which many residents of those districts were carried free of charge by the kindness of Mr W. Jackson, the contractor for the construction of the line. The first train from Yarmouth was laden with children accompanied by the mayor (Mr James Blake) and left amid great cheering from a large concourse of spectators. The arrival of the train at Freshwater was greeted by more cheers. The journey was repeated several times during the afternoon. It was stated that a number of the rural residents conveyed on this occasion had never before travelled by rail, or indeed, seen a railway train, and their delight and astonishment may be imagined.

On 16th May, 1887 the Board heard that Mr Barbenson had left the Island following the death of his wife. Consequently a certificate of work had not been signed so that the Board could pay the contractor - some cash was handed over on account. Progress was evidently not swift enough for the FYN Board and on 28th December there was discussion about the need to open to a temporary station at Freshwater. Mr Jackson took the opportunity to express his dissatisfaction with the manner in which the Engineer performed his duties.

In February 1888 the IWC, successor to CNR and RNR, approved the provision of a temporary connection at Newport for the contractor's use and within a month work at that point was in progress. The *County Press* complained:

> Railway engineers and contractors in the prosecution of their work are no respecters of picturesque scenery or of buildings 'hoary with high antiquity'. The house of the venerable prior of St Cross, Newport - a spot interesting indeed by reason of its old associations - happened to be in the way of the new line of railway from Freshwater to Newport, and the enterprising contractor is making short work with it, a considerable portion of the building being already destroyed . . . the pickaxes of the contractor's men are now busy with stones which were laid more than seven centuries ago.

Ironwork for the viaducts at Calbourne and Newport was supplied by the Darlington Waggon & Engineering Company. There is a persistent rumour that a Ryde Pier Company steam tram locomotive, one of two sold to the local gas company in 1886, was used in the later stages of construction. The FYN had sent a letter to the IWC in February 1888 giving notice that rolling stock to work the Freshwater railway would be needed within three months - it proved a rather optimistic forecast. This was followed by the issue of an unsigned Engineer's report to a meeting of shareholders on 15th March:

> I have much pleasure in informing you that since I last reported the Works have progressed favourably. Nine miles and a half of the permanent way are now laid and ballasted, the fencing, cuttings and embankments finished and all the Bridges erected on that length.
> The junction with the Isle of Wight Central Railway has been made, the whole of the Ironwork for the Viaduct over the Town Bridge at Newport has been delivered and is to be erected and completed by the 30th April.
> The Electric Signals supplied by the Automatic Electric Co. are in course of erection and will be in working order by the end of April.
> You will be pleased to hear the heaviest portion of the line has been completed, and the remaining portion is very light in formation so there is no difficulty (as regards the Works) in completing your railway by the 1st June.

CONSTRUCTION AND OPENING

On 10th May, 1888 the FYN Board finally resolved '. . . to cancel the engagement with Mr Barbenson' and two days later decided '. . . that Mr William Lidstone be appointed Engineer to the Company in terms of his letter of the 10th inst. to commence from the 14th May inst' for the sum of 50 guineas. One of his first tasks was to set out plans for the junction with the IWC at Newport. On 12th May the *Isle of Wight County Press* described a trial trip, part of which read:

> . . . on Thursday last, through the courtesy of Mr Jackson, the Contractor, I formed one of a party who had the pleasure of a railway trip from Carisbrooke to Freshwater and back. When I say 'Carisbrooke', the point whence we started is in that parish, and on arriving there we found the train in readiness for us, the said train consisting of the 'Freshwater' engine and two 'saloon' carriages, very comfortably, even tastefully, arranged and fitted. The party who made that first railway journey from Carisbrooke to Freshwater consisted of the Deputy Governor of the Island (Mr A. Harbottle-Estcourt), Mr F.B.T. Goldstone, with Miss Goldstone and Miss Marina Wilkins, and the writer hereof, and they were accompanied by Mr Jackson, and his able second in command, Mr Bullmore . . . At Yarmouth there was a halt, and we took on board the Mayor and Corporation of that town, the rector and other friends . . . [At Carisbrooke] his worship of Yarmouth delivered a short speech. He said he was glad he was to have seen that day when the first train from the neighbourhood of Newport had come into Yarmouth. He regarded the line as a most important one, and he believed it had a prosperous future before it . . . The line will probably be opened for traffic early in July (1888).

The occasion was marked by the taking of a photograph showing *Freshwater* in charge of two wagons filled with the great and the good. The construction of Town gate viaduct at Newport was under way and on 26th May it was reported that two 40 ft main girders had been erected across the road at Hunnyhill. The rails across the viaduct were connected up on 10th August and at about 3.45 in the afternoon, the locomotive *Freshwater* crossed to the Newport side for the first time. As the *County Press* later reported, it then took several important locals on a trip from Newport to Freshwater and back:

> A single wagon, comfortably equipped with seats, and lined with baize, accommodated the first passengers, who consisted of the contractor for the construction of the line, Mr Jackson: the Company's engineer, Mr Lidstone, CE; Mr Martin; Dr Groves; Mr Brannon; and Messrs Bullmore, Wildman and Knight, the contractor's agents. At 4.39 the party started from the Newport extremity of the line, close to the junction with the Central Company, the engine being in charge of the train. Town Gate Viaduct was crossed at a fair speed with a smoothness of motion and absence of oscillation that gave conclusive evidence of the thoroughness of workmanship and the stability of the structure. Amidst charming scenery Carisbrooke Station, which is situated at the back of Priory Farm, and is to be approached by a new road between Carisbrooke House and Church, was soon passed, as were the stations for Calbourne & Shalfleet, and Ningwood. After passing Calbourne is a small viaduct similar to that at Newport. Yarmouth Station was reached at 5.04, and at 5.08 the train reached the Freshwater terminus, which is situated near School Green. Here the party alighted and inspection was made of the electrical signalling system in use on the line. The run throughout had been most comfortably accomplished, and the absence of any jolting again testified to the excellence of the workmanship with which Mr Jackson has carried out his contract. As previously mentioned in our columns, a somewhat winding course has been given to the line, by which means unnecessarily steep gradients have been avoided. The only remaining

The contractor's locomotive *Freshwater* was photographed when making a trial run from Carisbrooke to Freshwater and back in May 1888. The locomotive bears a lined green livery with its name painted on the tanks in shaded lettering. The primitive dumb-buffered wagons are thought to be lettered with the name of J. Firbank, their previous owner.
J. Mackett Collection

CONSTRUCTION AND OPENING 33

work of importance to be done on the line is the brickwork at the stations, and the ballasting of a mile or two at the Newport end, for which the material to be used is already stacked at Newport Station . . . The return journey was made in an equally agreeable manner to that from Newport. The start was made at 5.33, and the whole distance accomplished within less than half an hour.

Ten days later *Freshwater* left the rails; Mr H.W. Miller who, then a boy, kept a diary noted '. . . she had on 4 empties, and 15 of ballast, I being in one of the empties'. Having finally been connected with the remainder of the Island railway system, the first two trucks of coal left Newport for Freshwater on 1st September, 1888 and the line opened for goods traffic on Monday 10th September worked by *Freshwater*. By then a run-round loop and single siding existed at Freshwater, Yarmouth had a siding and Ningwood its crossing loop but no siding.

William Lidstone wrote his first and last report for a meeting of shareholders on 1st September:

> I have the honour to report that the Works upon this line are approaching completion. The rails have been laid from end to end and the Contractor's Engine makes daily running from Freshwater through to Newport. The Ballasting is in a forward state, and the Viaduct, Bridges, Culverts and Fencing are practically finished.
>
> There remains to build the Five Road Crossing Lodges, to erect the Stations and lay out the Station Yards and put up gradient and quarter mile posts.
>
> The Stations at Freshwater and Yarmouth are already in hand and the others will be commenced forthwith.

The Directors added their usual platitudes and reported '. . . negotiations are pending between the Isle of Wight Central Railway and the Company for settling the Plans for the junction at Newport'.

Construction of the station and other buildings was let out to local builders, that at Yarmouth being a Mr St John. That did not prevent the public from sampling a trip along the line. On 6th October the *Isle of Wight County Press* published an advertisement by the IWR for a 'cheap excursion' on Tuesday 9th October. It was timed to leave from Ventnor at 10.25 am, Wroxall 10.31, Shanklin 10.38, Ryde St Johns Road 10.30, Bembridge 10.28, St Helens 10.32, Brading 10.39 and Sandown 10.45. The return fares to Newport were 3s. first class and 2s. third but tickets had to be purchased no later than 9.00 am that day. A note added:

> Mr Jackson, the contractor of the Freshwater Railway, will provide at Newport a train of carriages, in which he will convey, free of charge, passengers desirous of proceeding from thence to Yarmouth and Freshwater, over the new railway, reaching Yarmouth about 11.45 am, and Freshwater about 11.55 am. The return train will leave Freshwater at 4.15 pm, and Yarmouth at 4.30 pm.

A week later the same newspaper reported:

> The Isle of Wight Railway ran a cheap excursion to the Freshwater Railway on 9th October. Only passengers from the Isle of Wight Railway Stations were conveyed, which caused some disappointment in Newport where local people had been unable to obtain tickets.

Freshwater had the dubious pleasure of hauling the 14 carriage IWR excursion train over the line on 9th October, 1888. Here it is seen with an impressive collection of IWR carriages including the two Bembridge branch six-wheelers. The small structure and post halfway down the train is thought to be the apparatus for the electric signals.

M. Brinton Collection

ISLE OF WIGHT RAILWAY
CHEAP EXCURSION TO NEWPORT
FOR
YARMOUTH and FRESHWATER
TUESDAY, 9th OCTOBER

CHEAP EXCURSION TICKETS will be issued from all Isle of Wight Railway Stations to Newport (via Sandown by the undermentioned train: – From Ventnor 10.25 a.m., Wroxall 10.31, Shanklin 10.38, Ryde (St Johns Road) 10.30, Bembridge 10.28, St Helens 10.32, Brading 10.39, Sandown 10.45. Fares to Newport and back (see note below), 1st Class 3s; 3rd Class 2s.

Note: Mr Jackson, the contractor of the Freshwater Railway, will provide at Newport a train of carriages, in which he will convey, free of charge, passengers desirous of proceeding from thence to Yarmouth and Freshwater, over the new railway, reaching Yarmouth about 11.45 a.m, and Freshwater about 11.55 a.m. The return train will leave Freshwater at 4.15 p.m., and Yarmouth at 4.30 p.m. Tickets can be obtained at the above stations up to 9 o'clock on Tuesday morning, 9th October, and up to Monday evening at Messrs Chaplin & Co.'s offices, High Street, Ventnor; High Street, Shanklin; and Esplanade, Ryde; also at Taylor's Library, High Street, Sandown.

Facsimile of an advert for an excursion in 1888.

The train was made up to fourteen carriages upon leaving Sandown, and was full, and to this long train, a further three vehicles were added at Newport for the local dignitaries who had been invited, and the train left Newport, hauled by the locomotive *Freshwater*, suitably decorated, shortly before noon. People turned out in force to see the train.

The event was marked by a photograph of the train with *Freshwater* at its head and despite the heavy load is said to have drawn its train at a good speed. On Easter Monday 1889 the Isle of Wight Rifles were transported to a field day at Afton Park.

Mr Lidstone mentioned the provision of electric signals in his March 1888 report. The *County Press* wrote that instead of conventional signals there were a number of what appeared to be 'pigeon boxes erected on light iron-work stands, with a bull's-eye light in the centre'. Nearby were two pillars, i.e. signals facing in opposite directions, and a small brick-built structure to accommodate batteries. A signal at the beginning of a section displayed a white light when the line was clear but when the locomotive depressed a treadle the current was broken in an electromagnet in the signal and a red disc fell to cover the lens. Upon leaving the section a second treadle was depressed to restore the circuit. The treadles, described as big curved iron springs, needed a weight of 15 cwt to depress them and could not be triggered by permanent way trolleys. The driver would obey signals on the right-hand side of the line whilst those on the other side applied to trains travelling in the opposite direction - it was said to be impossible for trains to 'come together'. Invented by a Mr Walter Walker, Manager of the Automatic Electric Signal Co. Ltd, similar systems were said to have seen use in France and Germany but they did not catch on in Britain. Apparently installed between Freshwater and Watchingwell, they were still not operational when inspected in July owing 'to the non-arrival of the relays from the manufacturers' but were said to have functioned perfectly when the excursion was ran over the line in October 1888. The company prudently decided not to rely on the system and Messrs Stevens were employed to install conventional signalling. An agreement was sealed with the Automatic Electric Railway Syndicate of Liverpool on 28th April, 1891 under which it would complete its system of signals between Calbourne and Freshwater within 12 months but it is thought that the equipment was removed or abandoned soon afterwards.

In early March 1889 it was reported that Mr Jackson hoped to open the railway (to passengers) in March or April but it was May before Major-General Hutchinson inspected the line on behalf of the Board of Trade. According to the *County* Press he was accompanied by Mr Stileman (IWC Engineer), Mr Lidstone, Mr Jackson, Mr Simmons (IWC Manager), Mr Fox (FYN Chairman), Mr Crowther (a FYN Director) and others. The newspaper added:

> The inspection commenced about 9.00 am at the junction at Newport, where about three hours were spent examining the works. The Town Gate Viaduct was tested, using the heaviest engines available. The viaduct was of iron girder construction, supported on steel trestles; there was a 40 feet span across the road, the other spans being 28 feet; the length was 800 feet long. There was another viaduct of similar construction about 400 feet long near Calbourne. Both structures were declared satisfactory. Lunch was take at the George Hotel at Yarmouth.

CONSTRUCTION AND OPENING

In the absence of a suitable source of supply, the contractor used burnt clay as ballast instead of gravel or stone chippings in making concrete for bridges. There was little experience of how the works would weather so the Board of Trade Inspector recommended that they be inspected again in 12 months time. Major-General Hutchinson was particularly concerned about the condition of concrete in the arches and abutments of Newport and Calbourne viaducts. He also gained the impression that the line would be worked with tender engines and requested the provision of a turntable at Freshwater and 'the other intended terminus of the traffic should one not now exist, there'. After listing a number of failings, the Inspector concluded that the line could not be opened with safety.

A return visit was made to the Island on 3rd June, 1889 when the Inspector reported that most of the requirements had been carried out. Even so, the FYN had to resubmit the concrete structures for inspection in one year, construct the turntable at Freshwater within three months and provide home, distant and starting signals at Watchingwell. The need for those signals seems to have stemmed from Jackson's plans to make the station a public one - why he wanted to do this is not clear. Major Hutchinson was quite prepared to sanction opening of the railway for passenger traffic, subject to a speed limit of 25 mph, but the company lacked a proper agreement for working its railway.

On 5th March, 1886 the FYN Directors concluded a working agreement with the CNR, the senior partner in the Ryde, Newport & Cowes Joint Committee after having failed to tempt the mainland companies to take on the operation of the railway. It obliged the FYN to complete its railway to the reasonable satisfaction of the CNR Engineer and Board of Trade before 26th August, 1888, maintain the line during the first 12 months after opening (in fact the contractor would maintain the line for 12 months as part of his contract) and carry out any alterations, additions etc. that increased traffic might later justify. In exchange the CNR undertook to maintain and work the line as part of its railway, provide locomotives, rolling stock and staff. Out of gross traffic receipts the CNR would receive 55 per cent, paid six-monthly, and could charge a rent for use of the joint station at Newport; the FYN received the balance and any income from advertisements, book stalls and refreshment rooms on its line. Either company could give notice to terminate the agreement at the end of seven years. Whenever the agreement ended the FYN had to purchase any locomotives and rolling stock bought to work the line.

By the time the Freshwater railway was approaching completion circumstances had changed. In 1887 the CNR and RNR merged with the IWNJ to form the Isle of Wight Central Railway. None of the Directors who signed the 1886 agreement with the Freshwater company remained in office and their successors had neither the time nor capital to expend on this upstart. In March 1889 the FYN Secretary wrote to inform the IWC that the railway was nearing completion and that the FYN would be invoking the working agreement. Acting on instructions from his Board, the IWC Secretary replied:

To R. J. Palmer, Secretary   9th April, 1889
Dear Sir,
    Referring to your letter of 14th March the Directors of this Company have received the Report of their Engineer, Mr Stileman, on the Freshwater Yarmouth & Newport Railway.

He states his inability to give any definite opinion of the sufficiency of the structural portion of the Railway, as the Company have not forwarded any specification or drawing shewing the works of construction, and have not submitted complete information of that portion of which plans have already been forwarded. Moreover the Line is still in an unfinished condition, requiring considerable additions.

Under the circumstances the Directors cannot take the responsibility of working the Line under the Agreement nor take any liability for the safety of the Public nor for the maintenance of the Railway.

The Directors are however willing to work the Railway for 12 months at prime cost.

Of course this proposal is subject to the Line being passed by the Board of Trade.

 Yours faithfully,
  (signed) F. L. Beard
  Secretary

The FYN Board had not anticipated any difficulties with the working agreement even though completion had been somewhat delayed! The shocked FYN Directors instructed their Secretary to write:

17 Gt George Street, Westminster
30th April, 1889

To F. L. Beard Esq., Secretary
Isle of Wight Central Rwy Coy Ltd
Dear Sir,

I am instructed by my Directors to acknowledge receipt of your letter of the 9th inst. the contents of which has caused them considerable surprise. You have known for some time past from the notices sent you that this Company was intending to have the Line completed forthwith so as to, if possible, open it for traffic for Easter and, if you wanted further information of the Plans already sent you, on application from you they would have been sent and will be now sent to your Engineer, Mr Stileman.

With reference to the Line being in an incomplete state of course my Directors would see that it was only handed over to you to work after it had been duly passed by the Board of Trade officials.

As to your Directors being willing to work the Line for 12 months at cost price my Directors fail to appreciate this offer as the existing working Agreement provides the terms upon which you shall work this Company's line, viz: 55% of the gross receipts.

I am, Dear Sir,
 Yours faithfully,
  (signed) R. J. Palmer, Secretary

The Central was unmoved and gained some additional ammunition when the Board of Trade Inspector expressed his concern about the condition of the concrete structures. After a lengthy delay, on 26th June the IWC proposed that the Freshwater company maintain the permanent way and structures for which an additional percentage would be paid out of the receipts:

in the second and third years 7½ per cent of gross receipts
in the fourth and fifth years 8½ per cent of gross receipts
in the sixth and seventh years 10 per cent of gross receipts

The FYN Board met the following day and agreed to the offer provided the two parties could settle on the wording of a supplementary agreement so that the railway could open no later than 6th July. No such agreement was forthcoming and on 28th June the Secretary was instructed to write:

CONSTRUCTION AND OPENING

Referring to the interview of Mr Bayliffe and Mr Lidstone with your Chairman yesterday it is perfectly evident that the principle of our Line being maintained by an other person than the Working Company is not feasible, we find there is no such case known in the whole Railway system of Great Britain. The discussion therefore based on the principle of this Company maintaining the line cannot be continued as it is transparent that no satisfactory 'heads of a supplementary Agreement' can be arrived at between the two companies.

As the season is advancing a heavy loss has already been made as, we contend, through your default, we have therefore to request a reply to this not later than Monday next as, if we cannot come to terms by that date, we shall have no alternative in justice to our Stockholders (to say nothing of the constant representations the Board are receiving from the Public) but to make arrangements to work the Line ourselves.

The Central Board was quite used to such letters and on 3rd July the Secretary wrote regretting that the FYN had not agreed to their terms and adding 'As you have now determined to work the Line yourselves we shall be happy to render you every facility in our power'.

Their bluff called, the FYN Board resolved '. . . it is not desirable to work the Line ourselves . . . that negotiations be reopened with the Isle of Wight Central Railway to work the Line on the basis of the terms suggested in their letter of 26th June, 1889 in this Company maintaining and the Central Company working the Line and that the Chairman and Solicitor be authorised to come to terms', this is what was agreed. Given the gulf that existed between the Boards of the two companies, one wonders why the IWC did eventually agree to work the line; perhaps it feared that the IWR, which had running powers between Ryde and Newport, would be tempted to do so!

The Board of Trade finally gave permission to open the line on 18th July, a working agreement with the IWC was signed on 19th July and the formal opening took place the next day, Saturday 20th July, 1889. Inevitably it was the main event in West Wight for many a year. A small crowd assembled at Newport and all along the line little knots of people waited to see the first train. The *Isle of Wight County Press* reported:

> The inauguration took place about 11.30 am Yarmouth and Freshwater were decorated with flags; several prominent local citizens were picked up at Yarmouth, including Mr James Blake who was the last Mayor of that town. Other local dignitaries met the train upon its arrival at Freshwater, including the Chairman of the Company, Mr Edwin Fox. Mr Fox called upon Mr Granville Ward to declare the line formally open. This was duly done, and the wish expressed that the opening of the extension to Totland be not long delayed. After the festivities at Freshwater Station, the guests were conveyed in carriages to the Totland Bay Hotel for lunch and the customary ceremonies.

Those attending the opening and subsequent junketings included representatives of the IWR, IWC, Southampton and Isle of Wight Steam Packet Co., the LSWR, LBSCR, the various local authorities and magistrates. Most of the local residents had to content themselves with a sight of their new railway in operation. Traffic on the first day was encouraging with large numbers of West Wight people journeying to Newport for the Agricultural Show, and remained at a promising level throughout the remainder of the summer.

Thus opened the Freshwater, Yarmouth & Newport Railway 'better late than never'.

Poster announcing the opening of the FYN.

Chapter Four

A Descent into Bankruptcy

Having signed the contract for construction of their railway in March 1886, the Board found itself almost completely in the hands of the contractor and his solicitor, Mr Hogan. The Board clearly lacked acumen in managing sizeable contracts and showed a remarkable lack of control over Mr Jackson's activities. The impression is given of a group of well-meaning individuals who were out of their depth. To be fair to Jackson, he had been a contractor since the 1860s but possessed little capital of his own and depended on financial backers who naturally wanted to make money out of the enterprise. The first turn of the screw came on 30th July when he asked that £42,000 of the capital be issued as preference shares; they took priority over ordinary shares whenever a company declared a dividend. His backers would find it easier to sell on shares that held out a better hope of a regular dividend. Mr Jackson received £8,000 in ordinary shares, the first of numerous payments; in October he wrote asking that a proportion of money owed to him be paid to Messrs Armstrong & Co., a London merchant bank.

Meanwhile there had been some changes in the composition of the Board. Charles Harvey '. . . was incapacitated by illness' but Edmund Granville Ward could not be elected in his stead because land taken by the railway had not been valued; the shares to be issued in payment would have given him the necessary qualification for a seat on the Board. Mr Ward lived on Freshwater Isle in Weston Manor House and was a highly desirable catch; the Ward family owned a large amount of land in the Island, particularly around Cowes, and wielded considerable influence. His help was badly needed as other individuals who had initially supported the railway were alienated when the route was diverted away from Totland and the works of the Yar Bridge Company. In October 1886 Messrs Norton and McPherson offered to resign '. . . on certain terms which were agreed to'; those terms included a settlement of money owed by William Jackson. When payment was not forthcoming Mr Norton burst in on a Board meeting on 12th February, 1887 claiming that he was still a Director - the Minutes merely recorded the Board's resolution to the contrary!

Samuel Pittis demanded the return of a £50 deposit he had paid for £100 preference shares because the railway passed right through his property near Newport instead of skirting it; the Board acceded to his request '. . . although he was legally bound to carry out his contract'. According to returns to the Board of Trade, by the end of 1886 £39,100 ordinary shares and £3,957 in 5 per cent preference shares had been paid up.

Replacements for the resigned Directors came in the shape of Herbert A. Whitaker and Capt. G.P. Heine who joined the Board on 22nd October, 1886 - both had connections with the merchant bank. The Board approved the wording of a Prospectus inviting subscriptions for ordinary shares and finally decided to open a bank account. In November the first shares were allotted to applicants whose addresses were scattered throughout Britain, few were local people. Mr W.C. Heaton-Armstrong was appointed to the Board giving the financiers a majority.

ISLE OF WIGHT.

THE FRESHWATER, YARMOUTH AND NEWPORT RAILWAY.

SIX PER CENT. PREFERRED ORDINARY STOCK.

FORM OF APPLICATION.

To the Directors,

GENTLEMEN,

Be good enough to have transferred to me the following portion of the above Stock, £_____ at par.

And I hereby agree to accept the same (or any less amount), subject to the conditions contained in your Prospectus, dated August, 1889.

I enclose herein the sum of £_____, being the required deposit of 25 per cent. on the amount applied for, and engage to pay the balance on allotment.

Name_____

Address_____

Date_____

This form to be sent entire with the Deposit payable thereon to the Secretary, at the offices of the Company, 17, Great George Street, Westminster, S.W.; or to The Capital and Counties Bank, Limited, 39, Threadneedle Street, E.C.

ISLE OF WIGHT.

The Freshwater, Yarmouth and Newport Railway.

BANKERS' RECEIPT FOR DEPOSIT

On Application for 6 per cent. PREFERRED Ordinary Stock.

RECEIVED this_____ day of_____ 1889.

from_____

the sum of_____ pounds,

being the Deposit of 25 per Cent. on Application for_____ SIX PER CENT. PREFERRED ORDINARY STOCK of THE FRESHWATER, YARMOUTH AND NEWPORT RAILWAY.

For the CAPITAL AND COUNTIES BANK, LIMITED,

£ _____ Signature.

An application form for FYN shares.

A DESCENT INTO BANKRUPTCY

By the beginning of 1887 William Jackson was having difficulty in securing a steady flow of cash from Messrs Armstrong to pay wages, etc. because the FYN had been unable to sell enough shares and make regular payments. Although the Minutes are understandably vague on the matter, certain members of the Board met with unusual frequency to sanction the issue of shares to the contractor, ostensibly in payment for work done. Since a certain proportion of the share capital had to be issued before a start could be made on the debentures, this had the effect of bringing forward the date when they could be issued; debentures paid a guaranteed rate of interest irrespective of profits and were the most highly prized of a company's capital. These rather dubious dealings came to the attention of the other Directors and a well-attended meeting of the Board took place on 18th March. Armstrong & Co. were paid off by the issue of £21,600 in debenture stock, Messrs Heaton-Armstrong, Whitaker and Heine resigned and their shares were transferred back to Mr Jackson. George H. Hogan, Jackson's solicitor, joined the Board. Richard Palmer, Secretary to the company, who had been criticised for his management of the company's affairs and forced to resign in February 1887 in favour of a man who worked for Messrs Armstrong, was rehabilitated and returned to office without loss of salary.

A Prospectus for the issue of preference shares was approved by the Board in June 1887 and within a month the first were allotted to applicants. Issue of the remaining preference and some debenture stock was authorised in October - £18,500 in debentures were quickly issued. By the end of 1887 issued capital had totalled £55,600 in ordinary shares, £22,550 in preference shares and £40,300 in 5 per cent debenture stock.

In February 1888 another Prospectus was approved and so well were preference shares selling that a few went at a premium of 5s. a share. It should be remembered that the contractor's backers were paying the debenture interest and giving the impression that the railway was a very good investment in direct contrast to the true position. The capital was badly needed; Jackson owed several landowners for land taken by the railway. This included Mr Pittis who was owed £4,500 for his property near Newport; in January 1888 he agreed to accept £3,000 on account with the balance to follow in 12 months, plus interest of course. Amongst the applicants for debenture stock was a Mr Edwin Jones JP of Cannon Street, London who was allotted £4,000 on 15th March - we shall meet him again.

Following the resignations from the Board in March 1887 only Edwin Fox and George Hogan regularly attended meetings. By 12th May, 1888 Mr Ward still did not possess enough shares because the amount of his land required by the railway had not been agreed.

Within 12 months shareholders began to appreciate the true financial state of the company. At a meeting on 1st September, 1888 they sanctioned the division of ordinary shares into preferred and deferred half shares as provided for in the 1880 Act. This entitled holders of preferred shares to 6 per cent in priority to the deferred half shares, *if* the Board declared a dividend. On 5th February, 1889 a special general meeting was held to vote for a Bill authorising yet more capital - it had to be adjourned twice before their approval was obtained.

Meanwhile, William Jackson made an agreement with financiers William Alfred and Clement Crowther. They were duly elected to the FYN Board at a shareholders meeting on 7th June. Capital expenditure totalled:

	£	s.	d.
in the years to 31st December, 1887	113,200	0	0
in the year ending 31st December, 1888	62,620	2	8
plus 'paid to Totland Bay Hotel Co. on account Wm Jackson'	500	0	0
further expenditure on the contract was estimated at	12,479	17	4

Mr Jackson's financial problems did not disappear and following the opening of the railway the Board received a bill from Totland Bay Hotel for the festivities - the contractor normally funded the feast. He also owed £473 7s. 0d. for the signalling work at Newport; the IWC deducted it from the traffic receipts so the FYN Board promptly demanded reimbursement from Jackson's backers!

On 26th July, 1889 the Board approved a draft Prospectus for the issue of £48,000 preferred 6 per cent stock to coincide with the opening of the railway. Having exhausted the preference stock held by the FYN, Messrs Hogan and Crowther released a quantity of stock held by William Jackson so that allotments could be made to applicants; the money received was promptly handed over to Jackson's financiers. The shares and debentures in circulation soon exceeded public demand.

A Board meeting on 15th August, 1889 was attended by Mr Jackson's brother Henry, William being in 'ill health'. This illness might properly be regarded as diplomatic as the first item on the agenda was a letter from the contractor. William wrote that he could not complete the line or continue with its maintenance without further financial assistance and suggested that he be paid in Lloyds Bonds that would be redeemed in 12 months - left with a quantity of unsold stock the Crowthers had become reluctant to continue funding him. In September the Board discussed the financial position with W.A. Crowther who agreed to pay outstanding bills for land purchase and fund the completion of the line subject to certain conditions. The Board had just allotted £9,520 in preference shares to applicants and apart from a sum retained to pay for maintenance the proceeds were shared out between the Crowthers and Mr Hogan who was acting on William Jackson's behalf. Within weeks the agreement broke down.

On 28th November, 1889, Mr Lidstone, the Engineer, reported that William Jackson was '. . . not proceeding with the Works necessary to complete his contract' nor was he doing anything to satisfy the requirements of the IWC, Board of Trade, Isle of Wight Road Commissioners (who had complained about the state of the level crossings) and landowners who had not been paid for land. A letter was dispatched to Clement Crowther complaining that he had not advanced the money as the agreement specified and asking if he proposed to pay the £1,182 10s. 0d. in debenture interest that would fall due on 1st January, 1890. The next day William Jackson dismissed his workmen and by the end of the year was bankrupt. The FYN Board had been warned of William's situation and arranged with Henry Jackson that he would re-employ sufficient men to keep the permanent way in order pending a formal contract to maintain the line and complete the outstanding works; payment was in Lloyds Bonds. Henry was an established contractor but his involvement with contracts on the mainland meant that he relied for his information about the railway on second-hand information from his men on the spot.

The financial position was less easy to resolve. By the end of 1889 £46,774 in preferred ordinary stock, the same amount in deferred ordinary stock, and all the

£42,000 preference and £47,300 debenture stock had been issued; only some of the unattractive ordinary stock remained. William Lidstone advised that it would cost a further £3,800 to complete the outstanding work which the Board considered to be the responsibility of William Jackson. The contract with William Jackson was formally terminated by the FYN Directors on 20th December, 1889 and a fresh contract let to Henry Jackson for maintenance covering the six months to 20th July, 1890 at £35 a week; this was reduced to £25 a week when it was renewed but in practice the contract became open ended; Between March and August 1890 the company issued Henry Jackson with £3,600 in Lloyds Bonds for work done, a further £2,200 followed between August and November and £1,500 by the end of March 1891 - none were redeemed for many years.

On 28th March, 1890 the FYN Board set out a detailed list of its claim against William Jackson:

Cost of completing the railway. Estimated	£3,850
Cost of keeping railway in repair until 20th July, 1890 say £35 a week from cancellation of contract	£1,155
Payment until completion of contract of interest to debenture holders and preference shareholders one year	£2,500
Payment to land owners for land, costs, charges and expenses	£5,000
Losses by company in respect of bad workmanship in the contract, including the liability of the company to maintain the line for the period of six years in consequence of the working company refusing to maintain the line for the above reasons	£4,000
Solicitors, costs, charges and expenses, say	£1,500
Engineers, ditto say	£250
Secretary, office expenses and auditors	£200
Culvert & bridge on Fletcher Jones land not included within estimate - say cost	£350
	£18,805
Less: Value of plant and balance of purchase money of engine	£700
Total	£18,105

Mr Jackson's representative refused to accept the claim and there was a threat of court action. This proved to be an empty threat but the FYN was forced to instigate proceedings to prevent the sale of the contractor's locomotive *Freshwater*. The Directors claimed that the plant used by the contractor became the company's property upon completion of the contract. On 3rd June, 1890 Jackson's creditors in the London Bankruptcy Court heard him attribute his failure mainly to the FYN shares that were not worth their face value. As a footnote the FYN Minutes for 31st March, 1892 recorded the results of a court action between the Blaenavon Company and Mr Jackson's representative over an unpaid bill for rails. The suppliers gained a judgement ordering the FYN to hand over ordinary shares in lieu of cash for the debt - within months they had been sold on.

Hitherto the contractor's financiers had paid the preference and debenture interest but when the contract with William Jackson ended, the company had to find the cash to continue the interest payments. To pay the interest on 1st July, 1890, a £1,000 loan was obtained from the Capital & Counties Bank, the railway's surplus land being used as collateral. More cash was borrowed from the Property Securities Company using 1,000 ordinary shares in the Didcot & Newbury Railway that William Jackson had lodged with the FYN as security. The Property Securities Company had been formed in 1884 for the purpose of loaning money in exchange for securities; the principal shareholders included Edwin Fox and Richard Palmer. Neither the land nor the shares, when sold, raised enough to pay off the loans.

On 15th September, 1890 the Board resolved not to fill the seats vacated by the Crowthers 'who have retired from the Board'. This had consequences at the next shareholders meeting on 27th September when Benjamin Woodward, William Jackson's representative, and W.A. Crowther sought to adjourn the meeting for a month. Records of the meeting failed to record all the arguments but George Hogan objected to W. A. Crowther's right to vote as a large parcel of shares were held jointly in the names of Hogan and Crowther; the Chairman ruled that only the first named had the right to vote. Even so, not enough preference and debenture shareholders voted in favour of issuing the capital in the 1889 Act. That paralysed the company's finances bringing to an end hopes of extensions and purchase of the Totland Bay Pier & Hotel Company.

By June 1891 virtually all work to complete the railway had ceased and only essential maintenance was being carried out. At a meeting of the Board Henry Jackson claimed that he was unable to sell on the Lloyds Bonds and asked for 'a further discount of 10 per cent' to which the Board agreed 'for the present'. Jackson promised to complete the signalling at Carisbrooke and Yarmouth but nothing was done.

Another Bill became law in 1891 authorising the issue of sufficient stock to raise £20,000. This stock could only rank before the existing stock for interest purposes if three-fifths of the share and debenture holders agreed - they did not. The £20,000 was for paying the costs of the Act, buy land and settle other debts.

The powers to issue additional capital was worthless if no buyers could be found for it. Henry Jackson proposed taking the 'B' debenture stock at a price of £70 for every £100 of debentures on which he would pay 5 per cent interest for three years equal to a price of £85 per debenture. Wishing to do better the Secretary wrote to three brokers. The following reply from Percy Mortimer, who happened to be an IWC Director, was typical:

75 Old Broad Street
October 19th 1891
I have consulted others about the proposed issue of Debenture Stock for the Freshwater Railway, but, our opinion is (in which I agree) that the balance over after paying present Debenture Interest is so slender, and as the new issue would require £1000 a year, that it would be hopeless to try and place them at present at any reasonable price. I fear you will have to wait until the Railway earns nearly enough to cover the interest on the proposed issue.

(signed) P. Mortimer

A DESCENT INTO BANKRUPTCY

The reason for the responses was clear. As long ago as June 1888 the amount of 5 per cent debenture stock issued had reached the authorised total of £47,300; this equated to an annual interest bill of £2,365, a sum that the railway *never* earned. The FYN Board had no option but to accepted Jackson's offer - the FYN was at his mercy.

During 1891 meetings of the Board were repeatedly adjourned as the health of Edwin Fox, the prime mover in the company, deteriorated. The last meeting he chaired was on 11th December and there then appeared a gap until 28th March, 1892 when E. Granville Ward took the chair, apparently in Monte Carlo, as the FYN paid for George Hogan and the solicitor to travel there! The meeting resolved to appoint Hon. Ashley Ponsonby to the Board and as Chairman in place of the late Mr Fox. Three days later Ponsonby chaired the next Board meeting at which Mr Ward's letter of resignation was read out.

Throughout 1892 the Board tried to issue the 'B' debenture stock to settle debts but creditors frequently refused to accept them, took the company to court and forced the Board to find cash to settle the inevitable judgement. Most cash came from Henry Jackson or Edwin Jones for which they received generous amounts of stock. In October Henry Jackson wrote:

181 Queen Victoria Street, 14th October 1892
The Directors, Freshwater Railway

Gentlemen,
  With reference to my previous letter that I shall not be able to keep the Freshwater Railway in repair. I shall be glad if you can make arrangements to continue the same yourselves. I have done all I can to assist the Company under its present difficulties and regret that I shall not be able to continue doing so any longer. Any B. Debentures that I take for the extra Works I shall not be able to take at less than 50% Discount and this I would rather not do as I am unable to place them at that price.
    Your obedient Servant
    (signed) Henry Jackson

In December 1892 the IWC was asked to provide cash out of the traffic receipts to pay Jackson's men their wages. This played into his hands and more than once an increase in the fortnightly payments was gained ostensibly because of the need to employ more men on the work; it was not long before the harassed Directors were spending all the company's income on maintenance.

Despite having held Board meetings at which only two Directors attended for months, if not years, an entry in the Minute book suddenly announced that there was no quorum at a meeting on 7th February, 1893. The Secretary was instructed to obtain the temporary resignation of either Col Walker or Mr Ward so that two Directors would in future constitute a quorum, a curious entry as a letter of resignation from Mr Ward had been read out months earlier. At the next meeting on 23rd March Col Walker duly resigned and in April a similar letter was received from Mr Ward in Rome - neither had been attending Board meetings regularly.

The inevitable crisis came in the summer of 1893. On 14th June the IWC Board read a letter from the FYN asking for an advance on their receipts in order to pay interest on the debenture stock. The IWC offered £1,000 but this was quite insufficient and not all the interest could be paid when it fell due for payment on 1st July. An ensuing action in the courts resulted in the appointment of Hon. Ashley Ponsonby as Receiver on 9th August, a later order also made him Manager.

Chapter Five

The Railway in Use
1888 to 1893

The train service provided by the IWC was typical of that elsewhere on its system. Locomotive and carriage sheds were built by the FYN at Freshwater but were rarely, if ever, used because trains began or ended their journeys at the opposite end of the line. This was certainly the case from 1891 when the Central's locomotives were moved from Cowes to a new shed at Newport. During much of the year there were five trains taking approximately 35 minutes in each direction with an additional return working on Saturday evenings and three on Sundays. During the months of July, August and September a more frequent service operated. In 1894 there were eight return trains on weekdays and on Saturdays one short working serving Carisbrooke was continued to Ningwood to run round. On Sundays there were three trains and an unadvertised early morning mail and goods train to Freshwater and four in the reverse direction. The FYN 1880 Act laid down fares that were the equivalent of 3*d*. a mile first, 2*d*. second and 1*d*. third class; the actual fares between Newport and Freshwater were:

Single	First class	3*s*.	Second	2*s*.	Third	1*s*.	
Return	First class	4*s*.	Second	3*s*.	Third	1*s*. 9*d*.	

A 'Parliamentary' fare had been introduced as a consequence of the Railway Regulation Act of 1844; it obliged companies to operate at least one train a day stopping at all stations and charging no more than 1*d*. a mile. An Act in 1883 relieved companies of the need to run such trains if they made alternative third class accommodation available at the same fares. The IWC possessed no third class carriages but complied with the Acts by making second class compartments available to third class ticket holders on the first passenger train in each direction on weekdays. Other trains carried only first and second class passengers. The first batch of tickets printed for the line were to the same Edmondson design as those issued by the Central elsewhere on its system even to the extent of bearing only that company's title. Single tickets were printed horizontally but returns had a vertical layout. They also bore no printed fare, a requirement introduced by an 1889 Railway Regulation Act from 1st July, 1890, so staff had to hand write the fare until a second batch of tickets was produced - this time they bore both companies' names.

Publicity for the new railway promised a 'New Express Service with cheap excursion fares'. Through trains to and from Ryde and Sandown generated a healthy traffic, particularly on Bank holidays, when locals and visitors alike took day trips by rail across the Island to the beaches of West Wight. For those travelling in the opposite direction the frontage of the station master's house at Freshwater was adorned with the painted message 'The Family Route to London is via Ryde or Cowes: Frequent and Convenient Trains from this Station Without Change of Carriage - London in 4 hours'. The alternative route to London via Yarmouth and Lymington was ignored for obvious reasons.

No separate traffic statistics for the Freshwater railway have survived because they were included in IWC returns to the Board of Trade. A comparison of the Central's figures for 1888 and 1891 show differences that cannot be solely accounted for by the opening of the FYN.

Year ending 31 Dec.	Passenger traffic Numbers carried				Goods traffic	
	First	Second	Third	Season	Minerals Tons	General Tons
1888	24,331	190,504	195,917	745	70,335	24,070
1891	36,582	225,148	389,517	908	81,212	26,792
Difference	12,251	34,644	193,644	235	10,877	2,722

A record of traffic receipts appeared in the FYN Minute book for two years following the line's opening to passenger traffic. Weekly receipts varied from a nadir in January 1890 of £46 to a high of £262 in July 1890. Most income came in the months of April to October but only on one or two occasions did they exceed £200 and during the winter takings averaged just £60 to £70 a week. Income and expenditure for the years 1889 to 1892 were:

Year * ending 31 Dec.	Traffic receipts	Amount due to FYN	Permanent Way etc. costs	Profit	Capital expenditure on main line	Totland Bay branch
	£ s. d.	£ s. d.	£ s. d.	£ s. d.	£ s. d.	£ s. d.
1889	?	1,345 19 0	?	?	6,315 0 0	567 10 0
1890	6,508 3 8	3,579 10 0	nil	2,637 4 4	?	
1891	6,319 6 7	3,475 12 6	642 0 0	2,535 12 6	2,085 2 9	69 4 9
1892	7,047 7 10	3,876 1 3	2,205 8 5	92 16 3	815 5 10	69 4 9

So where did the users of the railway come from? Some passengers transferred from the handful of road coaches that operated to West Wight whilst others preferred the steamers from Lymington. Many visitors and a few locals had the money to pay for a railway journey from elsewhere in the Island to sample the delights of Freshwater, Totland, Yarmouth and Carisbrooke with its castle - the notion that easy and affordable transport generates business is not a new idea.

The principal goods traffic was in the carriage of coal from Medina Jetty. It was some time before Newport traders began using the railway to supply the area, whilst farmers were slow to begin sending their animals and produce by rail to the capital. Once they had discovered the advantages of the railway the FYN became the principal means of transport in West Wight. However, the lack of any large centres of population along its route meant that the company was destined never to generate sufficient income to service its borrowings, let alone achieve the financial stability of the IWR.

Plans provided by the FYN Engineer to the IWC showed certain items that William Jackson had not completed. Consequently the IWC considered that the FYN was incomplete and insisted that they be listed in a schedule to the working agreement listing the outstanding work:

---

* These figures were taken from the accounts and do not match the percentages in the working agreements because of various deductions for tax, etc. made by the IWC.

Carisbrooke station - a passing loop and platform, a proper station approach and the siding to be ballasted.
Ningwood station - a siding.
Yarmouth station - a passing place and platform.
Freshwater station - engine turntable, engine and carriage sheds, tanks and water column with water supply for locomotives, stationmaster's house to be completed.

The Central also expected the FYN to pay for furniture and fittings at each station. They were detailed in a second schedule and although the Central ordered them on 9th July, 1889 an arbitrator had to be called in to decide who paid the bill - he sided with the IWC:

Carisbrooke station - locked cupboard in booking office between fireplace and side of building enclosing three shelves for ticket stock, two shelves one foot wide over ticket windows, dating press, ticket case (not less than 150 tubes), two portable and fit platform seats. Office stool, necessary lamps for Porters and pair Station hand trucks for luggage, train staff and boxes in connection throughout the line.
Ningwood station - wide shelf under ticket window to form desk, three drawers under, one to be Cash till, book rack, two shelves foot wide and to end of room, dating press, ticket case 150 tubes, two portable and fit platform seats. Office stool, two hand lamps, pair Station hand trucks.
Yarmouth station - dating press, ticket case 150 tubes, two portable and fit platform seats. Office stool, two hand lamps, pair Station hand trucks.
Freshwater station - dating press, ticket case 150 tubes, three portable and fit platform seats. Office stool, two hand lamps, sack barrow and one pair Station hand trucks.

At a meeting of the Central's Board on 28th August, 1889 Directors discussed the provision of additional facilities at Freshwater. The locomotive and carriage sheds were under construction but there was a need for coal stores that the IWC Board decided the FYN should provide. On 20th November the IWC Board was informed that the siding at Ningwood had been laid out and the engine shed at Freshwater was almost complete. Marshland was filled, locomotive and carriage sheds erected and sidings laid. This work did not go smoothly as in January 1890 the locomotive shed was destroyed presumably by fire; it must have been the Central's fault because its Manager was told to get it rebuilt! The FYN Board resolved in November to erect a brick and tiled coal shed but months elapsed before it was completed.

Meanwhile a dispute was brewing over the rent for Newport station. To accommodate through trains connecting the Freshwater line with Ryde or Sandown the IWC constructed a loop road so that Ryde - and Sandown - bound trains could stand in the station at the same time, it was not planned to use the short bay road at the north end of the station for Freshwater line trains; there was also a considerable amount of expenditure on the construction of offices, locomotive shed and workshops. On 9th September, 1889 the IWC Secretary wrote enclosing a summary of his company's expenditure; he suggested that rent for the use of the station should amount to £872 15s. 6d. per annum but added that his Directors would settle for £500. Naturally the Freshwater Board balked at paying for facilities that were likely to benefit the IWC more than their own company.

THE RAILWAY IN USE, 1888 TO 1893

On 30th October they wrote that their Engineer considered that £200 was the maximum that should be paid in rent and with which they agreed! The £200 probably represented just the cost of providing the junction because Mr Jackson was billed separately for the additional signalling. A month later the Central threatened arbitration but the Directors responded that the rent was annual so there was no immediate necessity for a decision and the amount '. . . will be better ascertained after the expiration of the first year'.

On 22nd January, 1890 the IWC Board decided to deduct £250 each half year from receipts on account of rent. To keep up the pressure the Central also claimed a share of the income from advertising on the grounds that it had to do all the work to get it - the FYN refused. In March the FYN Board discovered the deductions but despite protests the IWC kept them up. On 20th May, 1892 the two companies agreed to refer the question to an arbitrator William Birt, General Manager of the Great Eastern Railway. His award dated 27th October, 1892 fixed the annual rent at £340 a year; it began with the delightful preamble 'To all whom these presents shall come I William Birt of Liverpool Street Station in the City of London, General Manager of the Great Eastern Railway Company Send Greeting . . .'

The first complaint about the permanent way was received from the IWC on 12th February, 1890 when it was added that the houses at stations and crossings were uninhabitable - there had been little money to fund their construction. Nothing had been done to complete the items listed in the working agreement so the IWC threatened to do the work themselves and charge the FYN accordingly. This was a hollow threat as it possessed neither capital nor the FYN sufficient income.

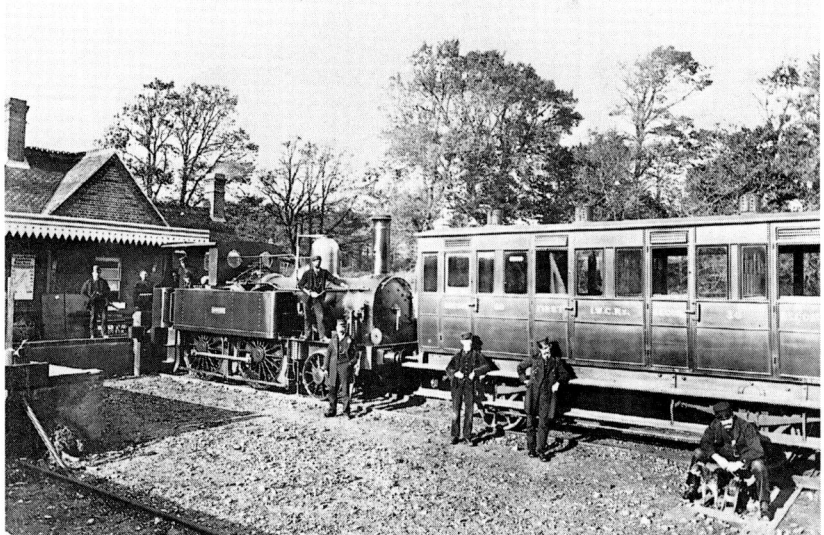

Soon after the opening of the railway, IWC No. 5 *Osborne* and its train of ex-IWNJ carriages stand at Freshwater in 1890. The man on the right seems to be perched on the hand lever that operated the points! *J. Mackett Collection*

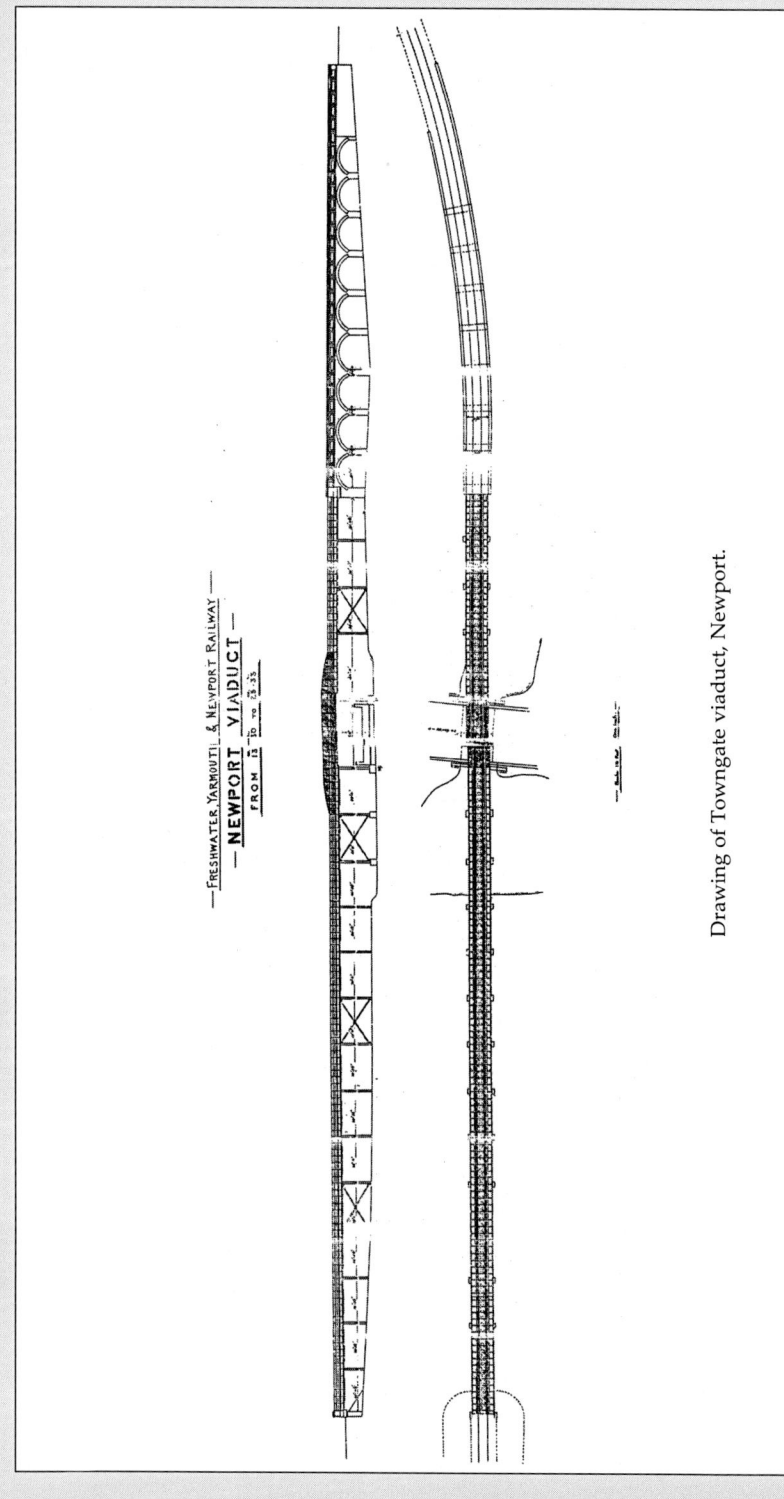

Drawing of Towngate viaduct, Newport.

THE RAILWAY IN USE, 1888 TO 1893

Major-General Hutchinson, the Board of Trade Inspector, made a return visit to inspect the concrete structures. He wrote on 13th August, 1890 that the concrete was perfectly satisfactory but a good deal of water was percolating through the arches at Newport owing to a poor covering of asphalt; there had also been some settlement at the eastern end of the viaduct that needed attention.
Richard Palmer, the FYN Secretary, wrote on 14th November, 1890 to the Board of Trade informing them of alterations at Carisbrooke and Yarmouth. Major General Hutchinson made a visit a month later when he looked at Newport viaduct as well as the two stations. He was satisfied with the viaduct and recommended that the Board of Trade confirm their authority to open the railway for passenger traffic 17 months after passenger trains actually began running. At Carisbrooke and Yarmouth the original lever frames had been replaced by others containing nine levers controlling the points and signals. The Inspector was not enamoured with the quality of the work and insisted on changes in the locking arrangements; it seems that one of Mr Jackson's men had connected up the levers because Messrs Stevens who installed the lever frames had departed from the scene because no-one paid their bill! Major Hutchinson also asked for check rails on the sharp curves at the ends of the loops, nameboards and fencing along the rear of the platforms. There was no money to pay for the work so the loops remained out of use.
According to a press report dated 25th January 1890, "The high winds of Friday blew down the engine shed at Freshwater Station, a structure of wood and corrugated iron about 40 ft long and 20 ft wide."
On 19th August, 1890 a train collided with and destroyed a platelayers trolley near Great Park Bridge causing damage to the engine. An identical collision at the same spot took place on 18th March, 1891. After a derailment near Newport, the IWC wrote that '. . . unless the Central Coy is authorised to repair the Permanent Way at the expense of the Freshwater Company, the Central Coy will stop working the line on the 1st November'. In a rare concession, the IWC Board decided to defer sending the bill when they heard that the FYN was putting its line in order. Certainly the condition of the railway left something to be desired as on 23rd August Newport magistrates ordered the company to put Park Lane bridge and its approaches in repair before 30th September; the FYN had to comply.
On 27th June, 1892 the IWC Board again had cause to discuss affairs at Freshwater; letters were sent asking that the water tank be connected to the mains supply and a goods shed provided. In August the IWC Manager reported that a siding to Lee brickworks, about half a mile east of Hill Place level crossing, had 'not been properly connected' to the main line by Jackson's men. The IWC promptly threatened to disconnect the siding but, after the usual exchange of correspondence, Mr Simmons was authorised to fit an Annett's lock so that it complied with Board of Trade requirements and charge the bill to the FYN. Henry Jackson subsequently wrote to the FYN Board taking the credit for completing Wellow siding.
On 2nd June, 1891 permission was given to the local water company to lay a water main along the line from Freshwater to Yarmouth in order to provide the latter with water - it was not clear whether Yarmouth station got its supply at this

time. There had been repeated complaints that sea water was polluting a well that supplied water to locomotives at Freshwater, but the FYN Board was reluctant to have the water tower connected to the mains supply. Inevitably the FYN refused to pay the bills which were sent to the IWC. There was the usual exchange of letters and then the IWC deducted the bills from FYN receipts - this exercise in brinkmanship happened time and time again. In October 1892 the FYN Secretary was told that a £79 9s. bill for chalk ballast supplied to Henry Jackson had to be paid - an IWC Director had supplied the ballast. A derailment of two coal trucks near Yarmouth on 5th October prompted Henry Jackson to write:

> *181 Queen Victoria Street, October 7th 1892*
> Dear Sir,
> I enclose you a copy of a letter I have received from my Agent this morning at Freshwater.
> As the 11.23 am train was going from Newport to Freshwater it had two trucks of Coal on the Carriages - when they got to Thorley one of them jumped off the road and pulled off the other. It was on a straight road and the road was in good order. Mr Simmons was there with some men and helped to put the road right. There was no one hurt, it cut up about 200 Sleepers. The Passengers were not delayed long because Mr Simmons brought out another train to take them on to Newport. There must have been something the matter with the truck for it mounted the rail in the straight road.
> I do not think it right to put Coal Trucks on a Passenger train. This ought to be seen into.
> Yours faithfully,
> (signed) Henry Jackson

The FYN Board had long since discovered that it was extremely difficult to get Henry Jackson to do anything beyond the most basic maintenance. He so bled the FYN of money that nothing was left for even the most minor improvement. Typical was a letter from a Mr Cole asking for help in making up a new road near Yarmouth station by providing chalk or gravel or both; the Board could only reply that they possessed neither and were in no position to buy any. In December 1892 a letter was received complaining about the unsanitary state of a house at St Cross, Newport occupied by a Mr Fallick. This sparked off a discussion whether this man paid any rent and it was decided to ask the Engineer to report on the collection of rents for houses owned by the company and what vacant land was available for disposal. This was not an easy matter as various landowners had not been paid and there were disputes about the ownership of properties at St Cross and Gunville.

Mr Lidstone's report in March 1893 mentioned that the loops at Carisbrooke and Yarmouth were incomplete. This prompted the FYN Board to write to Stevens & Co. asking them to complete the signalling to the satisfaction of the Board of Trade. There was no response because their previous bill had still not been paid. After the IWC wrote asking for additional coal stores at Freshwater Henry Jackson was prevailed upon to complete the stores in exchange for more debentures. The FYN Board signed up the first tenant on 17th May, 1893 but a letter from the IWC then reminded the Directors that an approach road and siding were needed; Jackson finally reported completion on 27th June. It was probably with relief to all concerned when the appointment of the FYN Receiver in August 1893 was reported.

Chapter Six

The Board of Trade step in

Normally the appointment of a Receiver would be followed by a cessation of meetings of the Board. In the case of the FYN this did not happen and a certain amount of business was carried out. On one occasion an offer of £400 was accepted from Henry Jackson for a parcel of land at Gunville but the transaction could not be carried through because '. . . the occupiers refuse to acknowledge the Company's right to the land'. This and a number of disputes involving rent supposedly owed to the company were referred to the Receiver.

The FYN continued to receive writs from landowners who were owed money but each was stubbornly defended by the company's Solicitors Booty & Bayliffe; they themselves asked for a lien on the surplus lands to cover their costs. Not all were successfully fended off as on 5th December, 1893 the Board agreed to pay £97 1s. 9d. to a Mrs Harvey because, according to a recent court decision, '. . . the landowner can seize the land and take up the rails and stop the traffic'!

Local newspapers continued to report a catalogue of minor derailments and accidents. One such occurrence took place on 16th September, 1894:

> Passengers by the last train from Freshwater on Sunday evening had an unpleasant and rather alarming experience. Nearing Carisbrooke Station shortly after 8.00 pm, instead of keeping to the main line, the train ran into the siding, crashing into five trucks of chalk standing there. The report of the collision could be heard a good distance around, and a number of people were quickly attracted to the scene of the accident . . .
> Mr EWH, a young man acting in place of the regular Carisbrooke Station Master who was sick, said he was perfectly certain the points were all right before he left the signal box to book passengers. He alleged someone must have tampered with the points during his absence from the signal box.

The staff were employed by the IWC so it had to find £20 to compensate a passenger and, more galling, replace two of Mr Jackson's ballast wagons 'at a cost not exceeding £10 each' - the IWC accounts recorded they actually cost £18. Somehow the accident escaped the attentions of the Board of Trade but the company was not so fortunate the next time. Mr William Bartlett, a well-known local letter writer, wrote to the Board of Trade enclosing a cutting from the *Isle of Wight County Press* about an accident on 30th March:

> On Saturday afternoon a somewhat alarming accident occurred to the Freshwater train. Soon after leaving the Newport station the front wheels of the first carriage ran off the line, and in this condition the train made its way over the Towngate viaduct to the Petticoat lane level crossing before being pulled up. The permanent way was damaged by the stray wheels, and some of the passengers were somewhat shaken. To make matters worse the train, which should have started at 1 pm, was an hour late in starting owing to a mishap on the Sandown line, and it was past 3 o'clock before the hapless locomotive got right away.

The 1.00 pm train had been delayed by an hour owing to the failure of an engine on the Sandown line 'from where the train came'. Locomotive No. 5

running chimney first and a five-coach train (plus a brake van) crossed Newport viaduct at about 12-15 mph but when it neared Petticoat crossing the first carriage was noticed to be off the rails. There was minor damage to the permanent way and a carriage suffered two broken leading springs and a right-hand carriage stay. Damage to the permanent way was described as trifling.

No reports concerning the accident had been received from either the IWC or FYN so the Board of Trade wrote asking for one. On 26th April, 1895 Mr Beard, the IWC Secretary replied that the accident was '. . . of so slight a character that being much pressed for work, our Manager forgot to report it to me'. Major Addison promptly made his way to the Island. Inevitably his enquiry focused on the permanent way. The Inspector heard evidence from the locomotive driver, Thomas Kemp, who made the telling comment 'I consider the road from Newport to Carisbrooke was not in good order, as the engine lurched a good deal at all times when running over it'. Charles Drower, the ganger on the three mile section from Newport to Park Bridge, stated that on 28th March he had found the line to be wide of gauge in several places, the worst being 1¼ in. and those more than ½ in. out of gauge were put right. He added 'The rails on which the run-off occurred were one inch out of gauge both on Tuesday and Thursday, but as they had not moved during that time I did nothing on the latter date'. George Drower's evidence read:

> I am permanent way inspector from Newport to Freshwater, employed by Mr Jackson, who is in charge of the line under the Receiver of the Newport-Freshwater Railway Company. I went over the road from Newport to Carisbrooke on the 26th with the ganger. We did not try the gauge. I remarked that some of the sleepers close to where the accident occurred were getting rotten, but that they need not be taken out for a few days. I was aware that the gauge was about 1 inch wide, but so long as it got no worse I did not attach much importance to that. It is impossible at present to keep the sharp curves of this line right to gauge, and to enable this to be done new sleepers and additional fang bolts are needed . . . During the last six months we have constructed side drains to drain the formation, and have put down a large amount of hard chalk ballast to improve the line, and in the last 12 months about 5,000 new sleepers have been used.

Major Addison concluded that the locomotive spread the track allowing the carriage to drop off the rails. He added:

> The evidence of the permanent way inspector and the ganger is of a somewhat startling nature, and a heavy responsibility will rest upon all concerned if the admitted defects are not remedied, and a very different standard of maintenance ensured in the future.

To make matters worse Major Addison inspected the railway to see if the provisions of the Regulation of Railways Act had been complied with - they had not. The IWC had undertaken to work the railway by train staff and ticket combined with absolute block telegraph system but the block instruments had got out of repair and the telegraph line connecting the block sections was unworkable. On 21st May, 1895 Major Addison wrote about the IWC's undertaking to work the railway in a safe manner:

THE BOARD OF TRADE STEP IN 57

This, it must be admitted, is a very serious state of affairs. An Undertaking to work a Railway in a definite way, entered into, signed and sealed by the responsible officers has hitherto been regarded as binding upon all concerned. If the Board of Trade cannot rely upon such an Undertaking being acted up to, the document is not worth ink and paper, and supervision over the safety of the travelling public is impossible.

There followed a flurry of letters from the IWC denying responsibility and from the FYN Receiver stating that he would have to apply to the courts for permission to spend money on improvements. In June 1895 Major Addison paid another visit when he reported that the crossing loops at Carisbrooke and Yarmouth were out of use (they had never been completed), abutments at the western end of Calbourne viaduct had been strengthened but the ballast was poor and in short supply whilst the sleepers were far from satisfactory. Major Addison concluded 'it is evident that a good deal remains to be done before the condition of the Railway can be considered at all satisfactory'.

In August 1895 the Board of Trade were informed that the block instruments were once again in use. After a further inspection on 12th September Major Addison wrote, to quote a note on the file, 'a strong report'. Block working had been re-established but several signals were not in working order, nothing had been done about Calbourne viaduct nor the crossing loops at Carisbrooke and Yarmouth. The sharp curves still lacked gauge ties:

> I am aware that there are great difficulties in obtaining money for work upon the Newport-Freshwater line but money *must* be expended if the line is to remain open for traffic. There are iron girders which will rapidly deteriorate if they are not maintained properly, being now greatly in want of paint; similarly, a little money spent on the locking frames in some of the Cabins will save a much larger expenditure at no distant date.

There was a real fear that the Board of Trade would order a cessation of services. Again the Central's Secretary sent a letter at the instruction of his Board denying responsibility for the maintenance of the line. Major Addison commented:

> The responsibility for the maintenance of the permanent way rests upon the Receiver of the Freshwater Railway. The Central Co. can, I think, only be held accountable for the mode of working the line: they have undertaken to work the line with train staff and ticket combined with Absolute Block system and certain signals are then of course indispensable. The Freshwater Coy have to pay for keeping those signals in order, but when they neglect them and they become unworkable the Central Coy is no longer in a position to comply with the Undertaking they entered into and they cannot wash their hands of all responsibility in the matter.

The FYN Receiver wrote to the Board of Trade on 4th November, 1895. The contractor had reported the arrival of 3,000 additional sleepers, 984 had been laid with new fang bolts &c. and 275 tie rods had been fixed on the worst of the curves. 'The block and telephone system has been placed in perfect working order. The curve at Newport Viaduct where the accident occurred has been put into gauge and properly strengthened with new sleepers, fang bolts, etc. The other works are being proceeded with as fast as the money comes in'. On 4th May, 1896 he wrote that the work was proceeding as fast as money allowed and the railway's whole income was being spent on the permanent way. This was with some truth as in January 1896 the IWC Board was told that, because of increased payments to Jackson for his men's wages, the FYN owed the Central £175 for the half-year!

On 3rd June, 1896 the Board of Trade was informed that changes were afoot in the management of the railway. George Perks wrote that his client Edwin Jones had gained the sanction of the High Court of Justice to replace the Hon. Ashley Ponsonby with George F. Colman, Manager and Secretary of the West Lancashire Railway. Mr Colman was appointed on 27th May; he was an experienced railwayman and precisely the right person for the task in front of him.

Immediately prior to his formal appointment Mr Colman visited the Island to make arrangements to put the railway into an efficient state before the summer season. One of his first acts was to sack Henry Jackson who had so lamentably failed to keep the railway in a satisfactory condition. He concluded a fresh working agreement with the IWC as the FYN Board had 12 months earlier given notice to terminate the existing one on 19th July, 1896 'in order that better terms may be made'. No improved terms were forthcoming and an agreement signed on 15th July repeated the previous wording with an added clause giving the IWC the right to cease working the line if it was not improved to the satisfaction of the Board of Trade and the Central's Engineer. To help the FYN pay for improvements the IWC agreed to pay £180 per month during the period of the agreement, the six months ending 31st December, 1896. Meanwhile, the IWC Board did its best to distance itself from the FYN and decided that tickets issued at Freshwater and Newport would henceforth bear only the title Freshwater, Yarmouth & Newport Ry.

Mr Colman reported to the FYN Board on 27th August, 1896 that he had carried out further work in order to comply with Board of Trade requirements. George Perks, newly appointed as solicitor to the company, listed the improvements in a letter to the Board of Trade on 8th October:

1. To correct gauge widening on curves 1,500 new tie rods had been put in.
2. Distant signals were being put into working condition and orders had been given for them to be regularly lit.
3. The two viaducts at Calbourne and Newport were being painted and the work would be finished that month.
4. The abutment at the west end of Calbourne Viaduct had been attended to; although not mentioned in the letter, a nearby earth slip was also put right.
5. The permanent way had been well ballasted and new sleepers put in where necessary.

Col Addison made another inspection in December when he found that the working of the distant signals were 'not all that could be desired' even though they were seldom if ever pulled off for a train. He had most to say about the loop roads at Carisbrooke and Yarmouth where the points remained spiked out of use and the connections to the signal box disconnected. Col Addison repeated that the loops should be brought into full use by reconnecting the points and modifying the interlocking as recommended in 1890, convert the loops into goods sidings or remove them altogether. On 5th January, 1897 Mr

THE BOARD OF TRADE STEP IN 59

Colman wrote to inform the Board of Trade that the crossing loops were ready for inspection. The IWC did not wait for this to take place and began using them immediately. Yarmouth parish council complained about the foot crossing between the platforms but the IWC refused a request that trains use the main platform claiming that the station was being worked in accordance with Board of Trade instructions. Col Addison wrote on 5th April that the arrangements were satisfactory at Carisbrooke but not at Yarmouth where check rails on the sharp curves had still not been fitted; the Board of Trade was also concerned that the platforms were not opposite each other and might present a danger to passengers. Permission to use the loop road was eventually given but Yarmouth never became a crossing point because the station was not a block post; the single line sections became Newport to Carisbrooke, Carisbrooke to Ningwood and Ningwood to Freshwater.

The working agreement signed in July 1896 was temporary as it obliged the FYN to bring its railway up to a satisfactory standard and since this had been achieved Charles Conacher, who had replaced Mr Simmons as IWC Manager, recommended a renewal for a period of 14 years. Naturally the IWC insisted that a schedule be attached to the agreement repeating the expectation that the FYN complete the loops at Carisbrooke and Yarmouth, a new approach road at Carisbrooke and various additions at Freshwater including a turntable, a 30 ft by 20 ft corrugated iron goods shed and water crane. Again the FYN did not comply with all these requirements.

The need for a more direct approach road from the village to the station at Carisbrooke was raised by Mr Perks at a Board meeting on 9th December, 1896. The local landowner had not been paid for land taken by the railway and approach road so was reluctant to co-operate further. It did not help that the new approach road would have passed through the churchyard. Eventually it proved cheaper to settle with the landowner and give up the idea of a direct approach to the station.

The company had also failed to settle a dispute with Sir John Stephen Barrington Simeon concerning his station at Watchingwell. The FYN had signed an agreement with Simeon on 27th April, 1887 in which the railway undertook to construct a level crossing adjoining Watchingwell farm house at the end of a lane leading from Great Park, and a station with a platform and cottage containing a waiting room, etc. for the use of Sir Barrington Simeon, his family, staff and anyone having business with him. The company was obliged to supply an attendant for the station and within three months construct a siding. The agreement also provided that 'such station shall not be used as a public station . . . and the Company shall at all times hereafter cause such station . . . to be kept in good repair and condition and cause all ordinary passenger trains to stop at such platform . . . on receiving reasonable notice'.

The existence of a station at Watchingwell was mentioned by the Board of Trade Inspector in May 1889 but it is thought little more than the platform had been built at that time. For some unknown reason a public station was proposed so the Inspector called for the provision of proper signalling - neither the signalling nor the station were completed. Simeon took the company to court and this led to a second agreement signed on 26th August, 1892. The FYN paid

£150 for permission to postpone completion of the station until 20th January, 1897 but had to provide the siding within six months. Although supposedly under construction during 1893 the siding was not finished and Sir Barrington Simeon issued a writ for breach of contract.

It seems that the existence of the agreement and the writ were unknown to the Manager, George Colman, and to the company's solicitor, George Perks. Mr Perks reported to the Board of 2nd March, 1897 that it was not until the working agreement with the IWC had been settled that he received a letter from Simeon's solicitors reminding him of the undertaking. He was somewhat peeved that neither Mr Palmer, the FYN Secretary, nor the IWC told him about the matter even though they knew about it!

Mr Perks approached the Board of Trade that month for advice on the facilities to be provided bearing in mind that the station was to be a private one. It was agreed that normal Board of Trade requirements as regards platforms, buildings and signals could be dispensed with.

However, it was one thing to build a station but quite another to get the IWC to stop trains there. After an exchange of letters an agreement between the FYN and IWC was signed on 5th May, 1897 under which the Central agreed to stop trains at Watchingwell from 8th May onwards when required. The Central extracted 1s. on each occasion and the wages of the crossing keeper at Watchingwell were deducted from the Freshwater company's share of traffic receipts - this cost the FYN upwards of £80 a year. Income from traffic to and from the station was divisible in the same manner as other traffic on the line. Sir Barrington Simeon had to agree the designs for the station but this seems to have been a relatively simple matter. Apart from a short platform the company constructed an attractive but small single-storey building behind which was a yard for road vehicles that also served a siding. According to a drawing prepared by a local surveyor, a two-lever ground frame was placed at the Freshwater end of the platform to operate a signal carrying arms in each direction that could be placed at danger when required - a second ground frame controlled access to the siding. On 24th November Lt Col Addison wrote that he had made an inspection of the completed siding and approved its use.

The original agreement with Sir Richard Simeon was one of several that had been negotiated with landowners as a way of securing land for the railway without having to pay for it. However, as the Southern Railway discovered, often land was not actually conveyed to the railway; typical was an 1891 agreement with Mr Taunton, owner of Lee brickworks near Wellow, in which the company agreed to pay for a siding to his brickworks in return for permission to build the line across his land. Elsewhere, William Jackson had bought some small plots in the years 1887 to 1889 but most of the land had not been paid for. All through the 1890s successive managements tried to regularise land ownership, a task that Mr Perks had been forced to take on. In 1902 he informed the Board that the purchase of all the land on which the railway ran had finally been completed.

Chapter Seven

A Change of Owners
1893 to 1905

If the debenture holders thought that the appointment of a Receiver in 1893 would improve matters they were sadly disappointed. After 2½ years a circular was sent to shareholders:

> Finding the line was in such a bad state of repair that it was highly probable that the Board of Trade would stop the running of trains, and having waited nearly two and a half years and there being no prospect of any interest being paid, the Debenture Holders became dissatisfied with the way in which the affairs of the Company were being conducted and decided to present a Bill to Parliament asking that the Board of Directors be reconstructed in such a way as to give them representation . . .

The Bill created a new Board with five Directors elected by the different classes of stockholders; each Director had to possess a minimum of £5,000 of stock. The proportion of representation would change if and when the arrears of interest was paid. The Receiver and Manager appointed by the High Court would be discharged immediately the Board was in place. The Bill also proposed to issue 4 per cent debenture stock to the value of £35,000 being £20,000 to pay the costs of the Act, landowners' claims, work required by the Board of Trade and any improvements to passenger and goods accommodation. The remaining £15,000 was for the purchase or hire of locomotives and rolling stock and buildings to house them whenever the working agreement came to an end. Debenture holders were barred from taking the company to court for enforcement of interest payments for five years.

On 20th July, 1896 the Bill became law; it was followed by a series of meetings when the following were elected:

Ordinary stockholders	1 Director	George Hogan
Preference stockholders	1 Director	George H. Sawyer
First debenture holders	2 Directors	Edwin Jones and William Cotterill
Second debenture holders	1 Director	William E. Jones

The first meeting of the new Board took place on 25th August, 1896 at the premises of Mr Perks, solicitor to Edwin Jones, at 9 Clements Lane, City of London. Previously meetings had been generally held at the address of the Secretary Richard Palmer at 17 Great George Street, Westminster. William Cotterill was elected Chairman and the Board then got down to business. Arrangements were made to issue the accounts for the 3½ year period to 30th June, 1896 and a half-yearly meeting was called for 4th September. The accounts made abysmal reading because Henry Jackson's bills for staff and permanent way repairs had eaten up virtually all the company's meagre income.

Freshwater, Yarmouth & Newport Railway
Timetable July - August 1894 until further notice

WEEKDAYS

		G	H	M		M		S		M	N S	S
Newport	Dep.	7.40	9.2	11.9	1.0	3.5	4.15	5.15	6.23		8.51	8.55
Carisbrooke	Dep.	7.45	9.7	-	1.4	3.10	4.21	5.21	6.29		A	-
Calbourne & Shalfleet	Dep.	7.57	9.19	11.24	1.15	3.22	4.33	5.33	A		A	9.11
Ningwood	Dep.	8.1	9.23	11.29	1.20	3.26	4.39	5.39	A		A	9.17
Yarmouth	Dep.	8.9	9.31	11.37	1.27	3.34	4.47		6.49		9.17	9.28
Freshwater	Arr.	8.15	9.37	11.42	1.33	3.39	4.52		6.57		9.25	9.33

		G		M		M		S		M		
Freshwater	Dep.	8.20	9.42	12.20	2.20	4.25		5.55	7.0		9.30	
Yarmouth	Dep.	8.25	9.47	12.25	2.25	4.30		6.0	7.5		9.35	
Ningwood	Dep.	8.33	9.55	12.33	2.34	4.39	5.55	-	A		9.43	
Calbourne & Shalfleet	Dep.	8.38	10.0	12.38	2.39	4.44	6.0	-	A		9.48	
Carisbooke	Dep.	8.48	10.10	12.48	2.51	4.56	-	-	7.28		H	
Newport	Arr.	8.55	10.17	12.55	2.58	5.3	6.16	6.23	7.34		10.3	

SUNDAYS

		H					
Newport	Dep.	11.38	2.50	6.57			
Carisbrooke	Dep.	11.44	2.56	7.3			
Calbourne & Shalfleet	Dep.	11.54	3.6	7.14			
Ningwood	Dep.	11.58	3.10	7.20			
Yarmouth	Dep.	12.6	3.18	7.28			
Freshwater	Arr.	12.12	3.24	7.32			

		H					
Freshwater	Dep.	8.40	2.5	3.45	7.39		
Yarmouth	Dep.	8.45	2.10	3.50	7.44		
Ningwood	Dep.	8.53	2.18	3.58	7.52		
Calbourne & Shalfleet	Dep.	8.58	2.23	4.2	7.57		
Carisbooke	Dep.	9.8	2.33	4.12	8.7		
Newport	Arr.	9.14	2.39	4.18	8.13		

A = calls by request. G = "Government" train. H = Carries first and third class, all other trains carry first and second. M = Mixed train. NS = Not Saturdays. S = Saturdays only.

Years 1 Jan. 1893 to 30 June 1896	Traffic receipts	Amount due to FYN	Permanent Way etc. costs	Profit	Capital expenditure
	£ s. d.	£ s. d.	£ s. d.	£ s. d.	£ s. d.
1893-1896	23,712 2 8	13,041 13 4	7,440 11 4	159 6 9	12,277 18 2

The election of George Hogan to the Board maintained some continuity with the previous regime and he proved useful in clarifying 'queries in the Balance sheet'. At the next meeting on 21st October, 1896 the Board heard that Mr Bayliffe had expressed disappointment that Mr Perks had been appointed solicitor in his place. Mr Perks offered to resign but the Board resolved '... that the appointment of Mr Perks as Solicitor to the Company made at the previous meeting be confirmed'. George Sawyer bought off the executors of Clement Crowther by acquiring £21,870 of preferred ordinary stock, £20,000 of deferred ordinary stock and £3,930 of 5 per cent perpetual debenture stock.

Messrs Booty and Bayliffe were not so easily dispensed with as they submitted bills totalling £5,907 that 'former Officials of the Company' had omitted to mention. The solicitor was instructed to seek persons willing to take up £20,000 capital authorised in the 1896 Act, a sum he reported would not be easy to raise. After some delay and an inspection of the line by a representative of investors the 1896 'A' perpetual debenture stock paying interest at 3½ per cent per annum was issued to:

	£	s.	d.
The executors of T. Chamberlayne for land in the Carisbrooke area	2,500	0	0
Booty & Bayliffe in part payment of their bills	1,250	0	0
Rock Assurance Company, investors	13,333	6	8
Edwin Jones	2,000	0	0

The stock was issued at 80 per cent of its face value so only £10,666 13s. 4d. and £1,600 respectively in cash was actually handed over. The FYN had to take out insurance against a failure to pay interest on the new stock and the Rock Assurance Company insisted on an undertaking from the executors of Mr Crowther that they would not take any action against the company for repayment of Lloyds Bonds in their possession. In exchange the FYN agreed immediately to hand Mr Crowther's executors £1,000, issue them with £3,000 'B' debenture stock and pay the remaining £1,000 owed when the sale of the company's surplus land was completed. Booty & Bayliffe also received £1,877 in 'B' debenture stock for the balance of their debt.

Not all creditors were treated so generously. On 2nd March, 1897 it came to light that the Secretary Mr Palmer was also Secretary to the Properties Securities Company. The properties company had claimed £300 compensation for losses it allegedly incurred when the FYN failed to buy certain property on the route of the Totland Bay extension. Since the land had originally cost £100 the FYN Board decided to fight the claim. Mr Palmer had clearly failed to tell the Board about all the company's liabilities and at the next Board meeting it was resolved that 'in view of the present condition of the company it would be desirable for Mr Palmer to send in his resignation . . .'. Mr Palmer was 'requested' to write up the company's books and after a brief interlude when Mr Colman acted as

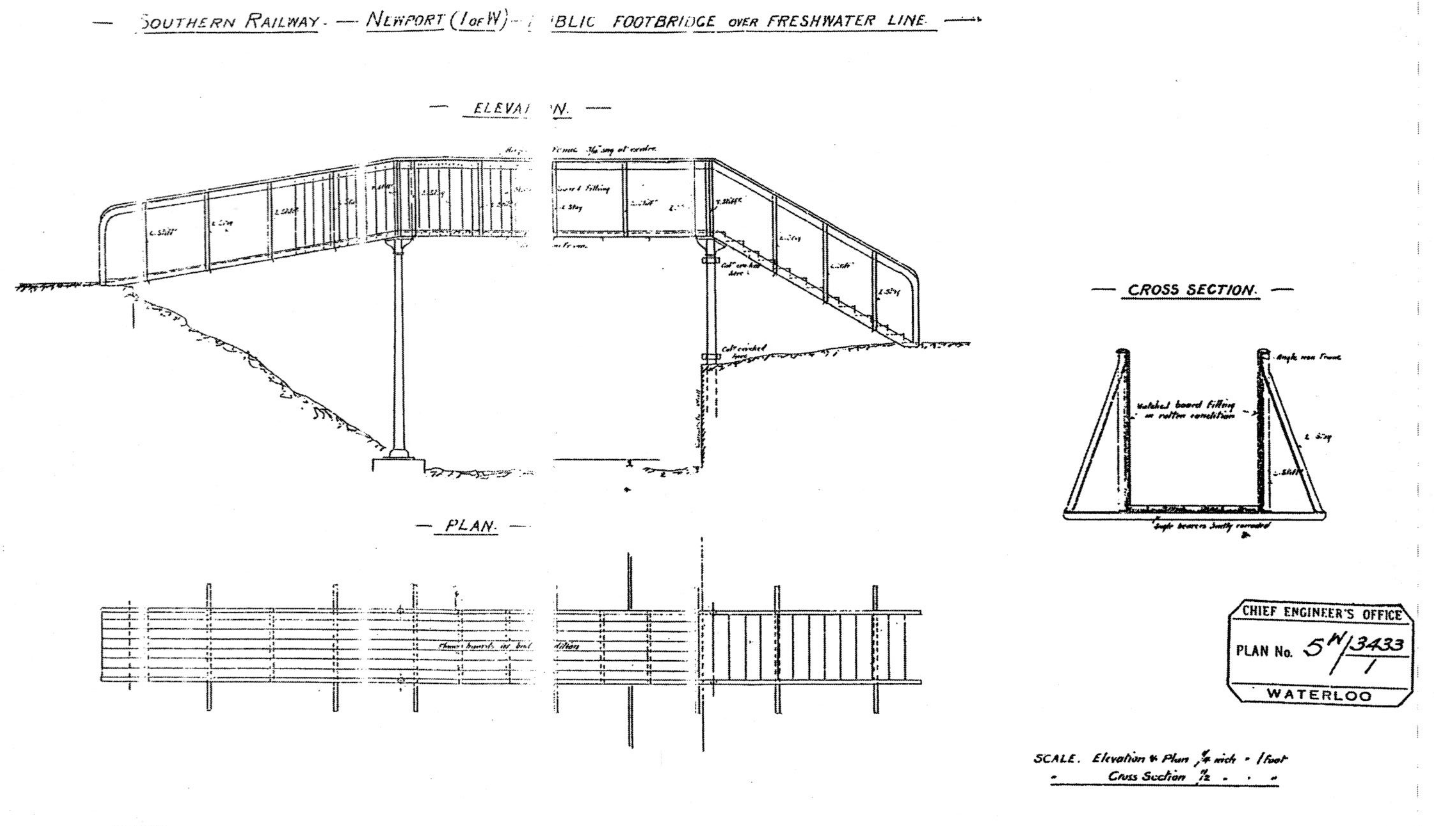

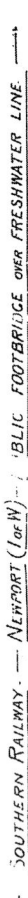

Drawing of the footbridge across the railway at Newport as rebuilt in 1898.

A CHANGE OF OWNERS, 1893 TO 1905

Secretary, Samuel Peck took over on a salary of £100 per annum. The dispute with the properties company was not mentioned again so presumably the solicitor saw them off!

Negotiations also reopened with another long-suffering creditor. Col Walker had almost given up seeing the return of £2,000 he had loaned in 1879 for the Parliamentary deposit and on 28th April, 1897 agreed to accept £1,000 in settlement; £500 was paid immediately but it was January 1899 before he received the balance.

For the first time the FYN possessed a manager in the shape of George Colman who understood how a railway functioned and had the interests of the company at heart. The Board was anxious to retain Mr Colman's services when his period as Receiver came to an end and resolved that he be paid a salary of £250 a year. Although the court discharged the Receiver on 27th May, 1897 the Board heard on 25th October that Mr Colman was going to work in Brazil - he left soon afterwards. The departure of Mr Colman was followed by William Cotterill, the FYN Chairman, but not in quite the same way. On 21st December the Board asked that he defer his retirement but by the date of the next Board meeting on 29th April, 1898 he had died. C.M. Cotterill was elected a Director and Edwin Jones became Chairman.

The more businesslike approach to the problems rubbed off on the IWC. Unfortunately, its Manager, Charles Conacher, was never given the freedom of action that was the norm for managers of other railways and the attitude of his Board continued to sour relations between the two companies. Typical was a proposal in April 1897 to carry mail to Freshwater by running an early morning train from Cowes in connection with the first boat from Southampton; the IWC Board refused because staff already worked long hours and there was no money to take on additional men. During the summer Mr Conacher suggested the introduction of 'omnibus communication between Yarmouth Station and Pier'; the Central Board was well used to such proposals and deferred a decision until the following year by which time the whole idea had been forgotten! This short-sighted decision had predictable consequences because locals put on their own horse-drawn conveyances between the pier and station, later running also to Freshwater, Totland and Newport.

The financial position had improved somewhat by 21st December, 1897 when the Board resolved to pay 1 per cent on the 5 per cent debenture stock on 1st January, 1898 in addition to the 3½ per cent stock; this unusually generous decision was rescinded at the next meeting when the 1 per cent was halved. The Directors clearly believed they should receive some reward for their efforts and asked shareholders to consider payment of Directors fees - they refused.

In 1898 Mr Fisk asked for the provision of a coal store at Calbourne; it was evidently built as several years later there was mention of its repair. A replacement footbridge across the railway at Newport was put in the following year. It took somewhat longer to provide a private siding for a Mr Manning at Gunville where there had been a brickworks since 1850. Regarded as the most important of the many brickworks along the Freshwater line, its chimney was a prominent local landmark for many years. The siding was said to have been ready for use in November 1899 but Conacher wanted the Board of Trade

Inspector to delay his visit until another siding elsewhere on the IWC was ready - as railway companies had to pay for inspections he was clearly trying to save the IWC some money. On 1st June, 1900 Lt Col Von Donop sanctioned the siding's use subject to an undertaking that the locomotive be at the lower end of the train because it joined the main line on a 1 in 66 gradient.

A derailment at Wellow on 20th September, 1898 generated a predictable exchange of correspondence. The FYN claimed £80 for permanent way repairs, the IWC responded by offering £21 10s. 3d. to which the FYN replied with a £75 claim and a report from its Engineer, Mr Lidstone. The Central duly obtained a report from the Brighton company's Engineer and when their revised offer of £25 was refused the two companies reached an impasse. The Central was equally adept at passing on responsibility for any matter that required expenditure. In February 1899 a claim for compensation was referred to the FYN with the allegation that the poor state of the fencing near Yarmouth resulted in the deaths of 11 sheep belonging to John Mills. A request to the IWC from the vicar of Calbourne for additional covered passenger accommodation met with the same response.

Business was evidently good enough for the LBSCR to open a booking and enquiry office at Freshwater Bay. Pickfords established an agency at Freshwater three years later and shortly afterwards the LSWR transferred its Freshwater parcels traffic to the Lymington-Yarmouth route, fortunately without much loss of income to the FYN. Most of the local coal merchants in the Freshwater and Yarmouth areas were individuals who usually owned no more than a single horse and cart. This changed in the early years of the new century when larger firms began extending their business into West Wight, a change evident throughout the Island. Messrs Bradbury of Southampton began supplying coal but after the IWC refused to reduce its carriage rates there was a hiatus until the FYN gave the firm free use of stacking grounds at its stations and so kept the traffic on the railway.

If the FYN Board considered its railway to be in a satisfactory state they did not take the same view of the service provided by the IWC. In July 1900 the FYN Secretary wrote complaining about the condition of the rolling stock used on the Freshwater line; trains had just begun running to Ventnor and the Central was using its best stock on that route. Later that year the Secretary had cause to complain about the deletion of certain early morning trains from the timetable.

In June 1900 George Sawyer resigned from the Board and was replaced by Harry Silk. The Directors were told that the balance of the 3½ per cent pre-debenture stock had been issued to Mr Chamberlayne's trustees (the landowner at Carisbrooke) in settlement of rent and interest owed. By then all other routine matters were being set aside whilst the Board awaited the outcome of discussions concerning a proposal to sell the railway. At a special meeting of the Board in October it was resolved to accept an offer of £90,000. To regularise capital in advance of the sale a Bill was placed before Parliament applying for authority to convert the arrears of interest into 5 per cent debenture stock. The Bill became law in August but its provisions were never implemented. The company's capital then stood at:

	Authorised Stock or shares	Loans	Created and issued Stock or shares	Type	Loans	rate
	£	£	£		£	%
1880 Act	100,000	33,300	100,000	Ordinary	33,300	5
1883 Act	42,000	14,000	42,000	5% Preference	14,000	5
1889 Act	36,000	12,000	-		-	
1891 Act	-	20,000	-		24,077 *	5
1896 Act	-	35,000	-		20,000	3½

The £100,000 ordinary stock had been converted after issue to £42,008 Preferred 6 per cent ordinary stock and £50,078 Deferred ordinary stock. By 1st January, 1901 the two classes of debenture holder were owed £16,318 10s. 0d. and £2,303 17s. 0d. respectively.

Management of the railway devolved on the Secretary. Mr Peck made numerous visits to the Isle of Wight where he walked the line with the permanent way inspector Mr Drower. At intervals C.R. Walker, a qualified engineer, was asked to inspect the line. The permanent way men received regular supplies of sleepers and rail fixings and on one occasion painting of the buildings was put out to a gang supervised by Mr Drower.

A serious accident at Yarmouth on 5th February, 1901 came to the attention of the Board of Trade. The conditional goods from Newport to Freshwater was being shunted at 9.25 am when the station master was seriously injured - a wagon ran over his right leg. The Central management claimed that the accident was his fault because he had been trying to couple wagons before the train had come to a halt. The IWC did not use coupling poles because most of the goods stock had old fashioned D shackle and pin couplings that were too stiff for the coupling poles; the Board of Trade Inspector recommended their replacement.

The Board of Trade might have been equally concerned had they heard about a derailment on 8th June, 1901 at Wellow involving the Central's newest locomotive No. 8; delivered in May 1898 it had been in traffic almost continuously since then. Refusing to believe that the locomotive might be at fault the IWC alleged that the permanent way was in poor condition; the FYN complained about the speed of the Central company's locomotives and sent a bill for alleged damage to the permanent way caused by the locomotive at Hare Lane on the following day 9th June. The predictable stalemate was reached when the Central attempted to keep quiet the admission that the locomotive's worn tyres had contributed to the incident. After this exchange, the Minutes fail to record any disputes between the two companies for over a year. That silence was broken in June 1903 by an accident at Petticoat Lane crossing which resulted in the death of the lady keeper, the only known fatality on the line; the Central contributed to funeral costs but denied any liability and surprisingly the matter did not come to the attention of the Board of Trade.

The sale dragged on through 1901 apparently because the buyers were reluctant to go ahead until their scheme for the Solent tunnel was further advanced. Tired of the delays, in November the FYN Board decided to seek the views of shareholders. The following month the *Isle of Wight Observer* reported the issue of a circular announcing a proposal to sell the undertaking for £85,000

* Raised £18,503 in cash.

The Freshwater, Yarmouth & Newport Railway Co.

Particulars of the cost of purchase of lands by the Company so far as can be ascertained from the Conveyances in the Company's possession.

	Date of Conveyance	Parish	Area A. R. P.	Purchased from	Amount of purchase price £. s. d.
1.	16 Nov. 1893	Freshwater	5. 1. 4	G. A. Jones	658.2.6
2.	15 April 1902	Freshwater} Thorley} Yarmouth &} Shalfleet}	13.3.9½	The Rt. Hon Wm. Frederick Baron Heytesbury & others	1,750.0.0
3.	22 June 1898	Calbourne} Shalfleet} St Nicholas &} Carisbrooke}	16. 2. 20	C. A Whitmore & others	2,500.0.0
4.	31 Dec. 1886	Shalfleet	2. 0. 29	Wm. Ash & others	249.10.0
5.	31 March 1887	ditto	3. 19	F. W Popham & others	£100.0.0
6.	7 Dec. 1887	ditto	1. 0. 13	James Eldridge & others	£120.0.0
7.	28 Aug. 1888	ditto	3. 0. 18	E. G. Ward	375.0.0
8.	18 Jan. 1889	ditto	21	Wm. Chessell & others	50.0.0
9.	19 June 1888	Carisbrooke	3. 3. 28	Henry Chessell	325.0.0
10.	26 June 1889	ditto	1. 34	J. P. Mew & another	250.0.0
11.	29 Aug. 1889	ditto	1. 2. 16	Rev Wm. Rowe & others	210.0.0
12.	6 Dec. 1893	ditto		Mrs M. N. Harvey	362.0.0
13.	11 April 1894	ditto	4. 0. 0	H. Wheeler & others	1,000.0.0
14.	11 Jan. 1901	ditto	5. 2. 9	C. E. Radclyffe & others	2,462.10.0
15.	8 April 1889	Newport	2. 1. 4	The Warden & c. of Winchester College	2,800.0.0
				Total	£13,162.2.6

Summary of land purchases by the FYN for its railway.

A CHANGE OF OWNERS, 1893 TO 1905

to the promoters of the South Western & Isle of Wight Junction Railway, i.e. the Solent tunnel. A meeting of shareholders took place on 11th December when the Directors recommended the sale; they regarded the terms as a bargain. The cash was to be shared out in proportion reflecting the likely dividend; preference and ordinary stockholders had little or no hope of receiving anything!

1s. 3d. in the £ on the Preferred Ordinary Stock.
7d. in the £ on the Deferred Ordinary Stock.
3s. in the £ on the Preference Stock.
14s. in the £ on the 5 per cent, 'B' Debenture Stock.
15s. 3d. in the £ on the 5 per cent, Perpetual Debenture Stock.
20s. in the £ on the 3½ per cent, Pre-Debenture Stock.

Whilst those attending the meeting voted to accept the offer, it was necessary to gain a positive vote from holders of three-quarters of each class of stock. This proved impossible and although the sale fell through the Directors issued a circular on 28th January, 1902 announcing that they proposed to sell their holding of £21,300 out of the £24,077 'B' debenture stock and that would give the purchasers a controlling interest in the company. At a Board meeting on 15th March the Directors awarded £262 10s. 0d. to the solicitor Mr Perks and £105 to the Secretary Mr Peck as special fees for their services in connection with the sale. More controversially they voted themselves £157 10s. 0d. each for past services and on account of the sale. The shareholders refused to confirm the decision probably because the fees wiped out the company's profits that year. In October the Directors met one last time to express their discontent and then walked out. The fees had been paid so the Secretary was instructed by the new Board to request their return. Mr Hogan protested vigorously but all the Directors eventually paid up and then disposed of their shares.

As the following summary shows, the Directors' efforts had improved the profitability of the company but this made little impression on the arrears of debenture interest. The profit for 1901 was reduced because of sizeable legal expenses.

Year ending 31 Dec.	Traffic receipts £ s. d.			Amount due to FYN £ s. d.			Permanent Way etc. costs £ s. d.			Profit £ s. d.			Capital expenditure £ s. d.		
1897	6,912	1	8	3,110	8	8	1,509	6	5	1,256	2	8	12,455	10	1
1898	7,234	13	3	3,255	11	8	1,416	12	8	1,688	1	4	437	6	9
1899	7,601	5	8	3,420	11	7	1,641	7	7	1,761	11	3	1,762	0	8
1900	7,614	11	8	3,426	11	3	1,798	17	8	1,384	6	8	1,719	12	4
1901	8,116	14	1	3,652	10	4	1,618	6	8	776	5	0	no record		
1902	7,926	18	3	3,567	2	4	1,897	9	9	1,540	19	6	no record		

During the final few months of 1902 a considerable quantity of stock changed hands. Most was purchased by Sir J.B. Maple Bart MP who, if the amounts quoted in the original offer were adhered to, expended something over £60,000 in buying the majority of the company's capital:

In this early view of Ningwood we see the signal box, waiting shelter and station master's house to the left of an impressive two arch road bridge - the north arch was never used by trains.

R. Silsbury Collection

The bookstall at Freshwater station contains an impressive array of literature on Saturday 26th March, 1904 when this photograph was taken. We see from the billboards the news of the day includes a gruesome murder and the war between Russia and Japan. *J. Mackett Collection*

A CHANGE OF OWNERS, 1893 TO 1905

	Purchased	Total issued
Preferred ordinary stock	£35,540	£42,008
Deferred ordinary stock	£47,180	£50,078
5% perpetual preference stock	£31,878	£42,000
5% 'B' debenture stock	£23,627	£24,077
5% perpetual debenture stock	£28,595	£47,300
3½% perpetual debenture stock	£15,583 6s. 8d.	£20,000

On 8th December, 1902 there was a meeting of a completely new Board of Directors. Present were R.W.E. Middleton (Chairman), P.G. Collins, F.G. Aman, A.E. Baker, W.P. Norton and the Secretary, S. Peck. Save for the death of Mr Middleton in 1905, his replacement as Chairman by Philip Collins and the recruitment of Charles Hodges the composition of the Board was unchanged until 1913.

The Directors inherited a railway that was in immeasurably better condition than had been the case a few years previously. It was fortunate that they had no expectation of profits as there were none; it was sufficient that the railway could be maintained in a fair condition until the completion of the Solent tunnel. Although not mentioned publicly at the time, the purchasers of the railway had the benefit of advice from Sam Fay, an experienced railwayman who rose through the ranks of the LSWR to become its superintendent of the line; for seven years he managed the Midland & South Western Railway and in 1902 was appointed General Manager of the Great Central Railway. We shall meet Mr Fay again.

The Board naturally wanted to reduce the company's fixed charges. During 1903 the Directors went through the working agreements with the Central company and decided to have the accounts checked - nothing adverse was discovered. The Board decided to raise the question of the water charges at Freshwater again; legal advice was obtained by both companies but there was no change.

Having failed to gain any further concessions from the IWC, business settled down to a routine if low-key existence. Amongst the few entries in the Minutes was a request by the Anglo-American Oil Company in October 1903 to rent land at Freshwater station for an oil depot to which the FYN responded positively; oil supplies were essential to the spread of road transport and many Island stations had oil stores. Trespassing on the railway was a recurrent problem as on 4th July, 1905 the FYN Board heard that children were getting onto the line from the recreation ground near Carisbrooke station; an order for 3 cwt of barbed wire was confirmed apparently as a consequence!

Hopes for refreshment rooms at Freshwater station finally died at this time. As long ago as 25th October, 1897 the Directors announced to shareholders that they proposed to erect refreshment rooms but numerous applications for a drinks licence were rejected by the local justices because the proposed accommodation was inadequate. In 1900 Mew Langton & Co. agreed to take a 60 year lease on land next to the station but this agreement foundered when a licence application was again refused. In December 1905 the Portsmouth United Brewery Co. expressed an interest in the 'proposed refreshment rooms'; it was left for them to make an offer but none was forthcoming.

Fares from Freshwater

To	Ticket		Departure time:	8.15	9.42	12.20	2.20	4.20	7.20
Newport	Single	First		3/-	3/-	3/-	3/-	3/-	3/-
		Second		2/-	2/-	2/-	2/-	2/-	-
		Third		1/-	1/-	1/-	-	-	1/-
	Return	First		4/-	4/-	4/-	4/-	4/-	4/-
		Second		-	-	-	3/-	3/-	3/-
		Third		2/-	2/-	2/-	-	-	-
Cowes	Single	First		3/6	3/6	3/6	3/6	3/6	3/6
		Second		-	-	2/4	2/4	2/4	-
		Third		1/2	1/2	-	-	-	1/2
	Return	First		4/6	4/6	3/-	4/6	4/6	4/6
		Second		-	-	-	3/4	3/4	3/4
		Third		2/4	2/4	2/-	-	-	-
Ryde	Single	First		4/6	4/6	4/6	4/6	4/6	4/6
		Second		-	-	3/-	3/-	3/-	-
		Third		1/8	1/8	-	-	-	1/8
	Return	First		5/9	4/-	4/-	5/9	5/9	5/9
		Second		4/3	-	-	4/3	4/3	4/3
		Third		3/-	3/-	3/-	-	-	-
Sandown	Single	First		4/6	4/6	4/6	4/6	4/6	4/6
		Second		3/-	3/-	3/-	3/-	3/-	3/-
		Third		1/9	1/9	-	-	-	1/9
	Return	First		-	4/-	4/-	5/9	5/9	5/9
		Second		4/3	-	-	4/3	4/3	4/3
		Third		3/-	3/-	3/-	-	-	-
Ventnor	Single	First		5/7	5/7	5/7	5/7	5/7	5/7
		Second		3/9	3/9	3/9	3/9	3/9	-
		Third		1/10½	1/10½	-	-	-	1/10½
	Return	First		4/6	4/6	4/6	7/6	7/6	7/6
		Second		3/3	3/3	3/3	5/7	5/7	5/7
		Third		3/3	3/3	3/3	-	-	-
				Third single and third return	Third return issued	Third return and second single no third single	Second return no third	Second return issued	Second single second return

Fares from Freshwater in November 1907.

A siding to Mr Dowty's brickworks about half a mile east of Ningwood station was first proposed in May 1903 but it was two years before the Board of Trade sanctioned its use. Mr Dowty was required to pay for its installation and guarantee £100 per year in traffic for a minimum of seven years. Although the traffic was forthcoming Mr Dowty was not quick to pay his bill for the siding's construction. On 21st March, 1906 he wrote to the IWC asking for a reduction in goods rates and '... objecting to stoppage of goods pending payment of accounts' but got a predictable reply. Mr Dowty was mentioned in connection with the use of a steam traction engine for haulage of bricks etc.; concerned about a possible loss of traffic to the railway and the engine's effect on the bridges and crossings the FYN Board tried to get its use stopped. He was not alone in using traction engines as in 1908 the Board heard that the approach road to Gunville overbridge '... was being cut up owing to Messrs Pritchett taking bricks from the adjoining brick-yard by their traction engine and not for conveyance over the Company's line'. The local authority refused to place a restriction on the use of the bridges and the FYN Board decided to do nothing more after the Engineer reported that there had been no apparent structural damage to the company's property.

It was, perhaps, the FYN that first appreciated the threat of road competition to the Island railways. On 3rd May, 1905 the Central Board read a letter from the FYN Secretary proposing that an IWC Director join the FYN Board and vice versa - the usual platitudes were expressed but nothing was done. The FYN would not let the matter rest and the Secretary then wrote suggesting a reduction of fares. The Central haughtily responded that '... the Board had the subject of such reduction under consideration, but thought that the competition could be best met by running more 3rd class trains' - they were promptly made available on four trains each way a day throughout the Central's system. Despite the greater availability of third class tickets passengers had to choose their journeys carefully because certain trains carried only first and second class whilst others carried first and third class. Whilst third class tickets bore the entry 'Parly 3rd Class' the 1d. a mile rate was honoured in the breach - a ticket for the two mile journey from Yarmouth to Freshwater cost 3½d. Unlike first and second class passengers, those travelling third class gained no advantage from buying return tickets as most were double the single fares. Statistics sent to the Board of Trade in respect of workmen's tickets demonstrated that all third class passengers suffered the same fate. The only relief was in the form of cheap tickets, including one issued at Freshwater called 'Evenings by the Sea' offering travel to Sandown or Ventnor, a curious title given that Freshwater was within a mile of the sea!

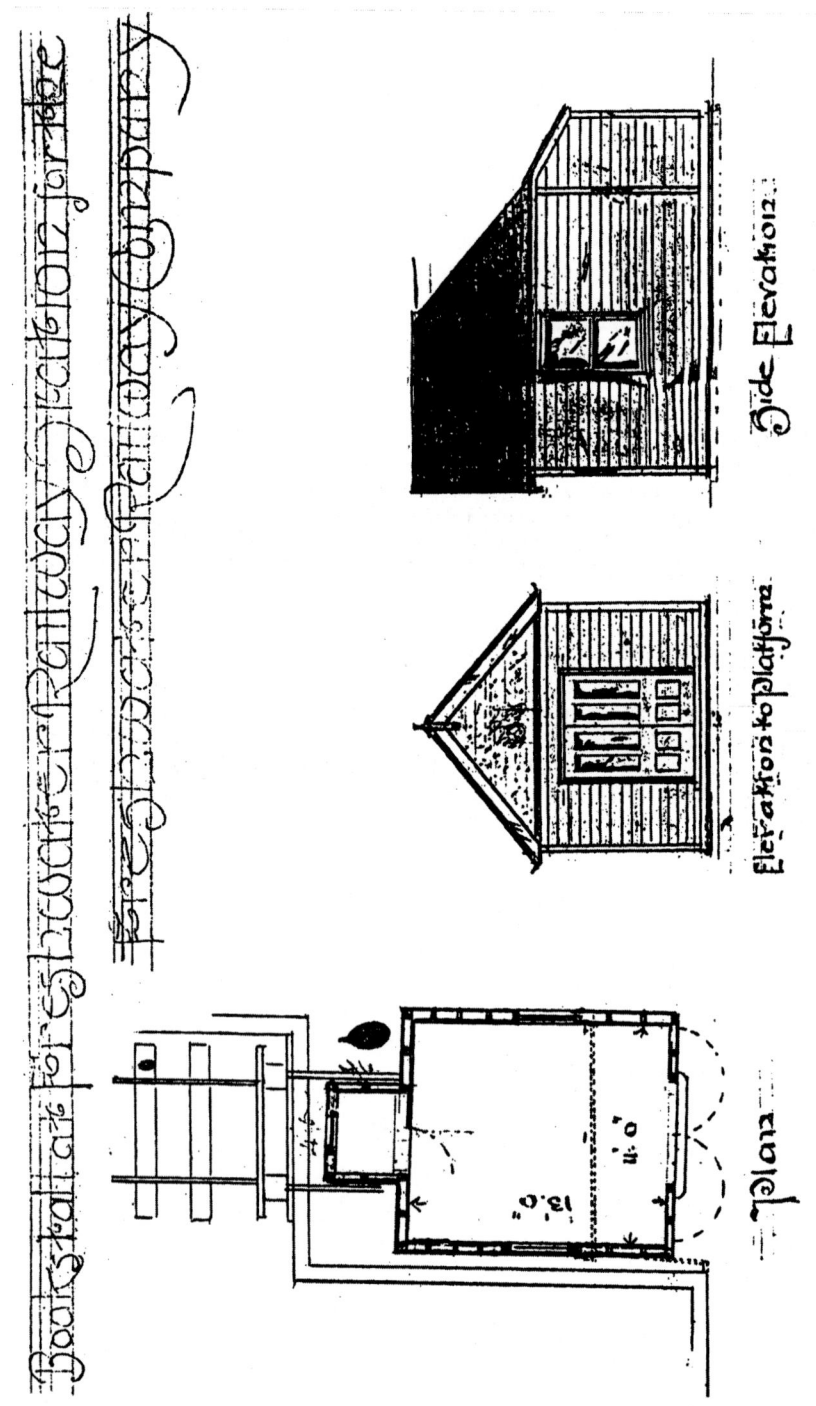

Drawing of new bookstall at Freshwater station in 1906.

Chapter Eight

1906 to 1911

On 8th May, 1906 the FYN Board discussed the appointment of William J. Waterhouse as local agent at a salary of £100 per annum. To a large extent he became the company's manager although was never referred to as such. Resident agent for the Totland Bay Estate, Mr Waterhouse had considerable local knowledge and being on the spot was able to negotiate directly with landowners and contractors. His constant stream of letters to the Secretary gave the FYN Board a much better appreciation of events on the ground and obviated some of the more tangled negotiations that the Secretary and Board had hitherto been drawn into; he even represented the interests of permanent way staff in improving pay and working conditions.

Following his appointment Mr Waterhouse went over the line with Inspector Drower. He found that the crossing keeper's cottage at Freshwater Causeway needed underpinning, the roof tiles at Watchingwell required attention and the water supply smelled badly because the tanks holding the rain water were full of dirt and needed cleaning - this sparked off a programme to connect the station and crossing keepers' cottages to a proper mains water supply. Telegraph poles belonging to the GPO had been erected on the company's land without permission and he met several people, including the local policeman, who were using the railway as a short cut. On 9th June Mr Waterhouse wrote that the permanent way men spent half their year in weeding but could be better employed if the company applied weed killer at a cost of about £45 for the whole line. The IWC had complained that the telegraph was defective but he found it to be in full working order.

To avoid having to draw up to the buffer stops at Freshwater, in October 1904 the IWC asked that the platform be lengthened and widened but this was resisted because the FYN did not own the necessary land. The back of the platform was bounded by a stream that formed the company's boundary and where the stream veered closer to the tracks the platform was consequently narrower. Mr Waterhouse discussed the purchase of more land with the adjoining landowner Sir Charles Seely and his agent and a few months later the FYN purchased a plot of land at an auction of the Hooke Hill estate. That plot was then handed to Sir Charles Seely in exchange for land adjoining the stream. In September 1907 the stream was diverted and the platform widened by William Wheeler, a local builder, at a cost of £111 6s. 0d., including replacement fencing and a gate. W.H. Paul supplied a new wooden bookstall for W.H. Smith for £38 10s. 0d. and the opportunity was taken to purchase cast-iron lamp standards for the platform and connect them to the gas supply. This had first been mentioned in February 1904 when the FYN Board agreed to contribute £5 towards the £9 15s. 0d. bill of replacing the oil lamps, provided the IWC paid £15 annual running costs. Even this arrangement generated friction between the two companies; the FYN later complained that Charles Conacher had kept the gas pressure turned down so far that the gas mantles for which the FYN had to pay were wearing out too quickly!

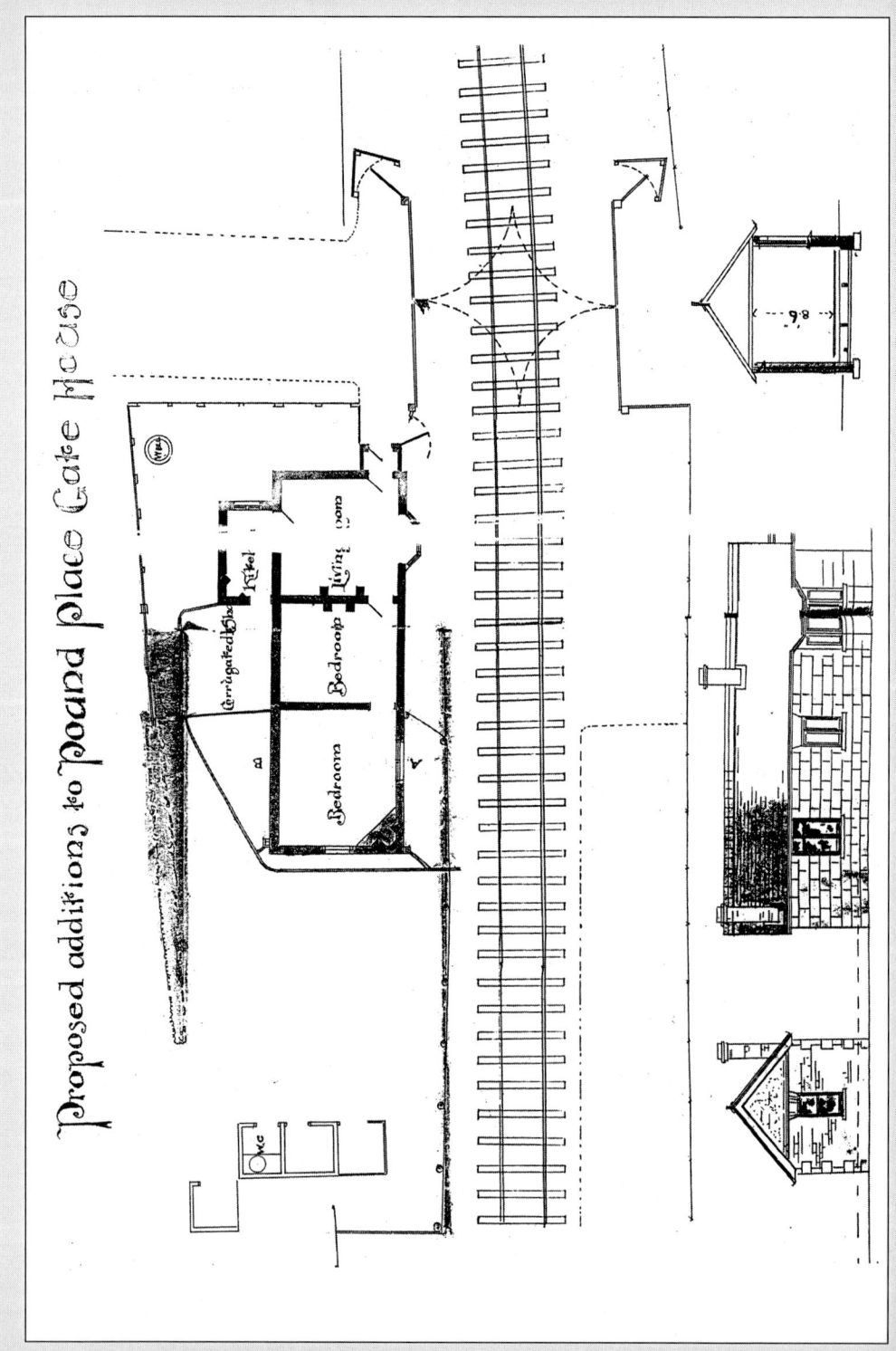

The crossing keepers' houses received some overdue attention. On 25th February, 1907 Mr Wheeler successfully tendered for the construction of an additional room at Petticoat Lane gate house to the same specification of one already added at Pound Crossing; his estimate of £61 8s. 0d. included the cost of taking up the floor and laying a damp course.

Between Freshwater and Yarmouth the railway passed along the banks of the River Yar. Enquiries were made as to whether it would be possible to acquire Yarmouth Tide Mill and some adjoining land for a quay. The tide mill, which dated from 1793, had been greatly affected by the construction of an embankment for the railway across the mill pond and although a steam engine was installed to power the machinery the mill had fallen into disuse. The company could not purchase the property without obtaining an Act of Parliament so Mr Waterhouse enquired whether a lease would be possible. He discovered that the company had little hope of securing the property at a reasonable rent as Lady Heytesbury, the owner, believed the promoters of the Solent tunnel would be willing to pay handsomely for landing materials needed for construction of the tunnel.

The FYN and IWC Minute books recorded several requests for contributions towards the cost of constructing a sea wall at Freshwater Bay. The River Yar rises in marshes just behind Freshwater Bay and there were fears that the sea would break through and flood a considerable acreage of land including the railway between Freshwater and Thorley; due to the Solent's double tides at certain times the sea level is about two feet higher at Freshwater Bay than at Yarmouth. The Central regarded the danger as so serious that in 1906 its Board contributed £10 and paid further small annual payments to keep the works in good order. When the working agreement between the two companies fell due for renewal a clause was inserted exempting the IWC from any liability should there be a breach of the sea wall!

The availability of crossing loops at Carisbrooke and Ningwood gave greater flexibility in the timing of trains but the overall service provided by the IWC did not increase; extra trains operated only in the months of July to September. This changed following the delivery of a steam rail motor in October 1906, one of the few purchases of new rolling stock by the IWC. Rail motor No. 1 had barely arrived before the FYN wrote asking for its employment on the Freshwater line especially on an early morning train from Freshwater to Newport connecting with a service to London. After more badgering, the IWC Manager Charles Conacher agreed to this after Easter 1907, but a trial trip run in March 1907 had to be abandoned when the rail motor was found to be 2 in. too wide for the viaducts. Rather than cut off a large number of bolt heads fouling the loading gauge, the Central modified the motor, the cost of the alterations being shared on the understanding it was used for additional early and late trains. Mr Conacher wrote:

THE FRESHWATER, YARMOUTH & NEWPORT RAILWAY

Newport, Isle of Wight
15th June, 1907

F.G. Aman Esq.
My Dear Sir,
    With reference to the letters we exchanged a month ago: I have now drafted our train service for the Summer Months, and have been able to give effect to your wishes for an early and late service on the Freshwater Line. The former will leave Freshwater at 7.50 am on Weekdays, reaching Ryde Pier Head an hour later in connection with the Fast Service due Victoria 11.50 am. We are bound to stop at all Stations to Newport for the Conveyance of Scholars, but the journey forward to Ryde should be made quickly.
    The 7.10 pm service from Ryde, connecting with the 5 o'clock trains from London will also work through to Freshwater every Weekday and be due there at 9.35 pm.
    We shall use the Motor for these trains and will require to stable it at Freshwater although at some extra cost in lodging and other expenses.
    Kindly arrange for the Engine shed to be placed at our disposal for the purpose although we have yet to test clearances etc. New springs are being made for the car adapted for your Newport Viaduct and we are promised delivery in ample time for the first proximo when the service commences.
    In addition, I have arranged to afford an extra train from Newport to Freshwater at 10.20 am with full local and mainland connections which will also be worked by the Car and an extra train from Freshwater to Ryde Pier Head at 11.15 am connecting with the London service due London Bridge 4.35 pm and Victoria 4.42 pm so that communication between Freshwater and London will be much improved this Season and I intend to make special announcement of the fact by posters and otherwise.
    I enclose extract from our Time Sheets shewing all the services that will operate, and I trust that you will agree that we have met you satisfactorily in the matter.
    I am, Yours faithfully,
        (Signed) Charles Conacher
49 Finsbury Pavement
London EC

Whilst the morning train carried passengers across the Island within a reasonable one hour, the worst excesses of the IWC made themselves apparent on the evening return journey when passengers had to endure a trip from Ryde to Freshwater of 2 hours 25 minutes. In order to accommodate the rail motor at Freshwater Mr Conacher wrote:

> Our Engineer has now examined the Shed at Freshwater in which it is proposed to stable the Motor Car from Sunday night next and except for the provision of suitable lighting, which I hope can be in the form of gas and the use of your portable vice when required no other fittings will be necessary as we intend to stable the Motor here on Saturdays for washing and repairs.
> The Engine Pit however is at the wrong end of the Shed to suit the Car and unless we are able to turn it, the construction of a small pit may be necessary. Please have two good paraffin lamps fixed in the shed from Sunday night next and I shall be glad if you will meet our requirements mentioned above.

Although the lodging turn at Freshwater was not popular with the crew the arrangements lasted for the summer season. The rail motor was also used on a 4.35 pm Newport to Freshwater service but that was a seasonal working and it was taken off during the winter. Within weeks the Central Board received a letter from the Island's Education Committee asking that it be reinstated, to which it agreed '. . . at an increased rate in the Scholars' tickets'. Whilst the rail motor was successful in satisfying demands for an improved service there were a number of other practical problems. It suffered from excessive vibration and oscillation that was aggravated when running over the light permanent way and many curves. Mr Waterhouse wrote:

> The inspection of the Permanent Way every week has resulted in the fishplate bolts being kept tighter than was formerly the case, and consequently the running is much smoother. Whatever vibrating or jolting now occurs it is mainly due to the rolling stock some of which is not of the latest design though it is serviceable.

By 30th September, 1907 a conventional train was on the line as locomotive No. 12 was hauling an early morning Newport-Freshwater working. Approaching Watchingwell at about 7.15 am, the fireman went forward from the footplate to attend to the sandpipe. He was stooping on the lower footstep trying to shake the pipe so sand would fall on the rail when his posterior came into contact with a bridge - fortunately he was only bruised!

A satisfactory summer season prompted the FYN Directors to press for a better service during the winter. At a meeting between representatives from the two companies in October 1907 the FYN suggested that the Freshwater line could be worked wholly by rail motor if a syndicate provided the necessary rolling stock. The Central responded that it was undesirable to sever the existing through trains, refused to reduce charges for the use of Newport station but offered to charge £35 a year for calling at Watchingwell in lieu of the 1s. for each stop; after staff wages had been added the bill to the FYN dropped from almost £80 to less than £50. Charles Conacher also persuaded his Board to revise the fares, those from Freshwater to Newport changed for first, second and third class single journeys from 3s., 2s. and 1s. to 2s., 1s. 6d. and 9d. The IWC refused to run more cheap third class trains claiming that they would result in a serious loss of income from second class passengers. The concessions did not impress Mr Waterhouse as in November he wrote:

> Twice I had occasion to get a ticket to Cowes the fares appears to have been altered, the 8.15 has been made a 3rd class returns train whereas the 7.50 am train was only a 3rd class single so that it was then cheaper to take a single ticket to Cowes and then a single back. The fares now do not seem so bad though. I cannot help thinking that it would save a lot of bother to have the same fares by every train. In the Summer the visitors complain constantly that they never seem to know what they have to pay and that it is so expensive to get about the Island.
> The last train might I think with advantage be made a 3rd return to come back the next day though as the first train in the morning is 3rd class and the return fare just double the single return fare would have to be reduced to make it any real advantage.

In anticipation of the steam rail motor's continued use, quotes were accepted from William Wheeler in October 1907 for repairs to Freshwater carriage shed together with the construction and erection of new doors. Anxious to retain the early morning service the FYN Board agreed to contribute not more than 10s. a week to pay for sleeping accommodation for the crew. The shed was ready in April 1908 '. . . but the motor was not yet in use'; it is doubtful whether the shed

IWC rail motor No. 1 ran on the line regularly between 1907 and 1910 so that is an excellent guide to the date of this view of it standing in Carisbrooke station. The lady in her summer dress and gentleman are evidently awaiting the arrival of an up train which must clear the single line before the rail motor can depart.
P.C. Allen

was used and the Freshwater line never saw the rail motor quite as frequently as had been the case during 1907. The 1908 summer season had eight trains each way plus an extra trip on Saturdays worked by the rail motor. This frequency did not last and in February 1909 the FYN complained that the service was no better than that during the winter of 1894! By October 1909 there was one fewer train on weekdays and eight on Saturdays including the mail and goods train that left Newport for Freshwater at 4.30 am. In the evenings there was a goods train in the reverse direction, that on Saturdays ran as a passenger train. Two Freshwater-bound trains could be run as mixed passenger and goods trains if necessary and no less than four in the opposite direction. On the single occasion when trains needed to cross they did so at Carisbrooke. On Sundays there were three return workings including the mail train.

In 1909 the FYN Directors agreed to increase the 'nominal sums' paid by coal merchants for use of the coal stores at Freshwater. They reckoned without the opposition of the merchants who took their traffic off the line. Rather than lose the traffic, the IWC paid the Freshwater company 1d. a ton in addition to their mileage rate on condition the FYN did not increase the rents, a rare victory for the FYN Board. A short-lived store was constructed at Ningwood for the Seely estate, the FYN charging a rent of £10 a year to which the IWC surprisingly agreed to contribute £5; in 1911 the FYN was still trying to extract payment from the IWC.

In January 1910 William Waterhouse reported that he had purchased a bulk load of red oxide paint probably for Totland Bay pier so the FYN took the opportunity to use the paint on the viaducts. A request from the IWC for a crane at Freshwater was refused as neither Cowes nor Newport had any - the Board quite reasonably concluded that if the Central possessed no cranes why should the FYN purchase one? Ningwood brickyard got new tenants who also rented storage space for their products in Freshwater goods yard. In June 1911 the Board heard that Gunville brickworks was closing, albeit temporarily.

During 1910 Honnor & Jeffrey of Freshwater took the IWC in front of the Railway Commissioners claiming that it levied additional charges for the delivery of parcels marked 'carriage paid' and the service was only performed if marked 'carriage paid to destination'. The Central claimed that parcels traffic to Freshwater did not justify a free delivery service and charges were made unless the label authorised delivery at the senders expense. Realising that the Commissioners were likely to rule in the complainant's favour the IWC announced that free deliveries were under consideration!

The new delivery arrangements prompted a demand for a larger parcels office at Freshwater. The only suitable site was behind the buffers where the bookstall had been erected so it was dismantled and moved to the opposite end of the concourse backing onto the stream. Construction of the extension to the parcels office was authorised on 1st November and it was in use by the end of the year. Mr Waterhouse wrote on 2nd January, 1911 reporting that the additional facilities had been particularly useful during Christmas week. He added:

Freshwater, Yarmouth & Newport Railway.

PERMANENT WAY DEPARTMENT,
CARISBROOKE, I.W.

January 14th 1911

Dear Sir,

As they was putting the 5 ballast waggons in Yarmouth Siding this morning. Mr Spunks went to put the brake down & slipped down. Broke his arm very bad & cut the side of his face. The doctor said it was very serious. They have taken him to Ryde Infirmary. There was nothing in the way so it was no fault of ours.

Yours Truly,
G. Drower.

W. J. Waterhouse Esq
The Estate Office
Totland Bay.

Letter from Inspector Drower, 14th January, 1911.

I am glad to say that there appears to be a better feeling amongst the passengers and customers of the line and I hope it will result in more traffic although the year just ended had been an unfortunate one for the management there being no Ashey Races and no fireworks during Cowes week and an exceptionally wet and rough time.

Income from the railway during the early years of the 20th century showed no great change apart from a slight increase in permanent way and other maintenance costs. The fixed charges including Newport station rent, stopping trains at Watchingwell and the water supply at Freshwater remained a burden.

Year ending 31 Dec.	Traffic receipts £ s. d.	Amount due to FYN £ s. d.	Permanent Way etc. costs £ s. d.	Profit £ s. d.
1903	7,769 8 8	3,496 4 11	1,832 15 2	1,517 14 1
1905	7,887 9 10	3,549 7 5	1,738 1 9	1,638 13 4
1909	7,389 12 7	3,325 6 5	2,605 18 5	677 16 4

More accidents at Yarmouth were mentioned in the Minute book. On 24th April, 1910 the mail train ran through the points but 'no harm was done'. More seriously the station master, Mr Spinks, lost his right arm in a shunting accident; the IWC paid his full wages of 28s. a week for several months and the local court later awarded him compensation of 5s. a week. Mr Spinks had joined the IWC at Cowes in January 1895 and worked as station master at Ningwood and Shide. The accident was no bar to Mr Spinks' career as he remained in railway employment until his retirement in 1933; latterly he had charge of Ashey, Haven Street, Wootton and Whippingham stations.

There were complaints from local landowners that a notorious band of poachers was trespassing on the railway in order to reach their property. Mr Waterhouse received a letter from the agent for Westover Estate informing him that a Yarmouth resident had been caught on 4th February, 1911 at 4.30 pm laying snares; he had got onto the estate by walking along the railway. The agent wanted the man prosecuted for trespass but the FYN Chairman decided not to do so; in fact the railway felt powerless to help as the permanent way men could not be present all the time and additional signs were ineffective. The man was convicted of poaching and fined 10s. with seven days prison in default.

In March 1911 Mr Hibberd, the new owner of Yarmouth Gas Works, refused to continue paying for permission to pass over the company's property; a meeting with Mr Waterhouse came to nothing and the railway company had to block off the access before he would give way. A siding from the station to the gasworks suggested by Mr Hibberd was never installed nor did the station receive gas lighting.

The loop and second platform at Yarmouth must have been regarded as a luxury especially as trains were not permitted to cross there. Charles Conacher wrote to the FYN Board in 1909 warning that a rearrangement was necessary to comply with Board of Trade requirements but nothing was done. The Railway Signalling Co. supplied plans proposing the transfer of point connections to ground frames and the addition of catch points at each end of the loop. Although the FYN Board discussed the matter neither the Freshwater end

Mr Drower and his workmen pose for the cameraman whilst renovating the metal part of the viaduct at Newport in about 1911. The raised central section of bridge across the Cowes road was apparently removed in SR days.
R. Brinton Collection

Yarmouth station in all its glory is seen in this superb sepia view of the station complete with a profusion of notices at some date prior to 1913. The station master is Robert White alongside his son Alfred (later a porter) and an unnamed porter next to the door to the booking office.
Blute/IWSR Collection

ground frame nor the catch points were provided. Instead the points were clipped out of use and the station master admitted trains from the Newport direction by displaying a green flag. On 24th October, 1911 Mr Waterhouse reported that the loop was no longer in use and trains in both directions were using the main platform, an arrangement he considered much more convenient.

The Central wanted to add more coal sidings to its goods yard at Newport and hankered after some FYN land. The two companies disagreed about the precise location of the existing boundary and the plans accompanying the 1889 agreement had to be checked - Newport North signal box was found to have been built half on IWC and half on FYN land! In August 1911 it was agreed to rent a strip of land to the IWC for £5 a year.

In the spring of 1911 Mr Waterhouse reported that the permanent way men were making good progress with the routine maintenance. Signal posts between Freshwater and Carisbrooke were repainted followed during the summer by the viaducts; Newport viaduct was expected to cost £125 10s. 0d. and Calbourne £48 10s. 0d. but some renewal of the timber was found necessary and that put up the cost. After Mr Walker wrote a critical report following one of his periodic inspections Mr Waterhouse responded with a lengthy list of improvements carried out between 1906 and 1909:

1. Apart from Freshwater Causeway, all the gate houses were improved, enlarged and put in good repair.
2. Timber decking on Newport viaduct was renewed and repairs executed to St Cross footbridge.
3. The approach road at Carisbrooke was improved and footpath fenced in.
4. Watchingwell station house was altered and improved, the platform lengthened and ramped to prevent accidents.
3. At Calbourne station, the accommodation was added to and water laid in.
4. At Ningwood, the general waiting room was enclosed and a store erected for Sir Charles Seely.
5. The approach road at Yarmouth had been put in order to the satisfaction of the local authority who had taken on its maintenance. A mains water supply was provided to the station.
6. Freshwater station platform was widened, improvements made to the booking office, a new bookstall built for W.H. Smith, gas columns provided, a cattle dock erected and accommodation provided for 'the famous motor'.
7. Generally concrete sills had been put on several bridges, fence posts were tarred from end to end, gates repaired and new telephone and block wire put up. There had been considerable work in lengthening the lock bars and improving the signal rodding.

The state of the railway at this time was probably better than it had ever been so it was hardly surprising that the FYN Directors had thoughts of working their railway themselves.

Station master S. Urry is photographed seated in front of the booking office at Freshwater *circa* 1910 flanked by two of his staff. Mr Urry's cap badge shows him still to be in the employ of the 'IWCRy', a career that had previously seen him working at Shide, Whitwell and Cowes. He transferred to the FYN in 1913 and on to the SR in 1923. The gentleman standing in the centre is thought to be Mr Waterhouse. *Mrs D. Cotton/J. Mackett Collection*

The neat station building at Carisbrooke was typical of the stations along the line. This view dating from about 1910 shows a bearded inspector Drower with two other railway staff on the down platform. Inspector Drower would then have been about 69 - he was age 82 when he finally retired in 1923! *J. Mackett Collection*

Chapter Nine

The Break with the Central

The inability of the FYN to pay the debenture interest was not to the liking of shareholders who expected the payments irrespective of the company's performance. The matter surfaced at a shareholders meeting on 10th November, 1903 when it was announced that the poor receipts prevented the payment of any debenture interest beyond that due on the 3½ per cent stock. Revd E. Dennett and Mr H. Dennett moved an amendment in protest but it was not seconded. Revd Dennett repeated his protests at later meetings and in letters to the Board. A proposal that the company amalgamate with the IWC was rejected by the Chairman on the grounds that it was desirable to retain the money in the possession of the company and there would be no object in capitalising the arrears of interest.

It was hardly surprising that the 5 per cent debenture holders were unhappy. Typical was William Mitchell, Solicitor to the Supreme Courts of Scotland, who had invested about £2,800 in 1888 on behalf of an officer's widow representing about half her capital only to find that it was not the safe investment he believed. Mr Mitchell wrote a pamphlet *The Isle of Wight and its Railways: its Risks and its Remedy* published in 1912 in which he tried to convince the Government that there was a risk of invasion and suggesting it fund the Solent tunnel, nationalise the Island railway companies (or failing that, just the FYN) and make use of the Island for military manoeuvres. All these activities would have generated income for the company's debenture holders!

On 2nd November, 1909 it was the turn of Mr Sanders when he suggested that the railway be operated as a tramway or with a motor service. Mr Sanders initiated a discussion at a shareholders meeting 12 months later but, 'It was pointed out to him that a motor service was not likely to develop the traffic to any great extent unless the special object was to work in conjunction with the main line trains and the through connections to different parts of the island over which this company had no control'.

The 1897 working agreement with the IWC was due to end on 31st December, 1910 and this gave the FYN an opportunity to press for more favourable terms. The Minutes for 4th January, 1910 recorded a resolution that the Secretary discuss a renewal of the working agreement with the IWC and Mr Aman would supply some facts and figures about independently working the line. Two months later Mr Peck was authorised to continue negotiations for a renewal of the agreement, including an option whereby the Central would maintain the line for a fixed percentage of gross receipts and incorporating the additional charges for Newport station, etc.

The IWC was wary of being drawn into additional commitments and asked its Consulting Engineer, Mr Elliott Cooper, to report on the condition of the Freshwater railway; in fact H.F. Stephens carried out an inspection. Then followed a meeting between the FYN Chairman and Secretary with the IWC Board on 21st June when the latter expressed a willingness to maintain the line for 15 per cent of gross receipts provided the FYN '. . . agreed to pay, and be responsible, for all structural works or repairs connected with the bridges and viaducts, all extraordinary renewals of rails, sleepers and all repairs in case of the sea breaking in at Freshwater'. The seven year agreement would have paid 60 per cent of gross receipts to the IWC.

On 5th July, 1910 the FYN Board considered the matter at their regular monthly meeting and decided to approve proposals that the IWC continue working the line '. . . subject to a proper understanding as to the responsibility for maintenance'. Mr Aman was clearly unhappy with this because there was an exchange of letters with the Chairman. On 23rd August, in Mr Aman's absence, it was agreed to accept the terms of the agreement subject to a reduction in its length from seven to five years. Mr Aman pointedly absented himself from the next meetings such that the Board had no quorum on occasions. The formalities were incomplete by the end of 1910 and the existing arrangements had to be continued for six months.

Letters between the two companies passed to and fro whilst the Central Board prevaricated. The Central's General Manager, Charles Conacher, resigned in March 1910 for a job with the Cambrian Railways and was replaced by George Henley, the company's accountant. Nothing was achieved before a meeting of IWC shareholders on 1st March, 1911 when Harry Willmott gained a seat on the Board. An experienced railwayman, he quickly ousted Percy Mortimer as Chairman and began to shake the company out of its torpor.

The appointment of Harry Willmott as IWC Chairman had unfortunate consequences for the FYN because he was not prepared to accept the terms of the proposed agreement. During April he inspected the line and had a meeting with the FYN Chairman Philip Collins. Mr Collins reported to his Board on 2nd May, 1911 when it was agreed to raise the offer to:

> . . . 70 per cent of the gross receipts to the Central Company to include the rent of Newport Station, Watching Well Station Stops, Water Supply at Freshwater and the proper maintenance of the line up to £1,700 per annum, this company bearing out of the receipts any necessary structural cost and expense or necessary maintenance beyond the £1,700.

Harry Willmott recommended an agreement for just 1½ years from 1st July during which the IWC would operate and maintain the line for 75 per cent of gross receipts once certain special works had been done by the FYN. The two Chairmen met again and the FYN Board gave their approval although 'Mr Aman dissented'. In a formal agreement signed on 11th August the key clauses were:

> In order to carry out certain works which have been agreed by the respective Engineers of the parties thereto the Freshwater Company have agreed to provide on the ground certain materials of the agreed value of £300 and the Central Company shall use materials or their equivalent in value in carrying out said works and shall also in addition expend on such works the sum of £450 which amount . . . shall be appropriated from the gross receipts . . . The Central Railway shall keep and maintain the permanent way, stations, bridges, offices, signal boxes, cabins and plant (including telegraph poles and apparatus) in a proper and efficient state and condition for the safe conduct of the traffic . . .

THE BREAK WITH THE CENTRAL 89

The FYN was obliged to carry out structural works in connection with buildings and viaducts, renewals and repairs 'due to Act of God, the King's Enemies, fire', flooding by the sea at Freshwater and work required by the Board of Trade because of previous neglect. In addition to 75 per cent of the gross receipts the IWC also collected '. . . 4*d*. per ton wharfage on coals etc. and 8*d*. a ton general goods from Medina Railway Wharf to stations on the Freshwater line'. The Central took over maintenance of the line on 31st July, 1911 when the permanent way men were transferred to the IWC, except for Mr Drower who was retained by the FYN on a salary of £1 a week plus the free use of a cottage - he was already of retirement age. The FYN Board also decided to dispense with the services of Mr Waterhouse at the end of the year

The FYN Directors were mistaken if they believed the agreement would solve the company's problems. The IWC drastically reduced the frequency of passenger trains during winter months and altered the fare structure. On 2nd October, 1911 Mr Waterhouse wrote about the changes:

> The 9.42 from Freshwater to Newport has no connection on to Ryde consequently passengers must either go at 8.15 or 12.20. From Freshwater by the former there is 30 minutes wait at Newport and 15 minutes by the 12.20. The County Council School Children will have to come out by 5.20 instead of 4.45 as formerly and as they leave school at 4 o'clock this means a long wait in Newport for them. You will remember that Mr Conacher for a time lost the School Children owing to his requiring I understand higher fares and he was afterwards glad to get them back at reduced charges. It is therefore possible that the C. Council may again resort to the road if the convenience of the children is not studied as they leave Freshwater at 8.15 it makes a long day for them.
>
> Of course one can hardly expect trains to be run at a loss but it is a question if any of the trains will pay unless the connection is good and eventually it may be found that the 9.42 does not pay.
>
> A good deal of money is being spent but if all the trains are so reduced it hardly looks as though the improvements are necessary. There seems to be an impression that the intention is to swamp the Freshwater Rly Co. so that it may be acquired on easy terms.
>
> I do not think the general Public understand the Railway fares which have apparently been changed about a good deal and they seem to give some dissatisfaction. One man I know was intending to go via Portsmouth but as he could not get the ticket he wanted he took a single ticket to Yarmouth and went via Lymington.
>
> The Permanent Way is still in very fair order but 4 Platelayers have been working in Newport Station Yard and as it is I understand the intention is to permanently curtail the number of men employed it will be necessary to keep the I. W. Central up to the mark in maintenance.
>
> As the line was handed over in good condition no doubt it can be maintained with a smaller staff at any rate for a time.
>
> A good deal of work is being carried out at Newport etc. and I still think it would have been better to have increased the rolling stock for Goods Traffic first and then to have done these additions after as the extra rolling stock would be of more benefit to our line than laying a lot of money in Newport Station Yard.

Mr Waterhouse was equally dismissive of the goods traffic:

> I ordered four or five deals [of timber] to come out from Newport which should have been at Freshwater on Thursday. They are not here yet and I shall have to cancel order unless delivered Monday.

It may not pay to bring the deals along on special trucks as owing to their length they probably would not go in the luggage van but as this is not very much material that I require it does not matter much but probably other people have a good many little lots and if they are to be kept waiting too long it will divert traffic.

It soon dawned on the FYN Directors that they had been duped. The Central was obliged to pay for upkeep sufficient for trains to run with safety but that did not apply to ordinary wear and tear nor any maintenance of structural works and buildings. The IWC could also charge for any work beyond routine maintenance of the roadbed and rails. Fortunately Mr Drower had continued to submit his regular reports on the condition of the permanent way; there was little activity to report as many of the gangers had been taken away to lay sidings in the Central's station at Newport. The FYN Board decided to have the line inspected by an engineer but it was June 1912 before Mr Walker's full report was made available.

A meeting of the FYN Board on 4th June, 1912 was crucial. The Secretary was instructed to use the contents of Mr Walker's report as the basis for a letter of complaint to the IWC. Despite the Board's previous decision to dispense with his services, Mr Waterhouse was asked to go over the line and compare its present condition with that when the IWC took charge. Following a resolution to obtain the services of someone 'experienced in railway matters', Mr Aman promised to communicate with a gentleman whom he thought would be suitable - that gentleman proved to be Sam Fay.

Meanwhile the IWC had been keeping up a constant flow of letters 'suggesting' additional work that it considered the FYN should pay for. The FYN Board refused a request to pay for halts at New Park and Thorley even though the Revd Marshall, writing on behalf of Thorley residents, said they were prepared to find half the cost. When writing about a broken rail at Carisbrooke, Russell Willmott, the IWC Manager, took the opportunity to warn that the whole line needed relaying with heavier materials - in fact the permanent way was not renewed until after 1923. Mr Waterhouse reported on a request that £120 plus labour needed to be spent on strengthening Town Gate viaduct; he found a way of achieving the same result at a cost of just £11 10s. 0d. As if the FYN Directors needed any additional evidence, the weakness of the working agreement became clear during 1912 when a lengthy spell of heavy rain played havoc with the bridges along the line. Although some minor repairs were carried out by the IWC, the FYN had to arrange and pay for most of the remainder. Typical was the payment of £64 to Mr Hart for rebuilding part of Ningwood bridge; there were also slips at Betty Haunt Lane, Thorley and Barnfield bridges that needed attention.

Negotiations for a renewal of the working agreement reached an impass after the FYN Directors demanded a more favourable arrangement for maintenance. On 19th November, 1912 the FYN Board approved the purchase of some rolling stock. This reached the ears of the IWC whose solicitors informed the FYN on 9th December that their clients would cease running trains over the Freshwater railway after the end of the year. To force the pace the IWC gave notice to staff working on the line and erected notices at stations warning of the impending change.

THE BREAK WITH THE CENTRAL

The FYN Board met in emergency session on 11th December, 1912 when the Chairman reported on events. After assurances of help from Sir Sam Fay (he had been knighted on 22nd July), it was decided to make arrangements to take over the working of the line from 1st January, 1913. That proved to be impracticable but on Monday 16th December the Chairmen of the IWC and FYN met with their lawyers to agree an extension of the working agreement for six months.

On 25th April, 1913 Russell Willmott reported to his Board that the FYN proposed to work the line themselves after 30th June and would not be using the Central's station at Newport. Sir Sam Fay had consented to act on the Freshwater company's behalf in making working arrangements and the Central management were asked to make an appointment to see him! The IWC offered to extend the working agreement for a further six months and reminded the FYN that they were obliged to buy certain rolling stock should it come to an end. Unless a satisfactory arrangement could be reached over the use of Newport station the IWC indicated it would make an application to the Railway and Canal Commissioners for a decision against the FYN.

An emergency meeting of the FYN Board was held on 21st May attended by the Directors and Sir Sam Fay. The accounts for 1911 and 1912 showed what the FYN had gained from the revised working agreement:

Year ending 31 Dec.	Traffic receipts £ s. d.	Amount due to FYN £ s. d.	Permanent Way etc. costs £ s. d.	Profit £ s. d.
1911	7,502 12 2	4,611 2 4	2,020 12 1	178 5 2
1912	7,020 0 4	5,265 0 3	192 14 4	1,196 6 0

IWC locomotive No. 8 and a train of LSWR carriages leave Carisbrooke with a Freshwater train in 1912. The neat little Stevens signal box stands adjacent to the down starting signal at the end of the main platform. *P.C. Allen/IWSR Collection*

Sir Sam Fay expressed the opinion that the company could work its line more cheaply and profitably than hitherto. Emboldened by his advice, the Board resolved to begin working the railway on 1st July, 1913, approved a contract for the construction of passenger and goods accommodation at Newport and authorised Sir Sam Fay to employ a Manager, take on staff and purchase locomotives and rolling stock.

The dispute between the IWC and FYN became a battle of strength. Harry Willmott, who had acquired some FYN debentures, instituted proceedings in the courts and obtained a judgement for £468 arrears of interest; another IWC Director, Sidney Herbert, and others gained judgements for a further £2,385. The FYN Directors, who amongst them held £180,000 out of the company's £225,000 capital, were forced to employ the Chairman's firm of Peake, Bird, Collins & Co., to institute their own proceedings for the appointment of Sir Sam Fay (who had also acquired some shares and debentures) and Frank Aman as joint Receivers from 4th July, 1913. Willmott complained that the FYN should not spend more of its capital on the new station at Newport but failed to gain the support of the court.

An extraordinary meeting of shareholders was held on 22nd July to sanction the issue of £15,000 debenture stock as authorised for in the company's 1896 Act. In a letter to shareholders issued on 3rd July the Directors wrote: 'Sir Sam Fay kindly agreed to advise this company the best course to adopt, and acting on that advice the Board have decided that it will be for the benefit of the Company to work the line itself'.

By then the FYN had taken back its railway. Russell Willmott gave a progress report to the IWC Board meeting on 28th July, 1913. Ownership of the station fittings, etc. were transferred for £50 and without prejudice to a formal resolution to their dispute, the two companies agreed to exchange the mail van outside the North signal box at 4.30 each morning. For the first few days the FYN locomotive shunted wagons destined for the IWC into its goods yard when no IWC locomotive was available but refused to continue doing this and it was agreed to exchange wagons at times convenient to each company. The Central's staff were handling parcels destined for the FYN and had begun carrying luggage etc. to the new FYN station. Russell Willmott complained to the Board of Trade about the lack of adequate access between the two companies' stations and enclosed a plan showing the narrow footpath used by passengers and inconvenient road arrangements. He added that one of the IWC porters had been summonsed for obstruction of the footpath with his luggage cart - deliberately, so FYN supporters claimed - the case was heard on 25th August but dismissed due to conflicting evidence. An official dismissed it with the comment: 'This letter is evidently written with the object of trying to induce the Board of Trade to refuse to sanction the use of the new station'. Sir Sam Fay wrote an equally robust letter; he maintained that the IWC had deliberately blocked a roadway between the two stations with coal and then demanded compensation for its reopening together with an indemnity for accidents that might occur from the road's use.

Col Von Donop inspected the FYN station in September 1913 following which he commented on the lack of arrangements for through passengers and:

THE BREAK WITH THE CENTRAL 93

Apart from the above question, the means of approach to this new station are adequate. The main approach is by means of a footpath, about 180 yards in length and of a very bad gradient, connecting the new station with the roadway leading to the Isle of Wight Central Station. There is also another approach from the further side of the line by means of a public footpath or of a cart track, both of which are of still greater length, and both of which lead to a footbridge over the Freshwater line. Neither of these approaches can be regarded as satisfactory, and I can only recommend the Board of Trade accept them as a temporary arrangement, reserving the power at any subsequent date to call upon the Company to provide a better means of approach.

Upon receiving the Inspector's report Sir Sam Fay visited the offices of the Board of Trade in London and expressed concern at the Inspector's caution. He emphasised that the majority of the traffic was local and would use a new road that 'may have been in a rough condition' when the Inspector saw it; only a handful of through passengers would use the footpath and there were many places in the country where there was worse access. 'The Central Co. have blocked up with a stack of coal the simplest means of access, and otherwise the land between the two stations belongs to a Brewery Company', the purchase of additional land for a new road or path would not be possible without a fresh Act of Parliament. Von Donop responded that he 'would still hesitate to recommend the Board to give more than a temporary approval to the present arrangements'. Although he intended making a second inspection the Great War put a stop to that and the temporary arrangements lasted until 1923. The Board of Trade was fully aware of the situation:

> If the Isle of Wight Central Company servants have as stated been prosecuted for obstructing the footpath between the two stations it would seem to be entirely that company's own fault for seeking to impose unreasonable conditions on the Freshwater Company . . . The quarrel between the two companies has brought about an absurd position and must involve some considerable further public inconvenience but I hardly think we are likely to do much good, at any rate while litigation is proceeding, by saying we wish they would be friends with each other.

Meanwhile the IWC had been active in the courts in an attempt to force the FYN to use the junction between the two companies. The Court of Chancery rejected its application but lodged a complaint before the Railway & Canal Commissioners asking to make an order that the FYN 'afford all due and reasonable facilities for the user of the two companies' railways at Newport (I.W.) as a continuous line of communication'. The IWC wrote that Parliament had not given the FYN powers to erect its own station at Newport and refused to give permission to build a footbridge connecting the two stations claiming that it did not constitute a continuous line of railway. When the FYN responded by asking for the provision of exchange sidings the IWC warned that the cost would have to be borne on the FYN. At a hearing on 17th and 18th November, 1913 a number of witnesses gave evidence as to the inconvenience resulting from the FYN's actions although one individual did agree that the service was much improved! Harry Willmott claimed that IWC traffic had grown 20 per cent because of the introduction of cheaper fares but through traffic to the FYN had fallen 10 per cent. He had no desire to place obstacles in the way of the FYN, was willing to run through trains if the Freshwater company would take off theirs and had no objection to the retention of the FYN station for local traffic.

Counsel for the FYN then opened the case for the defendants. The terms of the working agreement were said to be so adverse that the company was being starved out of existence. The whole object of the IWC was to 'skin the lamb' and if Messrs Willmott and Herbert had succeeded in being appointed Receivers 'we should have been finished . . . the object is simply to squeeze us almost out of existence and buy us up at a knock-out price'. Sir Sam Fay gave evidence that local traffic on the FYN had increased 43 per cent since 1st July. Through passengers between the two railways averaged only 16 per train during the height of the summer and nine in October. He admitted, however, that the FYN had changed its fare structure to encourage rebooking.

Whilst the commissioners reached no formal decision, they expressed the view that the FYN should not be forced run all its trains into the Central's station. The commissioners drew up a provisional timetable for through carriages into the Central station with haulage shared by each company. The hearing then adjourned in the expectation that the two parties comply with the judgement. That proved impossible and a further hearing took place on 2nd and 3rd February, 1914. The FYN maintained that it was the responsibility of the IWC to haul through carriages over its metals between its station and the point of junction between the two companies. The Central contended that this was incompatible with its working arrangements. The commissioners made an order asking the two companies to agree upon a timetable and ruled that the Central could not charge for the interchange of through carriages and the two companies had to share in their haulage 'so as to cause the least inconvenience to either company'. After a further delay the Central Board heard on 24th June that:

> Commencing Monday, 11th May, certain of the Freshwater Company's trains have been run into and out of our Newport Station: the work of the haulage between the Junction at Newport and our Newport Station has been equally shared by ourselves and the Freshwater Company without prejudice. The result has been fairly satisfactory but there is little doubt the simplest method would be for the Freshwater Company to work all the trains into and out of our Station themselves. As a general rule their engine when [we] work the train from their railway into and out of our station simply stands waiting for the train to be handed back to them and it would entail practically no extra work upon them to do all the haulage. They have done so on several days to suit their own convenience when using their vacuum fitted stock.

Within weeks, the squabbles between the FYN and IWC paled into insignificance when war broke out. One final entry appeared in the Central's minute book on 27th August, 1914:

> We continued up to the commencement of the War to do half the work of haulage between the Junction with the Freshwater Company and our Newport Station, except when the Freshwater Coy are utilising their Vacuum Stock which we of course cannot work. During the last week or two the through working was discontinued owing to military movements etc., but it has been commenced again this week.
> Pending negotiations and as a temporary measure we have accepted a nominal rent from the Freshwater Company for the use of our Station and conveniences excluding Junction Expenses and Water, of £5 per annum. If satisfactory arrangements are made with the Freshwater Coy, this nominal rent will probably be continued when the railways pass out of State Control. If not, we may seek to charge them a higher rent as provided for by the Freshwater Act 1880.

Chapter Ten

An Independent Railway
1913 to 1923

A site for a new terminus at Newport was pegged out by Mr Waterhouse on 20th May, 1913 approximately 100 yards from the IWC junction and next to a footbridge across the line. J. Ball & Son of Cowes contracted to carry out most of the work at a cost of £1,094 8s. 0d. By 7th June the firm's men were clearing trees and widening a cutting for a run-round loop, the spoil being dumped west of the footbridge to form a roadway and two goods sidings. The late Fred Hatcher remembered the felling of a horse chestnut tree during the construction of the goods yard much to his chagrin as he used to collect 'conkers'. On the south side of the run-round loop the contractor erected a wooden platform, nameboard, fencing, a waiting room, booking office, toilets and the foundations for a signal box supplied by the Railway Signal Company. Laying of the permanent way began during the night of 26th-27th June although Ball & Son were still providing men to assist with tracklaying up to 19th July. An approach road to the goods yard and station was created by widening a footpath leading from the Cowes road at Hunnyhill to the far side of the footbridge. Next to the entrance to the goods yard, the firm prepared the foundations and fitted out an office building, the structure for which was brought to the site in sections. A proposed footbridge connecting the two stations could not be built as it would have contravened Board of Trade regulations by crossing the IWC goods yard.

Lt Col Von Donop, the Board of Trade Inspector, visited the Island in September 1913 to inspect the station:

> The station consists of a single platform, 175 ft long, 3 ft high and of ample width. The platform is provided with shelter, Booking Office, lamps, nameboard and clock, and accommodation for both sexes is in course of construction. The arrangements are of a somewhat rough description, and it will be noted that, although a shelter is provided, there are no regular waiting rooms. As however the line is only 12 miles in length, and partakes of the nature of a Light Railway I think that the arrangements may be accepted.
>
> The points and signals are worked from a new box, containing a frame of 12 levers of which 4 are spare; the interlocking is correct.

Meanwhile, the local press had been following events. On 4th July, 1913 *The Freshwater, Totland & Yarmouth Advertiser* carried the news:

> The long talked of severance ... took place on Monday ... but the local company proved they were equal to the occasion, and Tuesday found new trains with much improved carriages running quite as punctually as of old. Passengers have nothing but praise for the new system ... through traffic may be slightly inconvenienced for a time, but this will naturally be adjusted as soon as possible. Mr Thomas has been appointed Station Master at Freshwater in place of Mr Hill, but all the other officials are being retained. We understand the Company also intends to do without the services of Pickford's, and to deliver the goods themselves.

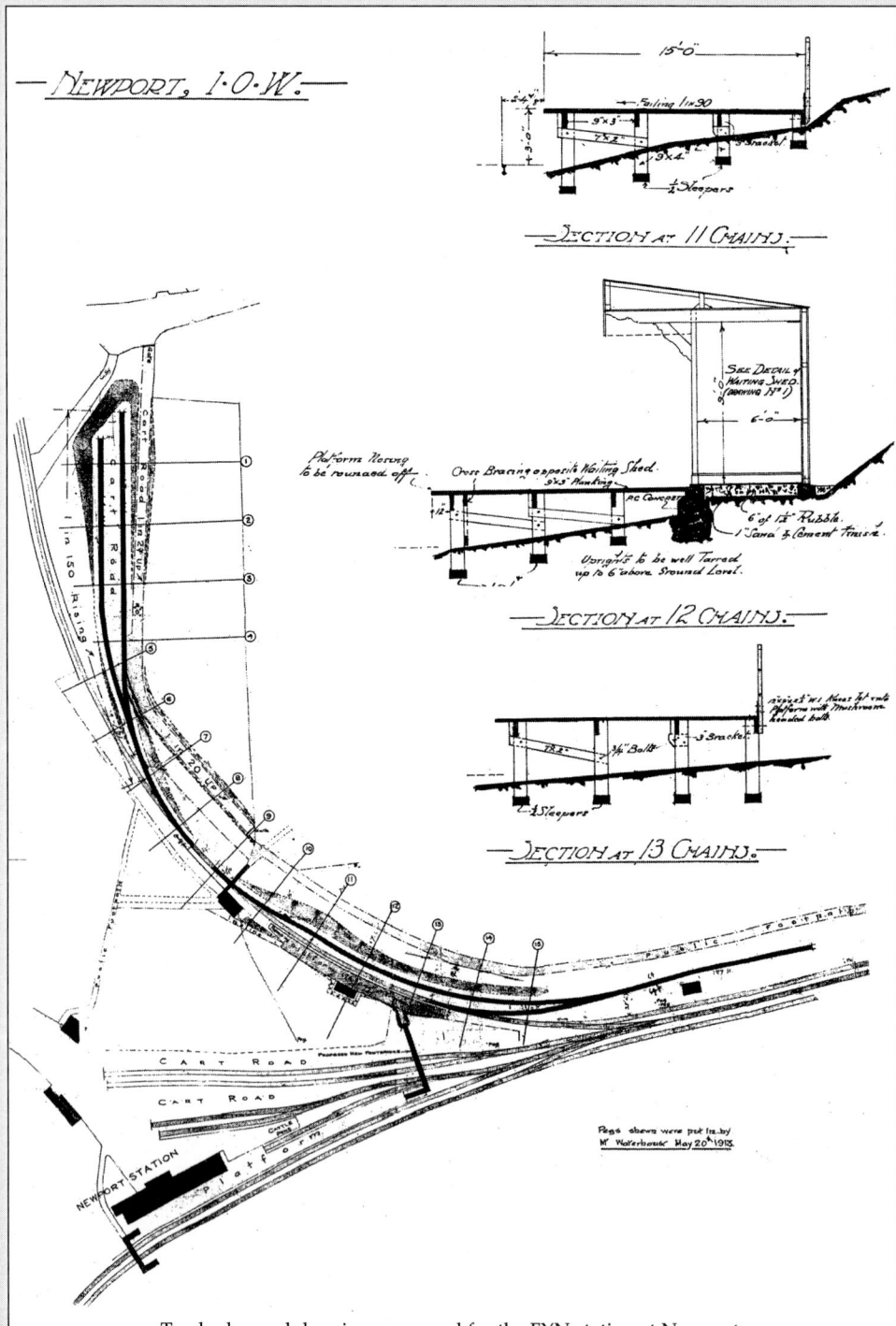

Track plan and drawings prepared for the FYN station at Newport.

AN INDEPENDENT RAILWAY, 1913 TO 1923

F_{reshwater,} Y_{armouth} & N_{ewport} R_{ly.}

UP-TO-DATE ROLLING STOCK.

Cheap Bookings: NEWPORT TO FRESHWATER.
Freshwater to Carisbrooke and Newport.

Connections with the mainland via Lymington, Cowes, and Ryde.

For Particulars of Train Service and Excursion Fares see bills, free on application.

Rail Motor Service.

On guarantee of a minimum of eight Third Class or four First Class fares, provided notice is given by 6 p.m. the previous day, a PETROL MOTOR CAR, which carries Twelve Passengers, will be run at any time when the line is clear.

The same Car will be run if required in connection with the Yarmouth-Lymington boats on similar guarantees and conditions, leaving Newport for Yarmouth at 6.35 a.m. (Mondays only), 8.10 a.m., 12.45 p.m., and 2.38 p.m., and leaving Yarmouth for Newport at 1.40 p.m. and 4.0 p.m.; and will leave Yarmouth for Newport each day at 8.15 p.m. for the convenience of Passengers from the mainland arriving by the 7.30 p.m. boat from Lymington.

Cheap Fares for Golfers.

Return Tickets (First Class only) are issued to Individual Golfers from any F.Y. & N. Station to Cowes, Freshwater, Shanklin, Sandown, Shide, Newport, Ventnor Town or Whitwell at a single fare for the double journey (minimum 1/-) on production of voucher signed by the Club Secretary.

Wheat Sheaf Hotel,

NEWPORT, ISLE OF WIGHT.

Oldest in the Town, but Modern in Service and General Comfort.

Nearest Hotel to Newport's Sporting Golf Links,

SPECIAL TERMS FOR GOLFERS.

ORDINARY DAILY 1.15.   LUNCHEONS.   TEAS.

TELEPHONE 453.   READ, PROPRIETOR.

A 1913 advert for the rail motor service.

Freshwater, Yarmouth & Newport Railway
Timetable from 7 June 1914

WEEKDAYS

		A								SO	
Newport	Dep.	9.4	10.25	11.42	1.15	3.20	5.17	6.45	9.0	10.25	
Carisbrooke	Dep.	9.8	-	11.46	1.19	3.24	5.21	6.49	9.4	10.29	
Calbourne	Dep.	9.19	-	11.57	1.30	3.35	5.32	7.0	9.15	10.40	
Ningwood	Dep.	9.23	-	12.1	1.34	3.40	5.36	7.4	9.19	10.44	
Yarmouth	Dep.	9.31	11.50	12.9	1.43	3.48	5.44	7.12	9.27	10.52	
Freshwater	Arr.	9.33	11.55	12.14	1.47	3.53	5.49	7.17	9.32	10.57	

										M	
Freshwater	Dep.	8.10	9.41	11.0	12.23	2.15	4.25	5.56	7.40	8.10	9.45
Yarmouth	Dep.	8.15	9.46	11.5	12.28	2.20	4.30	6.1	7.45	8.15	9.50
Ningwood	Dep.	8.23	9.54	-	12.36	2.28	4.38	6.9	7.53	J	9.58
Calbourne	Dep.	8.27	9.58	-	12.40	2.32	4.42	6.13	7.57	J	10.2
Carisbrooke	Dep.	8.38	10.9	-	12.51	2.43	4.53	6.24	8.8	J	10.13
Newport	Arr.	8.42	10.13	11.30	12.55	2.47	4.57	6.28	8.12	8.45	10.17

SUNDAYS

		B							
Newport	Dep.	10.20	11.48	2.30	4.25	8.15			
Carisbrooke	Dep.	10.24	11.47	2.34	4.29	8.19			
Calbourne	Dep.	10.35	11.57	2.45	4.40	8.30			
Ningwood	Dep.	10.39	12.2	2.49	4.44	8.34			
Yarmouth	Dep.	10.47	12.10	2.57	4.52	8.42			
Freshwater	Arr.	10.52	12.15	3.2	4.57	8.47			

		B					
Freshwater	Dep.	9.18	11.0	1.30	3.25	7.25	9.0
Yarmouth	Dep.	9.23	11.5	1.35	3.30	7.30	9.5
Ningwood	Dep.	9.31	11.13	1.43	3.38	7.38	9.13
Calbourne	Dep.	9.35	11.17	1.47	3.42	7.42	9.17
Carisbrooke	Dep.	9.46	11.28	1.58	3.53	7.53	9.28
Newport	Arr.	9.50	11.32	2.2	3.57	7.57	9.32

A = 13 July to 12 September only. B = 19 July to 6 September only. J = Calls when required to pick up or set down. M = Motor to carry 12 passengers only. SO = Saturdays only.

AN INDEPENDENT RAILWAY, 1913 TO 1923

The task of creating a fully operational independent railway was delegated by Sir Sam Fay to David Lamb of the GCR whilst W.H. Hunstone, another GCR employee, was appointed Manager. The changeover was fully reported by the *Isle of Wight County Press*:

> The working agreement of the Isle of Wight Central Railway Company on the Freshwater railway line terminated at midnight on Monday, and on Tuesday morning (1st July), the Freshwater Railway Company commenced working its own line, the only difference in the service at present being that the trains run to and from the new railway platform at Newport. Fog signals were exploded on the passing of the last 'Central' train from Freshwater which arrived at Newport at about 10.30 pm, and smooth working, having regard to the way in which the arrangements had hurriedly to be made for the change, the contractor's staff carrying out the work at the Newport Station having to work day and night on Sunday last, so that everything should, as far as possible, be ready for the alteration.
>
> In addition to the two fresh engines and a number of coaches which the Freshwater Company have imported for their service, a pleasing novelty in the way of a petrol rail-motor to carry twelve persons, has been introduced, and the trial trips with it have been pleasingly successful. Some inconvenience to through passengers has naturally been inseparable from such a hasty change, but this has been minimised as far as possible by Freshwater management ...
>
> An extended and much later service of trains and other improvements are likely to be introduced after the middle of this month. Mr W. Hunstone is the manager of the Freshwater line, and he has Mr J. Jenkinson as his deputy. The old stationmasters have been taken over, excepting at Freshwater, where Mr J. Thomas, of the Central Railway Company audit department for some thirty years, is temporarily acting, whilst Mr S. Urry, from the Cowes Station, has been placed in charge of the new Newport Station. Mr G.M. Button, of the Central Railway Company's staff, has transferred to the Freshwater Company in the manager's department.
>
> The work at the new station has been carried out by Messrs J. Ball & Son, Cowes. Sir Sam Fay, manager of the Great Central Railway, has been prominent in initiating the new policy of the Freshwater Company, and he has paid frequent visits to the Island of late.

The new management had simplified the fare structure based on a rate of 1½d. a mile first class and 1d. a mile third class. Those changes were reflected in the printing of a new series of tickets based on a design used by the GCR. The most noticeable change was in the layout of return tickets that henceforth were printed horizontally. Third class tickets continued to bear the abbreviation 'Parly' to indicate that they were issued at the statutory rate of 1d. a mile and after fares were increased during the war tickets appeared carrying the printed legends 'Actual Fare' and 'Revised Fare'.

To work the line, two locomotives were brought from the mainland with a petrol rail motor car and seven carriages. A further five carriages and some goods stock was bought from the IWC. The rail motor was quite a useful vehicle as it deputised on lightly-loaded passenger trains and in emergencies could cover for the unavailability of a steam locomotive or travel at short notice to Yarmouth to collect passengers whenever the ferry was delayed. It was also possible to hire the motor for the price of four first or eight third class tickets. Mrs M.B. Wheeler recalled seeing it at Newport in 1919 or 1920:

Soon the Freshwater train was signalled and we looked eagerly towards the footbridge to watch it arrive - but what was this strange vehicle approaching? Certainly no train, but something more like a small 'toast-rack' bus, sounding its horn, which was just like a motor horn, as it drew near on its small iron wheels and finally stopped. It was of course the Drewry petrol railcar . . .

My aunt at once moved forward to get in, but my father exclaimed in disgust, 'Surely you don't have to go in *that thing*, do you?' 'Oh yes!' she replied brightly, 'it's the Boat Train! It's lovely - you get such a lot of fresh air!'

You certainly did, for it had no sides! Fortunately this day was warm and sunny, but just imagine what it must have been like bowling along between the flat fields towards Yarmouth in a force 8 Sou'wester with the driving rain lashing down! Even with the tarpaulin curtains let down for protection (?!) against the elements, instead of being neatly rolled up under the edge of the roof as they were today, I could just imagine them in the howling gale - now bellying outwards, now flapping inwards from the force of the wind, as the rain drove in between them, soaking the luckless passengers within! Surely, this must have been a fine weather vehicle only!

My main impression of the railcar was how *low* it was. My aunt had to step *down* into it and my face was nearly level with the roof, although I was only a child at the time. There were three long seats extending right across it, all comfortably upholstered in black, buttoned leather, but I do not think it could have held more than 10 or 12 passengers. There were large, glass windowscreens at each end, and before starting off, the driver had to jump down on the track in front of it and keep swinging over the big starting handle just below the radiator, until - at last - the whole vehicle 'juddered' into life, vibrating violently. Then he leapt quickly into his seat, lest it 'conk out' and away it went! I can see it now, with my little aunt in her wide-brimmed hat, waving to us from the back seat, as it disappeared under the bridge and out of sight round the curve - just like some big, black beetle scurrying away to its lair!

Goods traffic was relatively unaffected by the change. The IWC would leave wagons on the FYN main line at a prearranged time and vice versa. Much of the traffic originated at Medina Wharf in IWC wagons so the goods stock was ample for the company's needs. Traffic passing off the FYN included a sizeable amount of milk and livestock that, in the absence of proper cattle wagons, was carried in converted open wagons.

Apart from a 1,000 gallon water tank, no accommodation had been made at Newport for the locomotives and rail motor until after their arrival. Since it was more convenient to operate trains from Newport, two short sidings were laid between the running line and FYN goods sidings giving access to a coal stage and wooden sheds for the two locomotives and rail motor. The points were worked from a ground frame locked by a key on the train staff. Knowing this, IWC staff would telephone the FYN shortly after a train had left for Freshwater with the news that there were wagons that needed to be collected urgently. This was only cured by making a separate key to unlock the frame without using the train staff - this dangerous piece of equipment was promptly taken out use after the SR took charge. Remarkably few mishaps were recorded at this time; the FYN was a long way from Westminster and officials soon had other diversions.

At the end of the summer season the number of passenger trains was reduced to six each way on weekdays, eight on Saturdays and four on Sundays. This was followed in October by a letter to the Editor of the *County Press*:

AN INDEPENDENT RAILWAY, 1913 TO 1923

... it is disappointing to find that not only are there exactly the same number of trains from Freshwater to Newport as last year, but that connections with the Central Company's trains at Newport have been apparently totally ignored. The 4.35 train from Freshwater to Newport which used to give such good connections to all parts of the Island, and to Portsmouth and Southampton, is cancelled, and the result is that the last train for Southampton and Ventnor Town leaves Freshwater at 2.15 pm and passengers for Ryde and Sandown have the doubtful pleasure of more than an hour's wait at Newport.

Although the letter may have been written at the instigation of the IWC the complaints were quite justified. Traders in Freshwater discovered that they were no longer getting the passing trade from day trippers as they walked from the station to the beaches near Totland. On 18th February, 1914 the Freshwater, Totland Bay and Yarmouth Tradesmen's Association wrote to the IWC asking it to do all in its power to run through trains between Ryde and Freshwater before Easter. Through trains to and from Ryde did not start again until after the SR took charge in 1923.

During the 1914 summer season there were 10 return workings on weekdays (including the early morning mail train) and six on Sundays. The summer season was cut short when war broke out in August and the Government assumed control of most of Britain's railways including the FYN under the terms of an 1871 Act of Parliament. Management was delegated to a Railway Executive Committee made up of the managers of the more important companies. The Freshwater company Receivers and staff remained at their posts. Some employees were called up for military service but the absence of any records makes it difficult to know precisely what happened - women were taken on to offset the resulting staff shortages.

Although local hoteliers tried to maintain 'business as usual', the requisition of many vessels plying between the mainland and the Island inevitably reduced the level of services that could be offered - in 1915 there were only five sailings on the Lymington to Yarmouth route in each direction during the week and none on Sundays. On the FYN, the winter timetable remained in force throughout the year with modifications to cater for workmen who travelled to Cowes to work in the shipyards and other wartime industries in the vicinity.

The dispute with the IWC faded following the outbreak of war but the FYN had not heard the last from the IWC. Russell Willmott wrote to the Board of Trade on 23rd December, 1914:

A few days ago three of the Freshwater Company's coaches left standing at their new platform, and ran away on to our run-round line near to our Box. I think we ought to be protected against future occurrences of this nature . . .

Mr Willmott might have added that there was no official means of communicating between the two signal boxes apart from the interlocking of certain signals; the block instruments to Carisbrooke had been transferred to the FYN box and signalmen had to shout to each other when exchanging trains! Whatever the merits of the complaint, Sir Sam Fay had more pressing responsibilities as he had been placed in charge of military and munitions movements in Britain; later he became Director-General of Movements and

Railways. He refused to apply to the courts for permission to spend money on changing the lie of the points; Mr Willmott responded that the IWC would not be responsible if such accidents repeated themselves. The only capital expenditure by the FYN during 1915 was £18 9s. 0d. on the provision of an electric light standard and wiring at Newport.

By 1916 the Government was discouraging travel for pleasure purposes. Tourist traffic disappeared altogether after the Government issued an order in January 1917 to abolish cheap fares and reduce train services. The train service rarely justified more than a shuttle service and the few additional trains could cross at Ningwood. At Carisbrooke the crossing loop was taken out of use and trains used the main platform. However, the Newport-Carisbrooke and Carisbrooke-Ningwood single line train staffs were retained so crews had to carry both; this duplication was solved in early SR days merely by welding the two together.

During the period of Government control companies received compensation if net income fell short of that earned in 1913 and if profits exceeded 1913 levels the excess had to be paid to the Government. There was no prospect that the FYN would make excessive profits but clearly a little creative accountancy took place to ensure that expenditure matched income - there were many ways in which some judicious expenditure could be incurred so that the Government would not receive the benefits! The profits were higher than in IWC days so Sir Sam Fay was right in his prediction. Income was sufficient to pay the interest due on the 3½ per cent debenture stock and an increasing contribution to the arrears of 5 per cent stock. The following figures were given in accounts issued by the Receivers (some of the entries for 1913 and 1914 might not be accurate to the last penny):

Year ending 31 Dec.	Traffic receipts £	s.	d.	Expenditure £	s.	d.	Balance £	s.	d.	Miscellaneous receipts £	s.	d.
1913	7,485	0	0	5,834	0	0	1,651	0	0	284	0	0
1914	7,822	0	0	6,169	0	0	1,652	17	2	248	3	5
1915	8,397	18	5	6,779	16	11	1,618	1	6	341	1	9
1916	9,028	9	2	7,409	5	6	1,619	3	8	358	13	7
1917	9,506	9	5	7,887	4	11	1,619	4	6	323	5	3
1918	11,421	14	0	9,802	9	6	1,619	4	6	378	19	5

No Board meetings were held for about two years following the appointment of the Receivers in July 1913 and when they recommenced proceedings were taken up purely with the transfer of shares; there were no meetings of shareholders until the final year of the company's life.

The signing of an armistice with Germany on 11th November, 1918 made no real difference to Britain's railway companies. The railways could expect compensation from the Government but that was unlikely to be sufficient to make good all the ravages of war and they lacked capital to make up the shortfall. The period of government control demonstrated that there could be economies if the number of companies was reduced. Some politicians favoured Nationalisation but attempts to pass an enabling Bill through Parliament in 1919 failed; that year the railways were freed of government control. This was of no

AN INDEPENDENT RAILWAY, 1913 TO 1923

consequence to the FYN as it remained in the hands of its Receivers. The GCR management had given way to Mr G.M. Button, a former IWC employee, but otherwise matters remained largely as before. In 1919 a writer commented:

> The Company possesses a single platform station at Newport, situated a little distance from that of the Central Company; and some little inconvenience is occasioned to passengers in traversing the uncovered path between the two stations, particularly on a wet day, especially when encumbered with luggage. The inconvenience has of late been somewhat mitigated by running the greater part of the Freshwater trains into the bay of the Isle of Wight Central Railway's station . . .

This inconvenience was not confined to passengers. On 16th June, 1919 the Board of Trade received a letter from Edward Parker on behalf of the Freshwater, Totland Bay and Yarmouth Tradesmen's Association. He referred to the 'gross laxity in transferring the luggage of through passengers from one station to another. Both companies blame the other . . . Lately a custom has sprung up of charging farmers and dairymen a fee for portering milk, meat etc., from one platform to the other . . .' Russell Willmott responded by giving details of the transfer arrangements that existed between the two companies. From May 1914 trains had been running into the IWC station at 9 am, 1 pm, 3 pm and 6.40 pm. Parcels etc. were transferred on those trains but if perishables were received at other times the FYN was told to come and get them by train or otherwise. He maintained that the complaint was about milk coming from the Freshwater line which was the responsibility of the FYN to transfer. Sir Sam Fay denied knowledge of any attempt to impose additional charges and asked that the tradesmen's association report specific instances. Nothing more was heard so the staff had evidently taken the hint! In June 1920 the local authorities repeated the complaints about inconvenience caused by the existence of two stations at Newport.

In common with other parts of Britain, the Isle of Wight experienced a considerable growth in road transport fuelled by the availability of surplus lorries and drivers; this was not confined to goods traffic as a number of firms began offering excursions using motor vehicles. In the Autumn of 1919 the FYN was caught up in a national strike of railwaymen - 'The Great Strike' as the *Isle of Wight County Press* put it. The dispute had its origins in pay rises given to railwaymen during the war but which the Government refused to consolidate into the men's wages - they had already conceded an eight hour working day. The *County Press* reported extensively on events within the Island:

> As far as the train service was concerned the West Wight was completely cut off from the remainder of the Island from midnight on Friday [26th September] until Tuesday evening . . . The whole of the staff of the Freshwater Railway were out, excepting the clerks and stationmasters at Newport, Yarmouth and Freshwater. The two engines were left at Newport in such a position as to prevent the use of the small rail-motor. On Tuesday a driver and a porter at Freshwater returned to duty . . . many residents assisted to get the engine into working order and run the first train out from Newport on Tuesday evening. The train carried mails and coal, which was getting short in the West Wight. It left Newport about 5 pm, and arrived at Yarmouth just before 6 o'clock, being heartily cheered both there and at Freshwater. On Wednesday a service of two trains each way was commenced . . .

TIME TABLES, 1st NOVEMBER, 1919, and until further notice.

WEEKDAYS.

Distance from Newport Jc.	DOWN.	1 Motor Mail.	2 Goods.	3 Pass.	4 Pass.	5 Pass.	6 Pass.	7 Pass.	8 Pass.	9 Pass. & Mail.	10 Pass.
m. chains.		a.m. See Note A	a.m. See Note B	a.m.	a.m.	p.m.	p.m. S	p.m. X	p.m. S	p.m.	p.m. S
0 6	NEWPORT (Central) dep.	4.30	5.30	9 0	11.00	1 8	3.15	3.15	5.14	6.45	8.45
	(F.Y.N.) arr.		5.35	9 4	11.04	1 15	3.19	3.20	5.18	6.48	8.49
	,, dep.	4.35	6 0		11.44	1 15		4.035		6.50	9 0
1 12	Carisbrooke ,,					1 19		4.39		6.54	
1 48	Gunville Siding ,,										
2 36	Watchingwell ,,		6.25	H	H	H	3H20	H	3H20	H	H
3 36	Calbourne ,,		H								
6 57	Dowty's Siding arr.		6.30			1.30			3H29	7 5	9 0
6 68	Ningwood dep.		6.40		11.55	1.34	3H34	4.34	3H33	7 9	9 4
8 17	Wellow Siding ,,										
9 67	Yarmouth ,,	5.30	7 2	9.27	12 7	1.42	3.42	5 2	5.41	7.17	9 12
11 69	FRESHWATER arr.	5.40	7 5	9.32	12.12	1.47	3.47	5 7	5.46	7.22	9 17

SUNDAYS.

	1 Goods & Mail.	2 Pass.
	a.m.	p.m.
NEWPORT (Central) dep.	5.50	6.30
(F.Y.N.) arr.	5.55	6.34
dep.	6 0	
Carisbrooke		
Gunville Siding		
Watchingwell		H
Calbourne		6.45
Dowty's Siding		
Ningwood		6.49
Wellow Siding		
Yarmouth	6.35	6.57
FRESHWATER	6.45	7 2

WEEKDAYS.

Distance from Freshwater.	UP.	1 Pass.	2 Pass.	3 Motor.	4 Pass.	5 Pass.	6 Pass.	7 Pass.	8 Pass.	9 Pass. & Mail.	10 Goods.
m. chains.		a.m.	a.m.	a.m.	p.m.	p.m. M	p.m. S	p.m. X	p.m. S	p.m. M	p.m. S
0 0	FRESHWATER dep.	8 5	9.40	11 5	12.20	2.25	4 0	5.35	5.52	7.35	9.45
·2 1	Yarmouth ,,	8010	9.45	11 10	12.25	2.55	4 5	5.40	5.57	7.40	10 0
	Wellow Siding ,,										
	Ningwood dep.	8018	9.53		12.34	2.33	4.13	5H48	6 5	7.48	10 10
4 23	Dowty's Siding ,,	8020	9.57		12.38	2.37	4.17	5H52		7.52	10 20
5 33	Calbourne ,,	H	H		H	H	H	H	6H20	H	H
8 24	Watchingwell ,,										
9 36	Gunville Siding ,,	8.33	10 8		12.50	2.48	4.28	6H3	6H20	8H3	10.20
11 2	Carisbrooke ,,	8.37	10 12		12.54	2.52		6 7	6.21	8 7	
11 77	,, (F.Y.N.) dep.	Stop	Stop	11.35	12.55	2H55	Stop	6 24	Stop	Stop	Stop
	,, (Central) arr.			Stop	1 0	3H0		6 29			

SUNDAYS.

	1 Pass.	2 Pass. & Mail.
	a.m.	p.m.
FRESHWATER	8.20	7.25
Yarmouth	8.25	7.30
Wellow Siding		
Ningwood	8.43	7.38
Dowty's Siding	8.47	7.42
Calbourne	H	H
Watchingwell		
Gunville Siding	8.58	7.53
Carisbrooke	9 2	7.57
NEWPORT	Stop	Stop

NOTES.

A. Motor leaves for Newport (Central), 4.40 a.m.	C. Conveys Live Stock for Lymington Boat.	E. Stops to set down only. H. Stops if required on notice being given to the Guard or at the Station.	S. Saturdays only. X. Saturdays excepted. R. Stops if required to detach or attach wagons.
B. Engine leaves for Newport Goods Yard (I.W.C.), 5.45 a.m.	D. Conveys Live Stock for Island Stations.	M. Mixed if required.	RR. Runs if required.

N.B.—The Goods train times are approximate only, and earlier running is permissible.

Extract from working timetable, 1st November, 1919.

Mr G.M. Button, the manager of the Freshwater railway, has received numerous offers of assistance . . . On Wednesday about two-thirds of the platelayers on the line resumed work, on the appeal of Mr G. Drower, the veteran permanent way inspector. On Thursday morning Admiral Sir Sackville Carden of Yarmouth, was amongst the large staff of voluntary workers assisting in running the first trains from Freshwater. The Admiral gave a hand with luggage at Newport and assisted the guard. The voluntary workers all wore brassarts on the arm bearing the letters F. Y. & N. Ry., followed by V. W. (voluntary worker). Yesterday (Friday) several platelayers who had returned to work earlier in the week, again joined their comrades on strike. About 40 per cent of the company's employees were out yesterday.

The newspaper gave details of the temporary passenger service; there was no Sunday service:

From Newport - 9.45 am, 4.35 pm (this train will depart at 5.30 pm today, 4th October)
From Freshwater - 8.30 am, 2.20 pm

The sudden start to the strike caused a considerable amount of inconvenience to the public including farmers who were unable to get their milk to market, the London newspapers and food distribution. Their needs were promptly alleviated by road vehicles so the damage had been already done by the time the strike came to an end on Saturday 5th October.

On 1st November a new railway timetable came into force. The introduction of the eight hour working day meant that one train crew could no longer work the long hours that had previously been the norm. An interesting solution was found in the employment of the rail motor with its driver to carry the early morning mails to Freshwater; it was timed to make a return working later that morning but saw no further use, a reasonable decision when the weather was likely to be inclement! A conventional train worked by a single set of men maintained a shuttle service at other times. Although running times had apparently been reduced this was illusory as the 32 minute Newport to Freshwater journey commenced at the FYN station at Newport and an additional 10 minutes was added for those trains starting at the IWC station. There were five return journeys on weekdays and one on Sundays.

Just as the 1919 strike had an effect on the FYN so other tragedies played their part. Inflation had forced up prices, wages and operating costs. This came to a head in January 1920 when the newly formed Ministry of Transport ordered increases of ordinary passenger fares to 75 per cent above pre-war levels, season ticket rates to 50 per cent higher and a doubling of goods rates. In the spring of 1921 a national miners strike threatened a shortage of coal and the Ministry ordered a drastic reduction in train services. No such restrictions applied to petrol and enterprising Islanders ran motor bus services; they outlived the end of the strike and quickly multiplied. Most operators targeted the other railways in the Island but the FYN was not immune as it had competition from the Yarmouth Touring Company. The end of the strike was followed by an order to again raise railway fares and in a rare moment of co-operation the IWC and FYN obtained Ministry of Transport permission to offer a limited range of excursion fares during the summer months; that was not enough to reverse a fall in traffic receipts in 1922.

WORKING OF TRAINS TO AND FROM NEWPORT (CENTRAL).

The engine of all trains scheduled to run into the Isle of Wight Central Company's Newport Station must run round the train at the Newport North Signal Box before drawing into the Station.

When leaving Newport (Central) the train must be propelled either from the Down Main Platform or the Freshwater Bay Line, as the case may be, to the Cowes Main Line beyond the Freshwater Junction at Newport North, and then drawn into the Freshwater Line Platform.

These trains must not exceed 8 vehicles.

The Brake Van must be run at the leading end of the train when propelled—that is, at the end opposite to the engine, and the Guard must travel in this Brake Van. No other duty must interfere with his keeping a good look-out when the train is being propelled.

MIXED TRAINS.

Nos. 5 and 9 Up trains may, when necessary, be run as mixed trains, subject to the following conditions:—

(a) That the Engine and Passenger vehicles of such mixed trains shall be provided with continuous brakes worked from the Engine.

(b) That the Goods Wagons shall be conveyed behind the Passenger Vehicles with brake van or brake vans in the proportion of one brake van for every ten wagons or fractional part of ten wagons.

(c) No "Mixed" train must exceed 25 vehicles, including the Passenger vehicles, Goods Wagons and Goods Brake.

(d) That the maximum average speed of any such train throughout the journey between stations shall not exceed 25 miles an hour.

(e) That all such trains shall stop at all stations, or at intervals not exceeding 10 miles.

(f) No dead-buffered vehicles or wagons loaded with coal, coke, bricks or other mineral traffic must be attached to a mixed train.

Extract from the Appendices to the FYN Working Timetable 1919.

(g) No wagons are to be attached or detached at intermediate stations without special authority from the Manager's Office, Newport.

Trains for the conveyance of Horses, Cattle or any other livestock, when vehicles are added for the conveyance of Passengers, shall be subject to the same Regulations and Conditions as apply to " Mixed " Trains. Drovers, Grooms or other persons travelling in charge of such stock shall not be deemed to be passengers.

SCALE.

Shewing what proportion of Unbraked Vehicles, fitted with Continuous Pipes, may be attached to a Passenger Train as provided in Clause (b).

To a Train consisting of BRAKED vehicles, equal to—	Four or six wheeled Carriages or Brake Vans UNBRAKED.		Horse Boxes, Carriage Trucks, Cattle Trucks or other four wheeled vehicles not carrying Passengers. UNBRAKED.
3 may be attached	1	or	2
3½ ,,	1	or	2
4 ,,	1	or	2
4½ ,,	1	or	3
5 ,,	1	or	3
5½ ,,	1	or	3
6 ,,	2	or	4
6½ ,,	2	or	4

Half vehicle means a Carriage Truck, Horse Box, Fish Van, Cattle Truck or other four wheeled vehicle not carrying passengers.

N.B.—It is permissible to attach not exceeding one Goods or Cattle Wagon, whether loaded or empty, to the rear of a Passenger Train without an extra brake.

MAXIMUM LOADS OF ENGINES.

Engine No. 1.—11 Mineral wagons, or 14 Goods wagons, or 22 Empty wagons, or 10 Passenger vehicles.

Engine No. 2.—10 Mineral wagons, or 12 Goods wagons, or 18 Empty wagons, or 9 Passenger vehicles.

Brake Van to count as 1 Goods.

Extract from the Appendices to the FYN Working Timetable 1919.

IWC No. 9 and its train of LSWR carriages stand in the platform at Freshwater. Note the water tower and sheds on the right.
A.B. MacLeod/IWSR Collection

Year ending 31 Dec.	Traffic receipts £ s. d.			Expenditure £ s. d.			Balance £ s. d.			Miscellaneous receipts* £ s. d.			Govt comp. £
1919	14,707	0	6	13,087	16	0	1,619	4	6	437	4	8	nil
1920	16,321	3	1	14,701	18	7	1,619	4	6	523	2	0	nil
1921	16,617	6	8	14,305	5	2	2,312	1	6	588	10	3	951
1922†	13,312	7	3	9,810	2	8	3,502	4	7	969	13	5	2,927

Year ending 31 Dec.	Passenger traffic Nos. carried				Goods traffic		Other Minerals	Total Livestock
	First	Third	Workmen	Season	Merchandise Tons	Coal Tons	Tons	No.
1919	4,788	156,256	8,916	179	2,429	187	734	2,223#
1920	2,410	150,640	10,840	175	1,942	107	1,246	3,174#
1921	1,637	134,517	6,058	62	1,036	258	2,872	2,609
1922	2,195	169,544	5,724	66	1,177	9,485	1,353	3,977

The detailed figures for 1919 to 1922 give an insight into the nature and variety of passenger and goods traffic carried by the FYN during its independent life. The decline in the numbers of wealthier first class passengers reflected a national trend evident since the opening of the railway; they were replaced by less well-off passengers who travelled third class. The significant number of workmen was a wartime traffic that gradually faded away. The low figures for coal is puzzling especially as there was a considerable increase in 1922; presumably it had been cheaper for merchants to receive their supplies by road from Yarmouth. The livestock traffic was soon lost to road transport.

An Act for the compulsory amalgamation of Britain's railways into four regional companies became law in 1921. In preparation for the creation of the Southern Railway Company the LSWR took on the task of purchasing the Island railway companies. Amicable settlements were reached with the IWR and IWC but an offer of £50,000 for the FYN was refused as its Directors wanted £70,000. They claimed that no account had been taken of the additional income that would accrue to the railway upon the opening of the Solent tunnel. As a consequence the FYN remained an independent company when the Southern Railway came into being on 1st January, 1923.

The 1921 Act ordered that a dispute should be referred to a Railways Amalgamation Tribunal. In order to save the time and cost of a hearing the SR increased the offer for the FYN to £60,000 but this was also refused. The last recorded FYN Board meeting took place on 25th April, 1923 attended by Philip Collins, Chairman, Charles Hodge and Frank Aman. They discussed a claim for compensation that had been submitted to the Amalgamation Tribunal and resolved to ask for free passes for life over the SR's system 'as had been done in the case of the Directors of the other Island Railway Companies'.

The tribunal met on 20th June, 1923 to hear the case. Sir Sam Fay repeated an opinion already voiced by the IWR Chairman that the SR would operate the line more cheaply than hitherto and that should be born in mind in reaching any settlement. Mr Bischoff, solicitor for the SR, countered that this was in direct opposition to previous utterances from the FYN. Frank Aman expressed the

---
* Miscellaneous receipts for 1922 included 'general interest' of £485 3s. 5d.
† For comparison, we have set out figures for individual stations during 1923 in a separate table.
# 1919 - 19 horses, 423 cattle, 157 calves, 1,208 sheep, 416 pigs; 1920 - 1 horse, 547 cattle, 119 calves, 949 sheep, 1,558 pigs.

110 THE FRESHWATER, YARMOUTH & NEWPORT RAILWAY

FYN No. 1 is pulling an up train as it passes the rarely-photographed crossing at Petticoat Lane on 12th May, 1919. The signals quite correctly stand in the clear position. *K. Nunn Collection*

FYN No. 1 stands with its train of carriages in the bay platform at the Central station on 2nd June, 1921. *H.C. Casserley*

Year ending 31 Dec.	Traffic receipts			Expenditure			Balance			Miscellaneous receipts*			Govt comp.
	£	s.	d.	£	s.	d.	£	s.	d.	£	s.	d.	£
1919	14,707	0	6	13,087	16	0	1,619	4	6	437	4	8	nil
1920	16,321	3	1	14,701	18	7	1,619	4	6	523	2	0	nil
1921	16,617	6	8	14,305	5	2	2,312	1	6	588	10	3	951
1922†	13,312	7	3	9,810	2	8	3,502	4	7	969	13	5	2,927

Year ending 31 Dec.	Passenger traffic Nos. carried				Goods traffic		Other Minerals	Total Livestock
					Merchandise	Coal		
	First	Third	Workmen	Season	Tons	Tons	Tons	No.
1919	4,788	156,256	8,916	179	2,429	187	734	2,223#
1920	2,410	150,640	10,840	175	1,942	107	1,246	3,174#
1921	1,637	134,517	6,058	62	1,036	258	2,872	2,609
1922	2,195	169,544	5,724	66	1,177	9,485	1,353	3,977

The detailed figures for 1919 to 1922 give an insight into the nature and variety of passenger and goods traffic carried by the FYN during its independent life. The decline in the numbers of wealthier first class passengers reflected a national trend evident since the opening of the railway; they were replaced by less well-off passengers who travelled third class. The significant number of workmen was a wartime traffic that gradually faded away. The low figures for coal is puzzling especially as there was a considerable increase in 1922; presumably it had been cheaper for merchants to receive their supplies by road from Yarmouth. The livestock traffic was soon lost to road transport.

An Act for the compulsory amalgamation of Britain's railways into four regional companies became law in 1921. In preparation for the creation of the Southern Railway Company the LSWR took on the task of purchasing the Island railway companies. Amicable settlements were reached with the IWR and IWC but an offer of £50,000 for the FYN was refused as its Directors wanted £70,000. They claimed that no account had been taken of the additional income that would accrue to the railway upon the opening of the Solent tunnel. As a consequence the FYN remained an independent company when the Southern Railway came into being on 1st January, 1923.

The 1921 Act ordered that a dispute should be referred to a Railways Amalgamation Tribunal. In order to save the time and cost of a hearing the SR increased the offer for the FYN to £60,000 but this was also refused. The last recorded FYN Board meeting took place on 25th April, 1923 attended by Philip Collins, Chairman, Charles Hodge and Frank Aman. They discussed a claim for compensation that had been submitted to the Amalgamation Tribunal and resolved to ask for free passes for life over the SR's system 'as had been done in the case of the Directors of the other Island Railway Companies'.

The tribunal met on 20th June, 1923 to hear the case. Sir Sam Fay repeated an opinion already voiced by the IWR Chairman that the SR would operate the line more cheaply than hitherto and that should be born in mind in reaching any settlement. Mr Bischoff, solicitor for the SR, countered that this was in direct opposition to previous utterances from the FYN. Frank Aman expressed the

---

* Miscellaneous receipts for 1922 included 'general interest' of £485 3s. 5d.
† For comparison, we have set out figures for individual stations during 1923 in a separate table.
# 1919 - 19 horses, 423 cattle, 157 calves, 1,208 sheep, 416 pigs; 1920 - 1 horse, 547 cattle, 119 calves, 949 sheep, 1,558 pigs.

FYN No. 1 is pulling an up train as it passes the rarely-photographed crossing at Petticoat Lane on 12th May, 1919. The signals quite correctly stand in the clear position.   *K. Nunn Collection*

FYN No. 1 stands with its train of carriages in the bay platform at the Central station on 2nd June, 1921.   *H.C. Casserley*

AN INDEPENDENT RAILWAY, 1913 TO 1923

opinion that the Solent tunnel was a very definite possibility and asserted that it could be built for £90,000 and would bring in a revenue of £30,000 a year.

On 11th August Sir Hugh Babington Smith and his two members of the tribunal decided that the original offer was fair and imposed a settlement of £50,000. Payment was made in SR shares distributed as follows:

Value	Stock	SR stock to be issued
£42,800	6% Preferred Ordinary Stock	cancelled
£50,073	Deferred Ordinary Stock	cancelled
£42,000	5% Perpetual Preference Stock	£21,000 Ordinary 'B' Stock
£24,077	5% 'B' Debenture Stock	£9,630 16s. Preferred Ordinary Stock
£47,300	5% Perpetual Debenture Stock	£37,840 5% Preference Stock
£20,000	3½% 'A' Pre-Debenture Stock	£17,500 4% Debenture Stock

A final shareholders meeting was held on 24th July to vote the Directors £400 compensation for loss of office. A report to the SR traffic officers mentioned that it had formally taken over the running of the Freshwater railway on and from Monday 27th August, 1923.

Meanwhile, the FYN summer service commenced on 9th July, 1923. Anticipating the impending change of ownership all FYN passenger trains worked into the bay platform at Newport IWC station and the FYN station closed for passengers that day - it remained open for parcels, etc. until 1st September. The mileage travelled by the rail motor had fallen significantly and it no longer figured in the timetable. Instead a shuttle service of eight trains a day ran from Newport to Freshwater and nine in the reverse direction; the odd number was balanced by an unadvertised mail and goods train at the start of the day. An additional train worked from Newport to Freshwater on Saturday evenings and there were five return workings on Sundays.

The weekday service required two train crews, a fact born out by a list of staff at the time. Mr Button had retired and been replaced by J. Thomas assisted by a clerk in the office, inspector Drower and 11 permanent way men. The locomotive department had two drivers, two firemen and a cleaner. The traffic department consisted of two guards, station masters at Newport, Carisbrooke, Calbourne, Ningwood, Yarmouth and Freshwater; they had no assistance apart from three staff based at Newport, one of whom was the rail motor driver. There were four women crossing keepers and a fifth lady in charge at Watchingwell - in all a total of 35 staff. Most staff joined the SR; an exception was Mr Drower who retired at the grand old age of 82.

So what conclusions can we reach concerning the FYN? It might be said in cruel economic terms that the railway should never have existed but that is to ignore the whole reason why many railways were built. The construction of the IWR encouraged development along the Island's eastern seaboard and whatever we may think of such unrestrained growth the IWR with its financial problems was turned into a relatively successful undertaking. By the time the FYN arrived on the scene it was too late; development was much slower in coming and never grew to the same extent as elsewhere. This left the company with financial problems from which it never emerged; the shareholders lost their investment and only a select few made money out of the FYN. Even so the railway brought to a remote part of the Island a rapid transport system where none existed before and in serving the local population achieved as much as any of the other Isle of Wight railways.

Traffic to and from FYN stations in 1923

Station	Carisbrooke	Watchingwell	Calbourne	Ningwood	Yarmouth	Freshwater
Annual receipts:		£	£	£	£	£
Passengers	no figures provided	60.4.6	331.13.10	556.12.9	1,321.17.1	3,955.15.5
Parcels		18/4	337.1.8	578.16.8	47.8.2	572.3.4
Goods		7/8	45.2.3	90.17.2	183.11.9	317.19.8
Various		-	-	-	3.19.4	15.19.9½
General goods tonnage (monthly):						
Forwarded		-	8 for year	1	15c	10
Received		-	644 for year	1	17t 7c	54
Coal and coke tonnage (monthly):						
Forwarded			-	-	-	-
Received		18t 3c for year	330 for year	1	122	500
Number of milk churns dealt with daily:						
Forwarded Summer		-	13	30	-	8
Winter		-	8	25	-	8
Transferred Summer		-	-	-	-	-
Winter		-	-	-	-	-
Received Summer		-	-	-	-	-
Winter		-	-	-	-	-
Number of regular season ticket holders:		2 summer 1 winter	5 scholars 1 adult	3	4	5
Number of staff employed Summer		1	1	1	2	4
Winter		1	1	1	2	4
Monthly number of passengers booked: (heaviest month in 1923)		263	858	1,080	4,691	6,581
Monthly number of tickets collected: (heaviest month in 1923)		not known	not known	1,023	3,258	12,500

Chapter Eleven

The Line Described

In the company's eyes the railway commenced at Freshwater. However, it was worked from the Newport end for most or all of its life so our description begins there. To avoid any confusion it is worth mentioning that *down* trains ran to Freshwater. The lengths of platforms and sidings are taken from a survey carried out by the IWC in the years 1911 and 1912. SR bridge numbers and mileages have been adopted as being the most reliable but we have largely ignored the numerous culverts and cattle creeps.

The Board of Trade Inspector's reports for the opening of the railway in 1889 contained the following information. The 11 mile 66 chain railway had gradients up to 1 in 60 and curves (at Newport Junction) of 9 chains. The viaduct at Newport had nine brick spans of 20 ft and 19 spans varying between 39 ft and 25 ft 6 in. with concrete foundations, piers and girder of wrought iron and a cross girder from rolled steel joists; the rails were carried on 20 longitudinals secured between angle irons bolted on the cross girders and a floor of iron plates. Calbourne viaduct consisted of nine spans varying between 25½ and 27¼ ft, with abutments in concrete and in all other respects similar to the Newport viaduct; the height from rail level to the bottom of the stream was 25½ ft. The widest of the nine overbridges had a span of 21 ft 8 in., five were in brick, one had concrete abutments and a wrought-iron girder top, one with concrete abutments and a timber top and two were in timber. One of the seven underbridges had a span of 33 ft built in brick with concrete abutments and a wrought-iron girder, two bridges spanning 8 ft and 10 ft had concrete abutments and a wrought-iron top whilst four had 8 ft spans and were entirely in concrete. The 11 culverts had concrete walls; four had spans of between 8 ft and 21 ft with wrought-iron girder tops and the remaining seven culverts had spans of between 4 ft and 8 ft with concrete tops.

The width of the formation level was 16 ft laid with 9 in. of washed gravel and coarse sand as ballast. The flat bottom steel rails in 24 ft lengths weighed 64 lb. to the yard fished at the joints and fastened to sleepers by fang bolts (and shoes) and dog spikes, there being eight of the former and ten of the latter in each rail length. The fir sleepers measured 9 ft by 9 in. by 4½ in. and were spaced 2 ft from centre to centre at the joints and 2 ft 9 in. elsewhere. Stations had been built at Carisbrooke, Watchingwell, Calbourne, Ningwood, Yarmouth and Freshwater, all with sidings except at Watchingwell and Ningwood; there were four level crossings at which houses were provided. Messrs Stevens supplied the signalling for the stations except at Newport where the North box and associated equipment had been provided by the Railway Signal Company. The line was worked by the staff and ticket system with Sykes simple one wire block instruments. Ningwood was initially the only crossing point and so the single line sections were Newport-Ningwood and Ningwood-Freshwater; Calbourne was a block post but not a staff station.

At Newport, the Freshwater junction was a few yards north of the station. If the provisions in the FYN's first Act in 1880 had come to fruition the junction

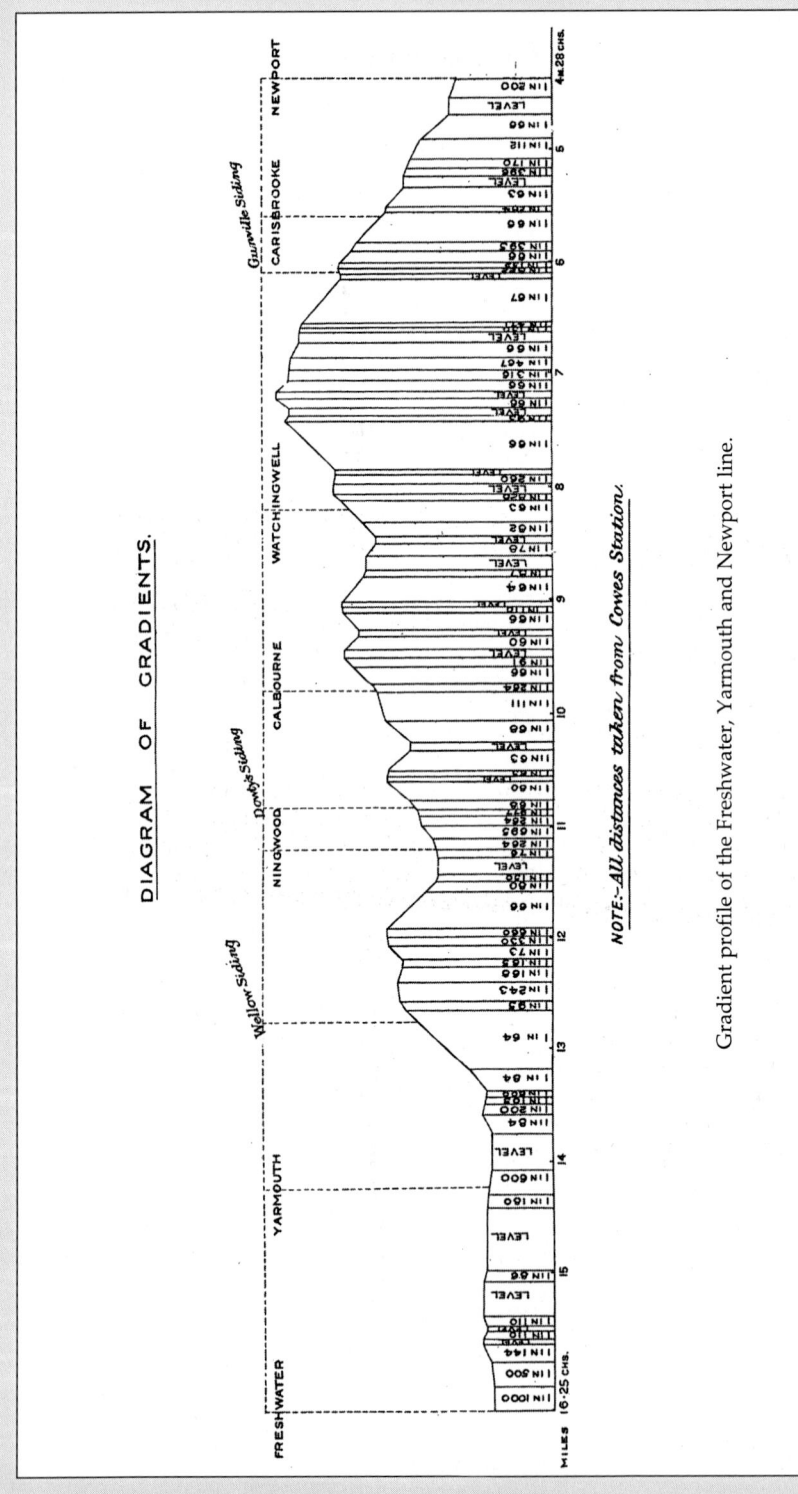

Gradient profile of the Freshwater, Yarmouth and Newport line.

THE LINE DESCRIBED

Looking north from the IWC station at Newport in 1920 we see that the FYN had extended its carriage siding behind the north signal box and, judging by the numbers, is home to most of the company's stock of carriages. The hefty bracket signal in front of the box was erected in May 1919.

R. Silsbury/IWSR Collection

The sharply curved junction between the FYN and IWC at Newport is seen in this view dated September 1920. The signal manufacturer's stencil 'Newport I of W' is still visible on the post to the right.

R. Silsbury/IWSR Collection

The IWC workshops and running shed dominate the background to the FYN station at Newport emphasising the proximity of the two railways. Looking east from the footbridge we can see the entrance from the footpath and the company's booking office.
Lens of Sutton

would have faced Newport but instead it faced Cowes, an awkward arrangement made worse by a Board of Trade requirement that locomotives run round each time trains entered and left the station. Double track was extended several hundred yards north of the junction where there was a new 35-lever signal box. Most trains worked in and out of the through platform roads. It was not until 1911 that the Board of Trade was asked to permit propelling of trains into the station but even then permission was not given to propel into the bay platform.

Leaving the junction with the IWC, the line to Freshwater began a sharp 9 chain curve towards the west on which was the station constructed by the FYN in 1913. At the eastern end of the 175 ft by 15 ft wooden platform was a signal box containing a 12-lever frame; key signals were interlocked but there were no block instruments governing movements between the IWC and FYN signal boxes. Next came a wooden and corrugated iron waiting shelter (measuring 23 ft by 7 ft wide and 11 ft high) that was later enclosed in wood and glass. Midway along the platform was a single large nameboard lettered 'NEWPORT' in black letters on a white background and at the far end a wooden building with a corrugated iron roof and canopy that did duty as a booking office. Passengers reached the station down a ramp from a footpath leading from the Central station. The footpath continued across the line on a cast-iron footbridge (bridge No. 1), renewed in 1898, to a newly built approach road from Hunnyhill. There was a run-round loop opposite the platform and a headshunt extending behind the IWC signal box as a carriage siding. Having become a single line under the footbridge, next to which was a water tower, a spur then branched to a goods yard with two sidings and a cattle dock. Two shorter sidings served wooden locomotive and rail motor sheds. Entry to the sidings was controlled by a single-lever ground frame locked by an Annett's key attached to the train staff. The company's offices were in a corrugated iron building next to the entrance to the goods yard at the foot of Hunnyhill.

A few yards beyond the points to the goods yard the railway crossed two bridges described collectively as Newport, Hunnyhill or Towngate viaduct (Nos. 2 and 3). The first bridge was partly on a curve of roughly 11 chains radius but the second was almost straight, 576 ft in length, they crossed the Newport to Cowes Turnpike and a tributary of Lugeley Brook.

The line began to climb as it curved towards the south through a cutting before reaching Petticoat Lane crossing. Although leading only to two small farms, it was described as a public road and was originally to have crossed the line on an overbridge. In June 1888 William Lidstone wrote to the Board of Trade explaining that it had been necessary to introduce a gradient at this point and the bridge would make the gradient worse. His request to substitute a level crossing and a gatekeeper's lodge was referred to Col Hutchinson who agreed to the changes but added '. . . on account of the cutting and course, signals interlocked with the gates'. A five-lever frame was provided to work home and distant signals in both directions. It is a reflection of the wages at the time that it was thought more economical to substitute a manned level crossing for a bridge. The line continued to loop to the south whilst still climbing on a low embankment for a short distance. A reverse curve then took the railway back to a westerly direction.

This view looking west from the footbridge shows the sharply curved lead into the FYN goods yard with its single lever ground frame on the right. By the date of this photograph in September 1920 there is a cattle dock and a locomotive shed inside which can be glimpsed locomotive No. 2. The down starter and up home signals on the same post were typical of FYN practice.
R. Silsbury/IWSR Collection

J. Ball & Co. erected this office building for the company in July 1913 next to the entrance to its goods yard at Newport. It remained in railway use until the closure of the Newport station in 1966!
R. Silsbury Collection

The country end of the viaduct is seen in about 1935 after the heavier class 'O2' 0-4-4Ts had taken charge of Freshwater line trains. W30 *Shorwell* is hauling a train of former London, Chatham & Dover Railway (LCDR) four-wheel carriages.   *R. Silsbury Collection*

Carisbrooke station (1 m. 13 ch.) was about half a mile north of the village and even further from Carisbrooke Castle, a significant source of tourist traffic. This was made worse by the absence of a direct approach road and once the omnibus became established the station lost most of its passenger traffic. There were two platforms each 198 ft in length flanking a 222 ft crossing loop. The platforms were originally built in brick with brick copings but, in common with other stations along the line were later rendered in cement. On the down platform was a single-storey red brick station house and a wooden signal box supplied by Stevens & Co.; a small waiting shelter matching the station building was on the up platform. The crossing loop saw some use in the years 1897 to 1913 but was not essential to the working of the line and thereafter it lay out of use. Beyond the loop was a 259 ft 6 in. siding facing up trains with a loading bank and little else. Leaving the station, the railway resumed its uphill climb that steepened as it approached Gunville bridge (No. 5) carrying a public road over the railway; it had a single concrete arch lined with brick and was typical of the overbridges on the line. Just beyond, on to the south side, was a private siding to Gunville brickworks added in 1899; the 175 ft siding faced down trains and was locked by Annett's key on the Carisbrooke-Ningwood single line train staff.

The railway continued to climb on a low embankment through farm land before looping to the south. Passing under Betty Haunt (or Ant) Lane overbridge (No. 8), the railway at this point was at ground level so embankments had to be constructed on each side to carry the road over the railway. A final spurt brought the line to its summit near Great Park farm 1½ miles from Carisbrooke. Then followed a steep descent passing under an occupation bridge before curving to the right and crossing Great Park bridge (No. 10), a wrought-iron structure on concrete abutments measuring 31 ft 4 in. on the skew and the scene of a serious derailment in 1939. A short distance beyond was the private station of Watchingwell.

Carisbrooke station.

Reproduced from the 25", 1908 Ordnance Survey Map

THE LINE DESCRIBED

Carisbrooke seen in 1920 also shows the disused crossing loop, signal box and siding in which stands one of the converted cattle wagons. *R. Silsbury/IWSR Collection*

By BR days the crossing loop and signal box had long gone but the up platform and its shelter still survive. *J.H. Aston/IWSR Collection*

A solitary wagon stands in Gunville siding during SR days, as is obvious from the bullhead track. The siding to the brickworks was added in 1899.   *A.M. MacLeod/IWSR Collection*

Watchingwell station seen on 18th September, 1953, just three days before closure, was little different from when it opened in 1897. In the foreground can be seen the ground frame that worked the signals. The SR erected a new name board, fitted distant arms to the signals and removed the siding.   *J.H. Aston/Lens of Sutton*

THE LINE DESCRIBED

Watchingwell looking towards Newport shows the road crossing at the end of the platform. *IWSR Collection*

Watchingwell station (3 m. 56 ch.) was for the use of the owner of Swainston Estate 'his family, friends, tenants and persons having business with him'. Situated next to a crossing to a nearby farm, the 95 ft 8 in. platform on the down side showed signs of having been extended at some date. The small single-storey house was somewhat plainer than the others on the line and was probably built in early 1897. Beyond the platform was a 132 ft goods siding facing up trains worked by its own ground frame locked by an Annett's key on the train staff. The two-lever frame on the platform was connected to two home signals sharing the same post; they could be put at danger to warn drivers that there were intending passengers. Leaving Watchingwell the line continued towards the west for a short distance before looping to the north. After passing under Hare Lane bridge (No. 13) the line rose and fell at gradients varying between 1 in 60 and 1 in 66 over Pound crossing and a second level crossing adjoining Calbourne and Shalfleet station.

Calbourne and Shalfleet station (5 m. 36 ch.) was situated halfway between the two villages but a hefty one mile walk from each. In the absence of any road competition the station was better than nothing but it could never compete with the bus. The station building was no bigger than the crossing keepers' houses and consequently there was no separate accommodation for passengers who had to use the resident's living room! The single 167 ft 11 in. platform was on the down side beyond which a 182 ft 8 in. siding faced up trains. The signal box next to the level crossing worked distant, home and starting signals in each direction; the station was an intermediate block post.

Continuing to fall, the railway passed through a cutting and along an embankment before crossing Calbourne viaduct (bridge 16) bridging a brook

Pound crossing was photographed in SR days as is obvious from the bullhead track. Note the unmade road surface, the wicket gate and the 'dropped' nature of the main gates. Also obvious is the extension to the crossing keeper's house added in the early years of the 20th century.
A.B. MacLeod/IWSR Collection

This is the only known photograph of Calbourne prior to 1923 and shows station master Henley who took charge of the station in 1903. After he had to retire due to deafness his wife was appointed stationmistress, a position she retained until 1944. *J. Mackett Collection*

THE LINE DESCRIBED 125

Calbourne gained a building from the FYN station at Newport in early SR days and is seen here with a new concrete name board occupying the end of the platform between the road crossing and station building.
Lens of Sutton

A little more of Calbourne station building can be seen in this view taken looking towards Freshwater shortly before closure in 1953.
Lens of Sutton

Judging by the individuals standing to the left the photograph of Calbourne viaduct was probably taken during one of Mr MacLeod's inspections of the line during SR days. Seen from the south-west, the neat design of the structure is impressive.　　*A.B. MacLeod/IWSR Collection*

The up platform at Ningwood contained one of the little brick waiting shelters identical to those at Carisbrooke and Yarmouth. Photographed in about 1921, the light flat bottom rails are all too obvious.　　*P.C. Allen*

Ningwood down platform contained the station building and signal box. The tall object at the end of the waiting shed is a stretcher cabinet that had been added during World War II. This photograph was taken shortly before closure in 1953. *IWSR Collection*

called the Caul Bourne, a tributary of Newtown River. A steep climb took the railway over an occupation crossing and past a private siding to Dowty's brickworks; situated on the south side of the line the connections faced up trains. Then followed a fall of about half a mile to Ningwood bridge (No. 17), a two-arch overbridge carrying the road across the line; one arch was used by the railway and the second by a local farmer.

Ningwood station (6 m. 64 ch.) was similar to that at Carisbrooke with a 192 ft crossing loop flanked by up and down platforms each 170 ft in length. The single-storey brick station building and wooden signal box were situated on the down platform whilst the up platform had a small matching waiting shelter. There was a separate station master's house on the up side fronting the road. A 306 ft 11 in. siding joined the single line at the Yarmouth end of the station; it faced up trains and was worked by a separate two-lever ground frame locked by an Annett's key on the train staff.

Leaving Ningwood the line rose and fell for about 1½ miles before passing Wellow siding. The 174 ft 6 in. private siding added in 1892 was on the north side of the line and led to Lee brickworks. A fall of about half a mile down Wellow bank took the line to Hill Place level crossing - unusually, it lacked signals. Then followed a largely level mile to Thorley bridge (No. 23), a wrought-iron girder overbridge on concrete abutments. The remaining section to Yarmouth was carried on a low embankment to keep the railway above the flood plain of Thorley brook.

Wellow siding, constructed in 1892, was removed by the SR during relaying of the line in 1929. Thereafter only the gate and trackbed remained to mark its existence.
A.B. MacLeod/IWSR Collection

0-6-0T No. W8, formerly FYN No. 2, arrives with a train of LCDR carriages at Yarmouth from Newport sometime between 1932 and 1936. The sidings have yet to be relaid in bullhead track.
P.C. Allen/IWSR Collection

Yarmouth in September 1920 has undergone a few subtle changes. The crossing loop is out of use but this is barely evident. On the up platform, the station name board has been renewed and there is an old van body placed there by the IWC in 1911. The company's haystack next to the siding is an unusual but by no means uncommon sight on the Island railways. *R. Silsbury/IWSR Collection*

Yarmouth station (10 m. 69 ch.) was situated at the back of the town half a mile from the quay and landing point for Lymington steamers - thankfully it was and still is a fairly level walk. The architecture had several similarities to Carisbrooke. The single-storey station building faced the approach road but on the railway side looked out on the Freshwater end of the 177 ft 9 in.-long up platform; one of Stevens' wooden signal boxes was at the opposite end. Immediately beyond the platform ramp at the Freshwater end was the sluice gate to Yarmouth Tide Mill that crossed the line at an acute angle (culvert No. 25) and as a result the loop road and 149 ft down platform were situated a few yards further to the east. The second platform had a small brick and tile waiting shelter identical to that at Carisbrooke. A spur at the Newport end of the station led to a 202 ft 10 in. coal siding and a short 9 ft 1 in. end loading dock; two kickback sidings off the coal road had fallen into disuse by 1908. Although the loop and down platform came into use in 1897 Yarmouth was not a block post and trains were not permitted to cross there. Trains reverted to using only the up platform in 1911 although the loop and signals remained.

Leaving Yarmouth the railway bore to the left on a low embankment as it crossed the mill pond before coming to the east bank of the River Yar. Heading south, it then followed the river towards Freshwater. A short distance from the terminus the railway crossed a public road on the level at Causeway Crossing. There was a single-storey house for the crossing keeper and a two-lever frame worked home signals guarding the crossing. On the west side of the crossing was a wooden footbridge that is thought to have been removed in early SR days. The line then swung to the west across what had become a narrow river (bridge 28) to the terminus at Freshwater.

THE FRESHWATER, YARMOUTH & NEWPORT RAILWAY

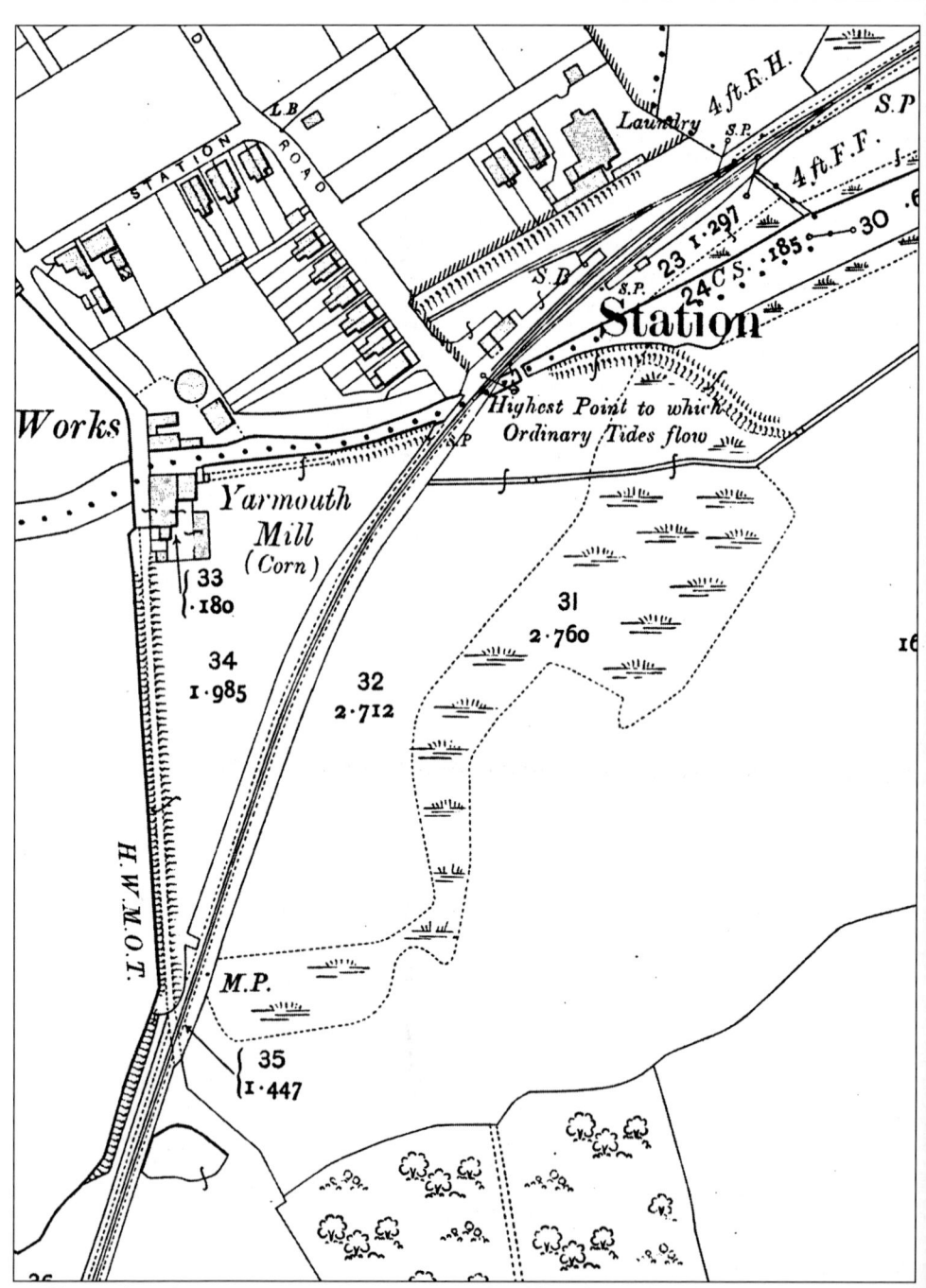

Yarmouth station. *Reproduced from the 25", 1908 Ordnance Survey Map*

Yarmouth station looking from the abandoned down platform in 1953. The station has lost its crossing loop, signals and signal box, the position of which is evident by the hole for point rodding in the front of the platform. *J.H. Aston/Lens of Sutton*

The FYN made several attempts to build a branch to the quay at Yarmouth. Seen in 1938, the tug *Jumsey* has just arrived with a tow boat from Lymington. The quay is being rebuilt ready for the introduction of the vehicle ferry *Lymington*. Today's ferries carry rather more traffic.

IWSR Collection

IWC No. 8 and a train of LSWR carriages run along the causeway with a train for Freshwater prior to 1911.
R. Silsbury/IWSR Collection

No. 2 and its train of LSWR carriages pass the crossing keeper's washing as it approaches Causeway Crossing with a train for Freshwater.
G.W. Tripp

This postcard by J. Welch & Sons of Portsmouth, showing the keeper's cottage at Causeway Crossing, was taken in about 1920 or 1921. The footbridge crossing the line cannot have seen much use and was later demolished. The brick-built house was clearly built in the same 'house' style as the station buildings along the line. *J. Mackett Collection*

Freshwater station (11 m. 70 ch.) was situated near School Green at a point where the deviation met the original line just before Hooke Hill. It was a lengthy walk from Freshwater Bay in one direction and Totland Bay in another. Given the company's plans to extend the railway to Totland, the abandonment of the remaining section of line towards Freshwater Gate was quite reasonable but it is fair to say that the selected terminus served no place in particular. The site itself was originally marshland that had to be drained and filled.

The original 1888 track layout consisted of a platform on the up side, a run-round loop and a single siding; it was at this time that signals and interlocking were installed. By the time passenger trains began running a year later a second goods siding had been added along with a short spur to an end loading dock and sidings to locomotive and carriage sheds. A kickback siding and a coal shed added in 1893 had to be shunted by means of a tow rope, a practice outlawed by the Board of Trade in 1900 but which was evidently still being used by the IWC in 1904.

At right angles to the platform was a single-storey brick station building joined at its south end to a two-storey station master's house. The extension to Totland would have diverged from the single line just short of the station and passed along the back of the platform and to the north of the buildings on the site of a stream. The platform was originally very short but by 1913 had grown to 316 ft in length, although varing in width because of the proximity of the water course. The signal box at the Newport end of the platform controlled key points and the signals but the additional sidings were worked by hand levers. One of the Central's few contributions to the railway was a carriage body dumped at the end of the platform in 1911 for a lamp room and an elderly van in one of the goods sidings.

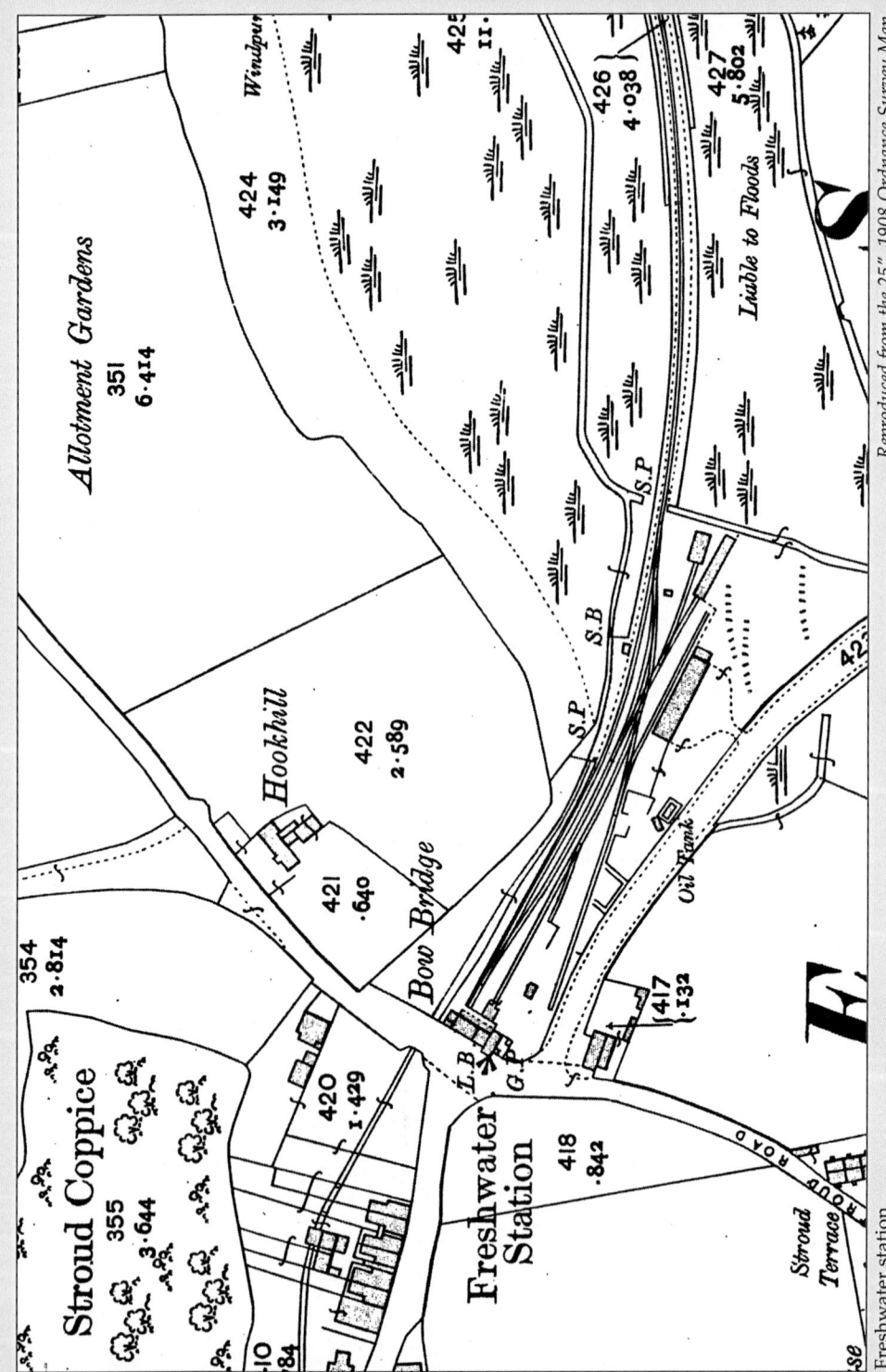

Freshwater station.

THE LINE DESCRIBED

Published as an Edwardian tinted postcard, the wooded surroundings to the front of Freshwater station are in stark contrast to the site of the station today. Note the large painted panel behind the ornate lamp advertising 'The Family route to London'. *R. Silsbury Collection*

The impressive frontage of Freshwater station is seen in 1953. The large *Southern Railway Freshwater* station sign partially covers the painted panel that advertised the 'Family route'. Apart from a reduction in the size of the covering to the station entrance the station looks much the same as it did when opened. *J.H. Aston/Lens of Sutton*

From the platform side, the buildings let onto a single and very modest platform that was progressively extended over the years. Two spare ex-LSWR carriages stand in a newly laid siding at the end of the run-round loop in 1912. The roof of the relatively new parcels office can be glimpsed behind the carriages. Note the ornate weighing machine on the right.
Portsmouth City Council Archive

Freshwater station is seen from the end of the platform in 1920. From left to right we see a row of goods vehicles including the FYN brake van, the wooden loading gauge, loading bank and cattle dock at which are standing two converted cattle wagons. The carriage body on the right was installed by the IWC in 1911 for use as a lamp room. *R. Silsbury/IWSR Collection*

THE LINE DESCRIBED 137

The alterations made at Freshwater in 1927 are evident in this view taken just before closure. Peeping out from behind the covered van is the signal box that had previously done duty at Newport FYN station.
IWSR Collection

No. 2 emits a large pall of smoke as it arrives at Freshwater. In front of the carriage shed can be seen what is believed to have been one of the few private owner wagons to run in the Island.
R. Silsbury Collection

Right: The Saxby & Farmer starting signal at Freshwater manages to obscure much of the signal box but we can see FYN No. 1 standing next to the coal stage and sheds. *R. Silsbury Collection*

Below: Former IWC locomotive No. 9 with the MSJ&A carriages arrive at Freshwater in about 1924. On the right can be seen the coal depot in front of which is one of the newly arrived LBSCR open wagons. *IWSR Collection*

Chapter Twelve

Locomotives and Rolling Stock

During the construction of the railway William Jackson employed a small 0-6-0T steam locomotive named *Freshwater*. It was built in May 1880 by Robert Stephenson & Co. but did not leave the works until 6th June, 1887 when sold to Mr Jackson at a cost said to have been £1,500. *Freshwater* was little heavier than the tiny CNR 2-2-2Ts but being a much more modern design seems well suited to its duties; it was painted green with the name in lettering on the tank sides.

Once rails had been laid throughout *Freshwater* made a number of special trips carrying dignitaries and in September 1888 began working goods trains. After taking a special excursion over the line on 10th October, 1888, it is said to have run to Cowes for wheel turning on 1st November perhaps because of its exertions that involved the haulage of 14 carriages on its own! *Freshwater* ventured further afield on race day at Ashey on 30th April, 1889 when it took a 10-coach train to Ryde and back. This trip proving successful, *Freshwater* worked trains on the IWC on 2nd May when two of the Central's locomotives (Nos. 5 and 7) were borrowed for bridge testing during the Board of Trade Inspector's visit to the Freshwater line.

Freshwater became the subject of a dispute between the FYN and its contractor. At a meeting of the FYN Board on 28th January, 1890:

> It was Reported that the engine had been sureptitiously [sic] removed by Mr Wm Jackson from the Engine Shed at Freshwater on the 24th December to the Works of the Isle of Wight Coy at Ryde under the pretext that repairs were necessary. The Solicitors reported that they had applied to the High Court of Chancery for an injunction against Mr Jackson and the Isle of Wight Railway Coy to restrain them from parting with the Engine otherwise than to this Company, this forming part of the Contractor's Plant now the property of the Company under the Contract. The application was not acceded to but leave was given to amend the affidavit and to bring the matter forward again in 14 days. The Solicitors further reported that Mr Jackson and the Isle of Wight Railway Company had agreed that the matter might stand over until the hearing of the action and that in the meantime the Engine should not be interfered with.

The outcome of negotiations between the parties was made known at the next Board meeting on 28th March when it was noted that the locomotive was then in the possession of the company, 'Mr Wm Jackson having pressed the Company to purchase the locomotive employed on the works for the sum of £800, £300 in cash and the balance to be credited to him in his account with the company'. Messrs Fox and Hogan had advanced the £300 and were authorised to sell the locomotive for the best price they could get, repay themselves and pay any surplus to the FYN. *Freshwater* was not mentioned again in the Minutes and no accounts survive showing for what or to whom it was sold. It may have passed into the hands of Henry Jackson as on 19th December, 1889 he reminded the FYN Board that it would be necessary to retain the contractor's plant in order to build the Totland Bay extension. In 1892 Jackson began hiring a locomotive from the IWC for ballasting work implying that *Freshwater* had left the line by then.

The former North London Railway 4-4-0T, IWC No. 7 stands in front of the water tower and locomotive shed in the early years of the 20th century. Sadly the names of the staff seen in the photograph are not known. *IWSR Collection*

The light permanent way is evident in this photograph of IWC 2-4-0T No. 7 and a train of LSWR carriages at Freshwater not long after its purchase in 1906. *IWSR Collection*

LOCOMOTIVES AND ROLLING STOCK

The whereabouts of *Freshwater* immediately following its departure from the Isle of Wight is unclear. The locomotive is said to have assisted in the construction of the Exeter to Christow line under the name of *Longdon* and the Weston, Clevedon & Portishead Railway when Henry Jackson was the contractor. After sale to the company in about 1898 it was photographed running as a 2-4-0T named *Portishead*. It had reverted to an 0-6-0T before being sold in 1900 or 1901 to the Renishaw Iron Company in Derbyshire where it lasted until broken up in about 1941.

William Jackson employed a number of wagons on construction works. A contemporary photograph showed two wagons bearing the name of the contractor Joseph Firbank which was apparently an indication of their former ownership - they had dumb buffers and no brakes. The IWC was desperately short of wagons and paid sizeable amounts for wagon hire to Jackson during 1888 and 1889. Some wagons were offered for sale in October 1889 and Herbert Simmons, the IWC Manager, was instructed to buy the six best for £10 each. A handful were retained by Henry Jackson for maintenance of the Freshwater railway, but they proved rather accident prone as one was destroyed in a collision in August 1890 and the IWC had to replace two more after an accident in October 1894. When Jackson was dismissed in 1896 six were purchased for £90 by the FYN but there were only five by 1st March, 1904 when it was reported that they were being dismantled at Ningwood; the FYN Board ordered that four be sold and the remaining wagon repaired - nothing more was heard of them.

The provision of rolling stock for the railway had been discussed by the FYN with the CNR when the original working agreement was drawn up in 1886. On 24th February, 1888 the FYN wrote to the IWC warning that rolling stock would be needed within three months, rather prematurely as it proved. The IWC Secretary replied that there was no provision in the agreement 'for producing designs of the Rolling Stock to this Company or that the Rolling Stock should be other than that now used in working the present lines'. This met with an immediate response from the FYN on 14th March pointing out that, during negotiations, the CNR said it had no surplus of stock and would have to provide new; since the FYN might have to buy the stock at a later date, the Directors felt it should be satisfactory to them. Although a new locomotive and two carriages were ordered during 1890, no attempt was made to allocate them to Freshwater line services. The FYN Board was undoubtedly surprised to receive a £35 bill from the LBSCR for painting and lettering some elderly carriages allegedly purchased for their railway - they had actually been bought by the IWC.

It is likely that virtually all the locomotives and rolling stock owned by the IWC ran to Freshwater at one time or another. The propensity of the Central to run mixed passenger and goods trains meant that the weak CNR 2-2-2Ts often encountered difficulties with the gradients and sharp curves leading to late running. More suitable were the Beyer, Peacock 2-4-0Ts Nos. 4, 5 and later the new No. 8. On occasions Nos. 6 and 7 were also used but this time the FYN complained that they were too heavy and damaged the permanent way; the same applied to 0-4-4T No. 2 after its purchase by the IWC in 1909. The FYN did approve of steam rail motor No. 1 and made strenuous efforts to get the IWC to operate it on the more lightly loaded passenger workings.

IWC railmotor No. 1 stands at Carisbrooke soon after delivery in October 1906.
P.C. Allen/IWSR Collection

Possibly on the same occasion, IWC rail motor No. 1 is being admired as it stands near the buffer stops at Freshwater.
G.W. Tripp

LOCOMOTIVES AND ROLLING STOCK

The coaching stock known to have been used on the line included a set of IWNJ four-wheel carriages in the early years. Two bogie vehicles built new for the IWC in 1890 were employed with an assortment of four-wheelers on the through Ryde to Freshwater trains. Latterly most trains were formed of LSWR stock. The FYN Board had a poor opinion of the condition of IWC locomotives and rolling stock, with good reason as there were numerous breakdown. The less said about the goods stock the better.

The first discussions by the FYN Directors about the purchase of locomotives and rolling stock took place during a meeting on 19th November, 1912. Mr Aman reported that two locomotives 'on offer' were to be inspected and reported upon. Negotiations for the purchase of passenger rolling stock was much further forward and the Directors decided to buy six carriages at £60 each from the Manchester South Junction & Altrincham Railway (MSJ&A) - the issue of a cheque for £360 was approved and signed. The accounts actually recorded the expenditure of £420 on seven carriages before the end of the year. The carriages were originally four-compartment second class vehicles dating from about 1880 that before delivery were converted to create:

one brake composite with one first, two third and one guard's compartment	No. 1
three thirds	Nos. 2, 3 and 5
two composites with two first and two third class compartments	Nos. 4 and 6
one brake third with two third class compartments	No. 7

The alterations were somewhat cosmetic as a commentator wrote that the only difference between the compartments was a rug on the floor for those travelling first class! The existing varnished teak livery was retained with the former company title replaced by the letters FYN.

Along with two locomotives, the carriages were transported by barge from the mainland to St Helens Quay on 25th June, 1913 and taken to Newport. The locomotives may have been the two that were mentioned in November 1912 but we do not know this for sure.

No. 1 was a Manning, Wardle & Co. class 'Q' 0-6-0 industrial saddle tank. It was one of several new locomotives supplied by Manning, Wardle & Co. to the contractors Pauling & Co. for construction of the Great Central and Great Western Joint Railway from Northolt Junction to High Wycombe. No. 56 *Northolt* was delivered in February 1902 and employed on various contracts until sold in 1913 to the FYN. By the time it reached the Isle of Wight the locomotive had been repainted in mid-green lined black and white lettered 'FY&N Rly', later altered to 'F.Y.N.' in gold on the tank sides; this was the livery carried by GCR passenger locomotives so Sir Sam Fay may have used his influence to get the locomotive overhauled and repainted in that company's workshops. The locomotive carried a steam brake, Westinghouse brake and vacuum ejector so could work trains fitted with either brake system. The small driving wheels gave it useful traction when hauling trains on the Freshwater line.

No. 2 was a LBSCR class 'A' 0-6-0T built in 1876 as No. 46 *Newington*. Several of the class became surplus to requirements by the turn of the century and in March 1903 No. 46 was sold with another to the LSWR for use on the Lyme Regis branch. The locomotive had its Westinghouse brake replaced with the vacuum

Locomotive No. 2 and the MSJ&A carriages were shipped by barge to St Helens where they were off-loaded onto the IWR's Bembridge branch. Here they are seen awaiting unloading on 25th June, 1913.
R.C. Riley Collection

During its unloading at St Helens we see that FYN No. 2 was still carrying LSWR livery.
R.C. Riley Collection

LOCOMOTIVES AND ROLLING STOCK 145

Locomotive No. 1 and some MSJ&A carriages has just drawn into the FYN station at Newport in July 1913 and is about to load up with passengers for Freshwater. Amongst the many intending passengers are several tradesmen wearing straw boaters and white aprons. Several workmen take a break from completing the construction of the station to watch the event.
P.C. Allen/IWSR Collection

Locomotive No. 1 stands at the Newport FYN station with former IWC stock on 12th May, 1919. The first carriage is brake third No. 9, the remainder are four- and five-compartment LSWR vehicles.
K. Nunn Collection

The MSJ&A carriages are best illustrated in this view of composite No. 4 as running in SR livery as No. 6358. *IWSR Collection*

During SR days a newly imported Brighton 0-6-0T No. W3 passes the Newport distant signal between Newport viaduct and Petticoat Lane crossing. The first carriage is the two-compartment MSJ&A brake carriage, No. 7. *IWSR Collection*

LOCOMOTIVES AND ROLLING STOCK 147

A lengthy row of the company's carriages can be seen in this photograph of FYN No. 1 running round its train at Freshwater on 2nd June, 1921. Most are MSJ&A carriages apart from the van on the right which is the Wright brake third No. 9.
H.C. Casserley

Locomotive No. 1 standing outside the FYN locomotive shed at Newport has been given a top class clean and polish in 1919.
K. Nunn Collection

FYN No. 1 looks a little more shabby as it stands at the company's station at Newport awaiting departure for Freshwater in 1920. Note the Westinghouse pump attached to the front of the saddle tank.
P.C. Allen/IWSR Collection

No. 1 and its train are seen just west of Petticoat Lane crossing as they head for Freshwater.
K. Nunn Collection

LOCOMOTIVES AND ROLLING STOCK 149

No. 2 did its share of work and is seen arriving at Ningwood in 1919. Unlike Yarmouth and Carisbrooke the signals at Ningwood were kept in full working order.
P.C. Allen/IWSR Collection

No. 2 is seen in the Newport station bay with a carriage clearly carrying the class number on its doors. *P.C. Allen*

No. 2 has just arrived at Newport with its train of MSJ&A carriages from Freshwater in 1920.
P.C. Allen/IWSR Collection

No. 2 bears a rather faded FYN livery as it stands next to the cattle dock at the neck of Newport goods yard.
R. Silsbury Collection

system brake, received the number 734 and a repaint in lined LSWR livery. No. 734 remained on the Lyme Regis branch only a short time and by 1909 had moved to Fratton for the Gosport and Lee on Solent services. The locomotive received a new boiler in 1912 displaying a number of Drummond features. According to the late D.L. Bradley, the locomotive was hired to the FYN until bought in February 1915 for £900. The LSWR livery was carried until the locomotive visited Ryde Works for overhaul in January 1916. The new livery was described as a bright light green with the black and white lining lettered 'F.Y.N.' on the tank sides and the number on the bunker sides; the coupling rods were painted red.

The third item of motive power was an unusual four-wheel petrol rail motor car. Built by the Drewry Car Co., it was landed in a partly dismantled state at Newport Quay and then hauled on a cart behind a steam traction engine through the streets to Carisbrooke where it was put on the rails. The date of arrival is uncertain but delivery was evidently prior to completion of the goods yard at Newport. In addition to the driver, it could carry between 12 and 15 passengers seated on leather bound reversible bench seats. Although it had a roof and glazed end panels, the sides were open save for roll-down weather sheets; the teak side panels were varnished, the words 'Freshwater Railway' being carried on the centre panel. The rail motor had a tendency to seesaw when travelling at any speed so in addition to being windblown and damp, passengers might also have felt rather queasy!

Under the terms of the working agreement between the IWC and FYN, the latter undertook to purchase locomotives and rolling stock bought for working the Freshwater line. The IWC claimed that it had provided two locomotives, six carriages and 33 goods vehicles. Sir Sam Fay was authorised to negotiate terms with the Central and whilst the FYN Minutes are silent on the matter, those for the IWC recorded that he purchased:

30 wagons and a goods brake van	£1,152
four carriages	£236
one passenger brake van	£54
Total cost	£1,442

Agreement could not be reached for either of the locomotives, said to have been IWC Nos. 4 and 6. Delivery of the goods stock was made on the evening of Sunday 29th June, 1913 and the carriages on the following Tuesday, the day that the FYN began operating its own trains. They included four carriages that had been built by the LSWR during the 1870s; Nos. 8 and 11 were four-compartment composites whilst Nos. 10 and 12 were five-compartment thirds. No. 9 was one of four built by Wright & Co. for the CNR in 1861 that by 1913 was running as a two-compartment brake third. The five were fitted with the Westinghouse brake and at first could not work with locomotive No. 2. Some flexibility was later introduced by dual fitting two MSJ&A carriages and a through vacuum pipe to No. 9. Although an IWC passenger guard's van was frequently seen on the line it is thought to have been one of the Central's mail vans that worked through from Ryde each day.

The goods brake van was also fitted with a through pipe so that it could run with the MSJ&A carriages. It was one of four goods brake vans purchased by the IWC in the early years of the century and was of Stroudley design. Technically a 'road van' in that it could carry small quantities of parcels etc., it was repainted after purchase

In 1913 the FYN purchased a petrol driven rail car from Drewry & Co. It is seen at the maker's factory before delivery.
R. Silsbury Collection

Delivered in partly dismantled state, the rail car was landed at Newport Quay and hauled on a cart by a traction engine to Carisbrooke where it was put on the rails. Presumably the roof came separately.
P.C. Allen/IWSR Collection

LOCOMOTIVES AND ROLLING STOCK 153

The rail car displays its charms in a posed shot at Freshwater *circa* 1913.   *R. Silsbury Collection*

The rail car was quite a useful vehicle as it needed only a driver. They wait at the home signal at Newport evidently waiting for permission to enter the station. One of the converted cattle wagons stands at the cattle dock on the right.   *K. Nunn Collection*

Most photographs of the rail car show it in good weather but that is evidently not the case when P.C. Allen photographed it in about 1920 standing next to the cattle dock at Newport.
P.C. Allen/IWSR Collection

The elusive FYN goods brake van No. 13 is being towed through Newport Central station by a freshly repainted IWC 0-6-0T No. 11 soon after the SR took charge. A newly-arrived LSWR bogie carriage stands in the loop platform.
P.C. Allen

LOCOMOTIVES AND ROLLING STOCK

and prominently lettered from top downwards 'Goods Brake Van', 'FYN' and the running number 13. The four covered vans, FYN Nos. 14 to 17, had been built by the IWC at Newport in 1911 on underframes salvaged from goods wagons; they were neat little vans with outside framing and sliding doors. The open wagons were five-plank open wagons conforming to the Railway Clearing House 1889 standard but this was no guarantee of their modernity as a high proportion possessed only a single-sided brake acting on one wheel. A few were lettered 'FYN' but the remainder kept their IWC livery and running numbers until 1923. The FYN goods stock livery was grey with white lettering about one plank high applied halfway up the body side with the letters 'FYN' applied to the left and the running number to the right of the door. The tare weight was applied near the right-hand end on the floor plank. The goods wagons were given running numbers 18 upwards. Nos. 18 to 22 were fitted with corrugated iron roofs and additional battens at waist level for carrying livestock, a crude but effective conversion.

By 31st December, 1914, £4,573 11s. 5d. had been expended on rolling stock. For this money the company had purchased two locomotives, one rail motor, 12 carriages, 26 open wagons, four covered vans and one goods brake van. Of the carriages, seven seated a total of 94 first class passengers and 140 second; the other five accommodated 220 second class passengers.

Services were so arranged that they could be worked by one steam locomotive and the rail motor. Running repairs were often carried out by IWC fitters who would do 'cash in hand' work for the FYN on a Sunday. At first the locomotives faced Newport but following heavy overhauls at Ryde Works in January 1916 were returned facing Freshwater; naturally the IWC charged for the passage of locomotives and stock over its railway.

By 1919 the second class seating in the carriages had been redesignated third class; the four aside seating was increased to five. There were then five composites seating 72 first and 100 third class passengers; the seven third class carriages seated 270. A writer in the magazine *Transport & Travel Monthly* reported that the FYN had found it cheaper to use the vacuum brake system and the four carriages fitted solely with the Westinghouse brake had been placed in reserve.

Amongst the few useful facts that could be gleaned from the accounts produced by the Receivers were summaries of miles travelled by the locomotives and rail motor. All ran quite a reasonable mileage in 1914 and 1915 but there then ensued a steady decline.

Year	Rail motor	Passenger locomotives	Goods locomotives	Total
1914	10,486	54,752	6,834	72,072
1915	8,694	47,652	6,402	61,748
1919	7,504	44,499	5,068	57,071
1920	8,158	45,079	5,306	58,542
1921	4,356	40,877	4,955	50,188
1922	24	45,005	4,728	49,757

With the possible exception of the rail motor, which may have been past its best, the Southern Railway found the locomotives and rolling stock to be in quite good condition and they served the SR faithfully for several years.

The four covered vans were rebuilt by the IWC from coal wagons in about 1911. The last survivor, van No. 15, was withdrawn in August 1930. It was then converted to tool van No. 438s gaining a small window in the side and is seen here standing at Ryde St Johns Road in the 1930s.
A.B. MacLeod/IWSR Collection

IWC No. 8 stands with an IWC train at Newport Central station but it is the wagon on the right that interests us. The FYN converted five open wagons to carry livestock in the manner shown.
P.C. Allen

LOCOMOTIVES AND ROLLING STOCK

By 5th November, 1928 FYN locomotive 2 had received SR livery and the name *Freshwater* but was still working on the Freshwater line. It is seen at Newport passing the remains of the FYN station - the building has yet to be moved to Calbourne. *H.C. Casserley*

After undergoing repairs at Newport and a repaint in SR green livery, locomotive No. 1 was appropriated for shunting at Newport and on Medina Wharf, where its good traction proved most useful, and gained an unofficial name *Papyrus* after the 1924 Derby winner. Ryde works carried out heavy repairs during the winter of 1928-1929 when the boiler was retubed and new cab sidesheets fitted. A repaint was followed by the affixing of nameplates to the tank sides bearing the name *Medina* below the 'SOUTHERN' lettering. This was no guarantee of long life as the locomotive was replaced by a LBSCR class 'E1' 0-6-0T in July 1932 and returned to the mainland a year later for breaking up. It should be added that No. 1 was the youngest locomotive to run in the Isle of Wight (ignoring IWC rail motor No. 1) and its replacement, although to a standard design, was appreciably older.

No. 2 became part of Newport's stud of Brighton 0-6-0Ts that found employment on Freshwater line services, the branch to Ventnor West, goods work and the Shide chalk trains. Early in 1924 it visited Newport works for attention when the vacuum brake was replaced by the Westinghouse system and the Brighton bunker extended to the rear of the frames in the same manner as the IWC quartet. By May it was one of the first of the former Island companies locomotives to be running in the SR sage green livery, albeit with the copper cap of its chimney painted over. Regularly rostered with IWC No. 8 or one of the Brighton 0-6-0Ts for Freshwater line services, it might otherwise be found shunting at Newport. The locomotive achieved another first in October 1928 when it left works after a repaint carrying a newly fitted nameplate *Freshwater* crowded with the 'SOUTHERN' lettering and running number on the tank sides; within 12 months the running number had been transferred

158   THE FRESHWATER, YARMOUTH & NEWPORT RAILWAY

to a more visually-attractive position on the bunker side sheets. In 1932 *Freshwater* entered Ryde works for a thorough overhaul; the Drummond boiler was replaced by a standard LBSCR class 'A1x' boiler and chimney, whilst the repaint included a renumbering as No. 8 following the arrival of the first of four LBSCR class 'E1' 0-6-0Ts. Although LSWR class 'O2' 0-4-4Ts later took over its duties on the Freshwater line, *Freshwater* was one of a handful of the class to stay in the Island for the Ventnor West and Shide chalk trains. It returned to the mainland in 1949 and after a change of identity to No. 32646 during an overhaul at Eastleigh Works it returned to service until withdrawn in 1963. The locomotive was not broken up and eventually returned to the Isle of Wight for service on the Isle of Wight Steam Railway.

The SR lacked any use for the rail motor but allocated a SR running number as a third class carriage. It was withdrawn from stock in December 1924 and transferred to departmental stock as an inspection vehicle, although probably seeing only intermittent use until condemned and broken up in 1927. This did not deter the SR from using Drewry rail motors because two new vehicles were obtained in 1927 for the Ryde Pier tramway.

Of the Freshwater company's rolling stock, the LSWR carriages were withdrawn with the last of their IWC brothers in 1926. The MSJ&A stock was considered amongst the best of the Island companies' carriages and lasted until 1930; one brake third remained in use as a mail van until 1933. The goods brake van was withdrawn in 1926; the other goods vehicles went for scrap at various dates between 1927 and 1932, somewhat later than much of the Central's fleet.

One of life's little mysteries can be seen in this photograph of No. 2 *Freshwater* soon after being renumbered 8 in 1932 as it stands in the bay platform at Newport. The grounded van body clearly ran on the Great Central Railway at one time but despite the obvious links between the FYN and GCR, it was actually one of several GCR vehicles purchased by the IWC from a dealer in second-hand rolling stock.   *R. Silsbury Collection*

Chapter Thirteen

A Solent Tunnel

Since the fortunes of the FYN were inextricably linked with a proposed Solent Tunnel it is incumbent on us to chart the convoluted history of the schemes for linking the Isle of Wight with the mainland.

In 1871 a proposal for a railway to Stone Point on the mainland prompted Charles Vignoles, an engineer, to advocate a tunnel under the Solent linking the railway with Cowes; trial borings were made but it was said that Vignoles was already too old to carry the scheme forward! Three years later a tunnel was mentioned after the Swindon, Marlborough & Andover Railway (SM&AR) proposed a railway to Stone Point. On 16th August, 1878 *The Globe* newspaper mentioned that Hamilton Fulton, Engineer to various Isle of Wight railway schemes, was trying to resurrect Vignoles' scheme. At the Island end, the tunnel would have surfaced in what is now known as Gurnard Bay before connecting with the CNR; Fulton claimed that the tunnel would only be two miles long with gradients of 1 in 82 and 1 in 55 on its approaches. Meanwhile, the SM&AR finally gained Parliamentary approval for a railway to Lepe in 1882 where there would be a pier. The necessary capital to fund the railway and pier was not forthcoming and the powers lapsed.*

Activity then shifted east to Spithead. In October 1886 the *Morning Post* mentioned the formation of a committee to promote the construction of a tunnel from Stokes Bay to Ryde. George Stulz Wells, Secretary, claimed that it was possible to build a fort halfway along the three mile tunnel and suggested that the Government might like to pay for one half leaving the promoters to built the remaining 1½ miles from the fort to Ryde; the response was predictable and nothing more was heard of the idea.

The possibility of a tunnel connecting with the western end of the Island was first mooted in 1885 but it was not until 1900 that the idea took root. A lengthy article in the *Daily Telegraph* for 21st November, 1900 commented that the journey from London to Newport took an average of four to five hours but a tunnel would cut the time to about 2¼ hours at a cost of no more than £750,000. A Bill to form the South Western & Isle of Wight Junction Railway became law on 26th July, 1901. It authorised the issue of £600,000 in £10 shares and borrowings of £200,000 for a railway and tunnel connecting the LSWR with the FYN. Lord Heytesbury, a local landowner and the only objector to the Bill, had been bought off by a generous offer of £6,000 for land needed by the company. Mr Granville Ward JP and T.B.H. Cochrane JP, Deputy Governor of the Isle of Wight, spoke in support of the undertaking. The Bill successfully passed its remaining hurdles in Parliament and became law. The first Directors were named in the Act as the Rt Hon. Augustus Arthur Earl of Egmont, Sir John Blundell Maple, Baronet, Frank Gerard Aman, Richard William Evelyn Middleton and Robert Cuninghame Murray. The Maple family were well-known furnishers; two of the other Directors later sat on the FYN Board.

---

* This is covered in more detail in *The Fawley Branch* by J. R. Fairman, Oakwood Press 2002.

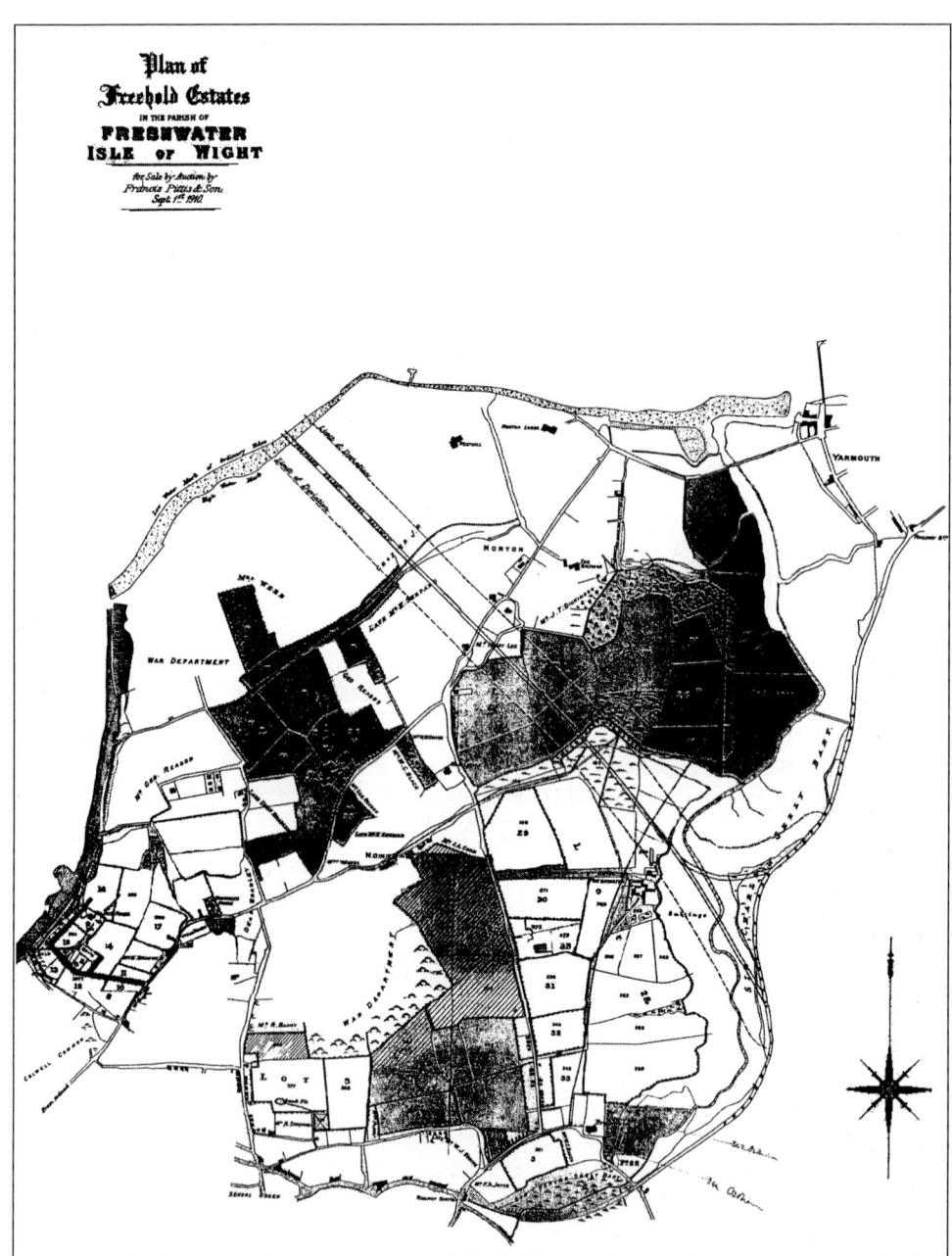

Proposed route of the Solent tunnel.

The railway began at a point on the Lymington railway about 2½ miles from its junction with the Bournemouth line. It headed south to the coast at Keyhaven where the line fell at 1 in 40 to the tunnel portal which was below high water mark. The 2¼ mile single track tunnel would have been brick lined at each end with an iron section in the centre, 46 ft below the sea bed at its deepest, above which was about 150 ft of water. A climb of 1 in 40 took the railway out of the tunnel just north of Freshwater farm. A quarter of a mile further on the railway split in two to cross the River Yar near King's Manor on separate viaducts. They connected with the FYN in each direction midway between Yarmouth station and Causeway Crossing, the west to north curve being on a tight 15 chain radius. The line was approximately 7½ miles in length and the tunnel 2½ miles.

At Keyhaven there would be a generating station to produce electricity for pumping, ventilation and working the line. Clauses in the Act granted the company powers to run over and electrify the LSWR from Brockenhurst station, the FYN and into the IWC station at Newport. Fares and charges were set at 150 per cent of standard Board of Trade rates. The Engineers, Messrs P.W. and C.S. Meik, estimated the cost at £550,000 of which £400,000 would have been spent on the tunnel. The *Isle of Wight Observer* mentioned on 27th April, 1901 that experimental borings were being carried out at Keyhaven but nothing was then heard of the project for some time. A supporter was said to have been Sam Fay who in 1901 was LSWR superintendent of the line but left the LSWR for the Great Central Railway the following year. Thereafter the LSWR Board, which had never been particularly enthusiastic about the undertaking, refused attempts to secure a working agreement. The LSWR had good reason to oppose the tunnel because of its considerable investment in the Portsmouth-Ryde and Lymington-Yarmouth ferries; one steamer had been added to the Yarmouth run in 1893 and a second in 1901.

In 1903 the tunnel company obtained a second Act. It authorised the construction of a half-mile railway on the mainland branching from the authorised tunnel line about 3½ miles from its commencement to the coast where a pier was envisaged - these facilities had been wanted by the LSWR. The idea was that ocean-going vessels would land transatlantic passengers at Keyhaven from where they would be transported by rail to London saving several hours in their journey. The company was authorised to issue additional £10 shares to a total value of £210,000. Five years was given for the completion of the extension railway and seven for the pier. The FYN was given running powers over the company's railway but the IWC could not do so without their consent.

In 1904 the company was forced to return to Parliament for an extension of the time limits. A petition in opposition to the Bill was presented by Lady Heytesbury and her husband's executors apparently in the hope of gaining some improvement in the agreed purchase price. When the Bill became law it extended the time limits for completion to 26th July, 1908.

A further Act passed in 1909 again extended the time limits, authorised more construction and the issue of another £390,000 in £10 shares and borrowings of £130,000. Plans for the pier on the mainland had been modified to an L shape about 170 yards in length with a 700 yard landing stage suitable for the largest ocean-going vessels. The company also gained powers to operate tugs. The 1909 Act also authorised the construction of a branch and pier at Yarmouth. Just

MOTORING IN THE ISLE OF WIGHT.

Loading Motor Cars at Lymington.

NO Motor Tour through England can be considered complete which does not include a run round the Isle of Wight (sixty miles). The most convenient point for crossing is at Lymington, on the South side of the charming New Forest, where the London and South Western Railway Company has provided efficient accommodation for such traffic, including slipways whereby cars can be shipped by their own power, on to specially constructed boats, thus entirely obviating the necessity of lifting, and removing a difficulty which hitherto has deterred many from visiting the lovely "Garden Isle."

The boats—towed by fast, powerful tugs—quickly negotiate the passage, which is the shortest and most sheltered, to the island. On Week-days (weather and circumstances permitting) the boats leave Lymington Town Station Wharf at 9*30, 11.30 a.m., 2.30 and 4.45 p.m. for Yarmouth, and leave Yarmouth at 8.*0 a.m., 12.30, 3.15 and 5.30 p.m. for Lymington. Cars should be upon the Wharf half-an-hour before these times.

* Prior notice should be given to the Station Master at Lymington in regard to conveyance by these boats.

Special passages can be arranged on Sundays upon arrangement being made with the Station Master, Lymington (Telephone No. 7), not later than the previous day, the extra charge being £1 per Car above the ordinary rates, which are 9s. for cars not exceeding half-a-ton, and 14s. for cars above 10 cwts., including wharfage and porterage at Lymington and Yarmouth.

BANK HOLIDAYS ARE TREATED AS ORDINARY WEEK-DAYS; GOOD FRIDAY AND CHRISTMAS DAY AS SUNDAYS.

Unloading Motor Cars at Yarmouth, I. of W.

Advert for the LSWR ferry service between Lymington and Yarmouth.

under ¼ mile in length, it would have begun about 200 yards east of Yarmouth station before curving to the north to a 400 yard-long pier on the coast; the junction of the line faced Yarmouth. Five years were given for completion of the railways and seven years for the piers. The LSWR could appoint a Director to the company's Board and provide an unspecified amount of capital.

In the *Isle of Wight County Press* for 1st February, 1913 a Southampton correspondent claimed that the LSWR had bought a site near Keyhaven for a dock and landing stage; it was rumoured that a train ferry to the Island was envisaged. That summer there was also a proposal for an electric tube railway between Stokes Bay and Ryde. Widely reported in the *County Press* and *Railway Gazette*, the four mile line would have cost £750,000 including land, generating stations and rolling stock, capital being raised in Paris - certainly no-one in the Island favoured it.

But to return to the Solent tunnel. In December 1913 an interview took place between the promoters and a committee of the Isle of Wight County Council. The promoters claimed that the tunnel could be built for less than £1,000,000 and were anxious to obtain a guarantee from public funds to pay half the interest on any debentures they might issue. Although the tunnel would undoubtedly improve the value of the Island from a trade and property point of view, members of the County Council refused to bind themselves to the undertaking and stated that such a guarantee could increase local taxes by 9d. in the pound.

In January 1914 the *County Press* reported that trial borings were being carried out near Fort Victoria when a depth of 260 ft was reached through a strata which was almost entirely clay. Right up to July there were hopeful reports of experiments and preparations for the start of construction. The *Isle of Wight Times* went so far as to pronounce that the scheme was backed by one of the largest financial firms in the world and they intended to develop the south and west of the Island.

During 1914 another Bill passed through Parliament authorising an extension of the time limits for completion and an increase in capital by a further £300,000 in £10 shares. Inevitably the scheme was deferred during the Great War but an effort was made to resurrect it when the war ended. On 27th June, 1920 a deputation from the Isle of Wight went to London for a meeting with Sir Eric Geddes, Minister of Transport, in the hope of gaining his support; Geddes claimed that the cost had risen to upwards of £2,000,000 and the Government wished to avoid subsidies. 'The answer might lie in a train ferry . . .'

The existence of proposals for the Solent tunnel was used by the FYN to seek a higher payment in compensation from the Southern Railway in 1923. In a hearing before the Amalgamation Tribunal Frank Aman claimed that Parliamentary powers for the tunnel had been extended to August 1924 and it remained a real possibility. The Solent tunnel scheme was last mentioned in 1927 when the Ministry of Transport informed the County Council that it did not anticipate an increase in traffic sufficient to justify the cost of its construction.

Official indifference did not see an end to the idea of a tunnel. In 1932 Mr C.F. Dendy Marshall wrote to *The Engineer* proposing an atmospheric railway with a three mile smooth-walled tunnel through which a single carriage would have been blown by powerful fans; aided by the approach gradient the carriage would accelerate to a speed of 60 mph. His scheme received no support, nor have a legion of subsequent proposals for a bridge or tunnel.

Chapter Fourteen

Life under the Southern Railway and its successor

We will be publishing a history of the SR and its successors in the Isle of Wight but to round off this book we should summarise events that affected the Freshwater Railway.

Beginning at the end of August 1923, the line reverted to a branch of the IWC system, albeit managed by the SR. The track layouts at Newport, Carisbrooke, Yarmouth and Freshwater were rationalised, bridges strengthened and the permanent way relaid using second-hand material sent from the mainland. The Freshwater line truly became an integral part of the Island railway system during the 1930s when, following the introduction of heavier locomotives and bogie carriages, through trains were introduced during the summer months to Freshwater from Ryde, Sandown, Shanklin and Ventnor.

Although there was a brief resurgence of traffic after the war, the railway's nationalised owners had no interest in branch lines and it was not long before rumours of closure became fact. The last train left Freshwater for Newport on the evening of Sunday 20th September, 1953. Removal of the permanent way and bridges began in 1956. British Railways sold all the buildings and land to the County Council following which the majority was auctioned off.

A class 'O2' 0-4-4T brings its train into Yarmouth station from Freshwater on 20th September, 1953. The concrete name board is a SR addition. *R.C. Riley*

LIFE UNDER THE SOUTHERN RAILWAY AND ITS SUCCESSOR

The Freshwater Railway Today

Considering that just about half a century has passed since the demise of the railway, sufficient has survived to give an impression of how it looked.

At the Newport end of the line there is nothing to see. The IWC station was demolished in 1971 and replaced by new roads and buildings; a filling station belonging to a well-known supermarket occupies the site of the FYN goods yard. Whilst the metal section of the viaduct was removed in 1958 the brick portion remained until recent redevelopment. An undertaking to preserve the structure was abandoned when it was declared 'unsafe', i.e. too expensive to restore!

There is no point in trying to follow the trackbed to Carisbrooke as so little is visible. The crossing keeper's house can be found at Petticoat Lane but the remains of the station at Carisbrooke vanished under housing and a school playing field. Gunville road overbridge was removed in 1967 and the site of Gunville siding built on. At the time of writing, the only railway feature in the neighbourhood is the bridge at Betty Haunt Lane which still carries road traffic over a non-existent railway. Much of the next section has reverted to farmland or nature but the station house at Watchingwell and the house at Pound crossing are still standing. There are remains of the abutments that supported Calbourne viaduct but Calbourne station has metamorphosed into a modern bungalow. At Ningwood the overbridge and approach embankments were levelled during road improvements whilst the station building and station master's house have become private residences. The crossing keeper's house at Hill Place crossing was demolished shortly after the line closed.

From Thorley a footpath runs along the trackbed to Yarmouth. The station building at Yarmouth still exists and a search through the undergrowth will uncover the remains of the second platform and shelter. The footpath becomes a bridleway that can be walked to Freshwater. This stretch shows the railway at its best with lovely views across the river and copses carpeted with primroses and other wild flowers in the spring. About half a mile from Yarmouth the remains of a landing place used by the contractor building the line can be discerned at low tide, but otherwise there are only a few fence posts to mark the passing of the railway. The crossing keeper's house adjoining Causeway crossing still exists and has been recently extended. The station buildings at Freshwater were demolished in 1963. The site of the station is occupied by a supermarket, garden centre and the 'End of the Line' cafe; the latter contains a collection of photographs of the railway.

Some relics from the FYN can be found at Havenstreet on the Isle of Wight Steam Railway. The Brighton 0-6-0T FYN No. 2 was saved for preservation and returned to the Isle of Wight in 1979. It is in regular use on the railway after having received a new boiler, one of the first to be built for a preserved locomotive. A MSJ&A carriage body survives in private ownership and the battered remains of the FYN goods brake van lie at St Helens Duver.

Appendix One

Directors and Chief Officers

Chairman	Edwin Fox*	1880-1892
	Hon. Ashley Ponsonby	1892-1896
	William Cotterill*	1896-1898
	Edwin Jones JP	1898-1902
	Richard W.E. Middleton*	1902-1905
	Philip G. Collins	1905-1923
Directors	Edwin Fox*	1880-1892
	Lt Col John Walker†	1880-1893
	William C. Harvey	1880-1886
	John Norton	1880-1886
	George G.L. McPherson	1880-1886
	Herbert Alston Whitaker	1886-1887
	Capt. G.F. Heine	1886-1887
	W.C. Heaton-Armstrong	1886-1887
	Clement Crowther	1888-1890
	William A. Crowther	1888-1890
	Edmund G. Ward	1888-1896
	George H. Hogan	1887-1902
	Hon. Ashley Ponsonby	1892-1896
	William Cotterill*	1896-1898
	Edwin Jones JP	1896-1902
	George H. Sawyer	1896-1900
	William E. Jones	1896-1902
	C.M.L. Cotterill	1898-1902
	Harry Silk	1900-1902
	Richard W. E. Middleton*	1902-1905
	Walter P. Norton	1902-1913
	Frank G. Aman	1902-1923
	Philip G. Collins	1902-1923
	Arthur E. Baker	1902-1922
	Charles Hodges	1905-1923
Solicitor	Alfred Bayliffe (of Booty & Bayliffe)	1880-1896
	George D. Perks	1896-1902
Engineer	Messrs Yockney & Son	1880-by 1886
	R.J.C. Barbenson	1886-1888
	William Lidstone	1888-1899
	Charles R. Walker†	1899-1913
Secretary	Jas H. Matthews	1880-1886
	Richard J. Palmer	1886-1897
	H.E. Rich	1887
	Samuel Peck	1897-1913
Receiver and manager	Hon. Ashley Ponsonby	9.8.1893-27.5.1896
	George F. Colman	27.5.1896-27.5.1897
	Frank G. Aman & Sir Sam Fay	4.6.1913-1923

The company's 1880 Act authorised six Directors but with powers to appoint any number from three to six. A quorum was to be three or two when there were three Directors.

* died in office. † engaged for inspections only when required.

Appendix Two

A Chronology of relevant Isle of Wight Acts of Parliament

This summary contains the name of the Act, a brief description and the Parliamentary reference.

Isle of Wight Railways (Extensions) Act 1865
Powers to build the Western lines from Newport to Yarmouth and Freshwater.
28 & 29 Vict. Ch. 224. Date of incorporation 5th July, 1865.

The Yarmouth and Ventnor Railway, Tramway and Pier Act 1871
To incorporate a company to build a railway between Yarmouth and Ventnor.
34 & 35 Vict. Ch. 56. Date of incorporation 16th June, 1871.

The Yarmouth and Ventnor Railway, Tramway and Pier (Deviations) Act 1872
To alter the route of the railway.
35 & 36 Vict. Ch. 28. Date of incorporation 27th June, 1872.

The Freshwater Yarmouth and Newport Railway Act 1873
To incorporate a company to build a railway from Newport to Yarmouth and Freshwater.
36 & 37 Vict. Ch. 136. Date of incorporation 7th July, 1873.

The Freshwater Yarmouth and Newport Railway (Abandonment) Act 1877
To abandon the railway and wind up the company.
40 & 41 Vict. Ch. 105. Date of incorporation 23rd July, 1877.

The Freshwater Yarmouth and Newport Railway Act 1880
To incorporate a company to build a railway from Newport to Yarmouth and Freshwater.
43 & 44 Vict. Ch. 186. Date of incorporation 26th August, 1880.

The Freshwater Yarmouth and Newport Railway Act 1883
To extend the time for completion, raise additional capital and confirm an agreement with the Totland Bay Pier & Hotel Co.
46 & 47 Vict. Ch. 196. Date of incorporation 20th August, 1883.

Freshwater Yarmouth and Newport Railway (Deviations) Act 1887
To alter the route of the railway and extend time for completion.
50 & 51 Vict. Ch. 133. Date of incorporation 19th July, 1887.

The Freshwater Yarmouth and Newport Railway Act 1889
To build an extension railway from Freshwater to Totland.
52 & 53 Vict. Ch. 185. Date of incorporation 26th August, 1889.

The Freshwater Yarmouth and Newport Railway Act 1891
To raise additional capital.
54 & 55 Vict. Ch. 167. Date of incorporation 28th July, 1891.

Railway Rates and Charges No. 9 (Isle of Wight Railway, &c.) Order Confirmation Act 1892
Revised rates and charges.
55 & 56 Vict. Ch. 47. Date of incorporation 20th June, 1892.

Freshwater Yarmouth and Newport Railway Act 1896
To reconstitute the Board of Directors, rearrange capital and raise more capital.
59 & 60 Vict. Ch. 143. Date of incorporation 20th July, 1896.

Freshwater Yarmouth and Newport Railway Act 1901
To raise more capital.
1 Edw. 7 Ch. 200. Date of incorporation 7th August, 1901.

South Western and Isle of Wight Junction Railway Act 1901
To incorporate a railway from Lymington to the Isle of Wight.
1 Edw. 7 Ch. 99. Date of incorporation 26th July, 1901.

South Western and Isle of Wight Junction Railway Act 1903
To build a short extension railway and raise additional capital.
3 Edw. 7 Ch. 244. Date of incorporation 14th August, 1903.

South Western and Isle of Wight Junction Railway (Extension of Time) Act 1904
To extend the time for completion.
4 Edw. 7 Ch. 69. Date of incorporation 22nd July, 1904.

South Western and Isle of Wight Junction Railway Act 1909
To revive the powers to build the railway and raise additional capital.
9 Edw. 7 Ch. 69. Date of incorporation 16th August, 1909.

South Western and Isle of Wight Junction Railway Act 1914
To extend the time for completion and raise additional capital.
4 & 5 Geo. 5 Ch. 145. Date of incorporation 7th August, 1914.

The Railways Act 1921
Reorganisation and further regulation of railways. Schedule 1 contained a list of constituent and subsidiary companies forming the Southern Group.
11 & 12 Geo. 5 Ch. 55. Date of incorporation 19th August, 1921.

Appendix Three

Signal Diagrams

The signal diagrams are based on a series of drawings at the Public Record Office in Kew and most date from the opening of the railway for passenger traffic in 1889. A list of the signal boxes is as follows.

Signal box	Built	Supplier	No. of levers	Notes
Newport	1913	Railway Signal Co.	12	installed in 1913
Carisbrooke	1888	Stevens	7	9 lever frame installed by 1897.
Calbourne	1888	Stevens	8	
Ningwood	1888	Stevens	8	
Yarmouth	1888	Stevens	7	9 lever frame installed by 1897.
Freshwater	1888	Stevens	6	

At Newport, two IWC signals could be pulled off only if FYN lever No. 11 was reversed; lever No. 9 was locked by a lever in the IWC box. The arrangements at Carisbrooke and Yarmouth show the signalling arrangements when the line opened. A second drawing shows Yarmouth following the opening of the crossing loop in 1897, but no drawing has come to light to show the arrangements at Carisbrooke although it is reasonable to assume it was virtually identical. By 1923 control of the siding at Calbourne had been transferred to a separate ground frame. The signalling at Freshwater had evidently been installed some months prior to the opening of the line and consequently the sidings were worked by hand levers rather than from the signal box.

Signals at the level crossings, goods sidings at stations and various private sidings were controlled by ground frames locked by Annett's key attached to the train staff. A typical arrangement is shown in the drawing of Causeway Crossing.

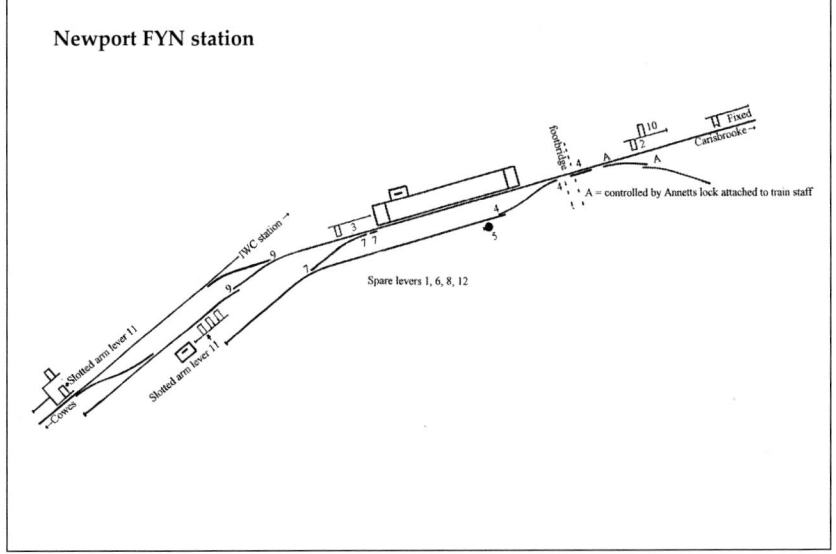

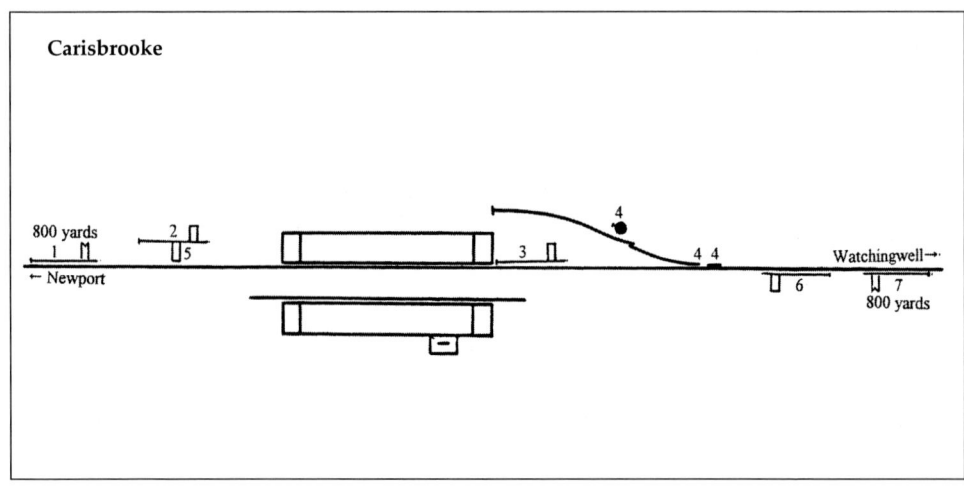

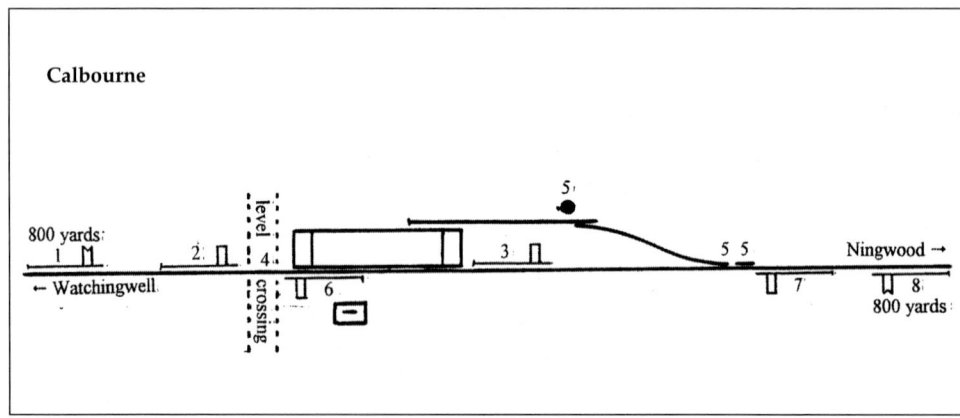

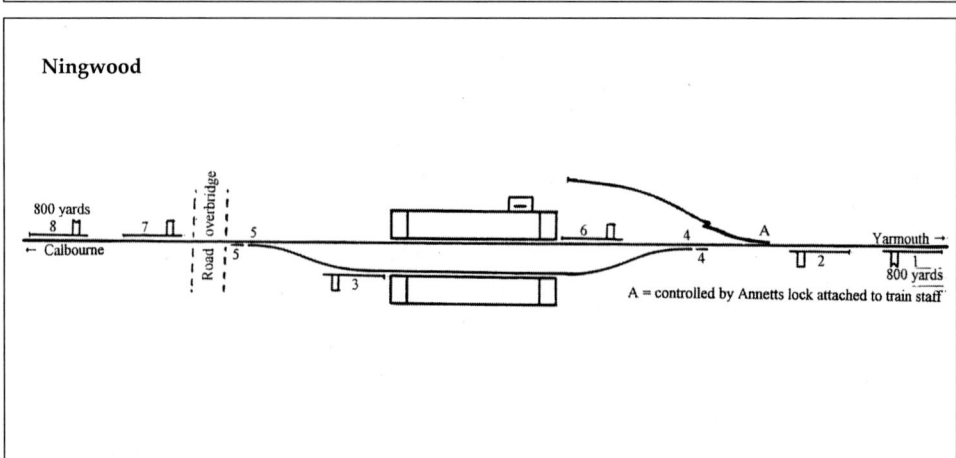

APPENDIX 171

Yarmouth

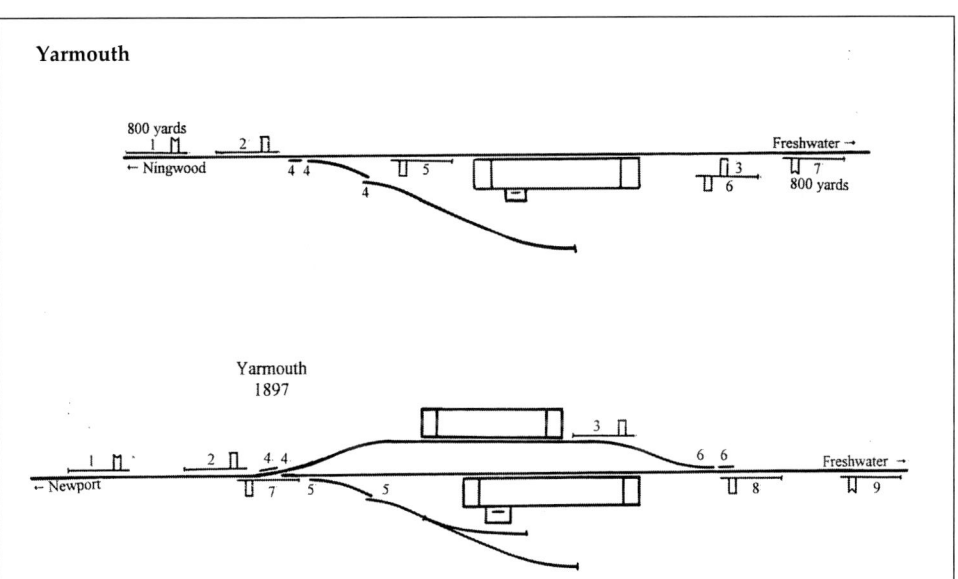

Causeway Crossing

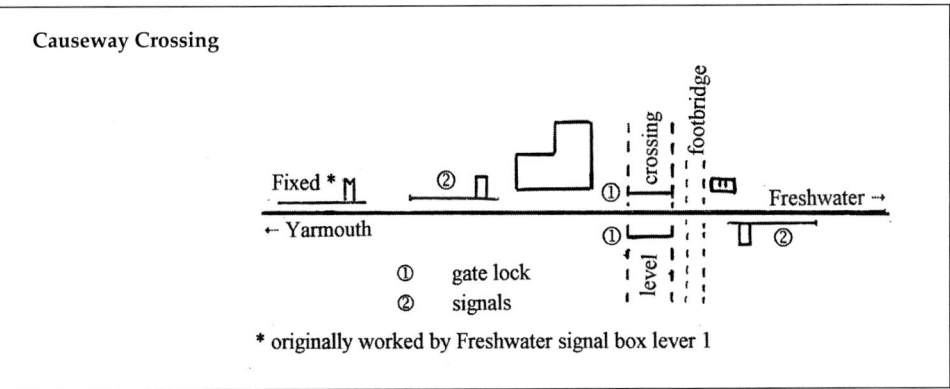

Freshwater

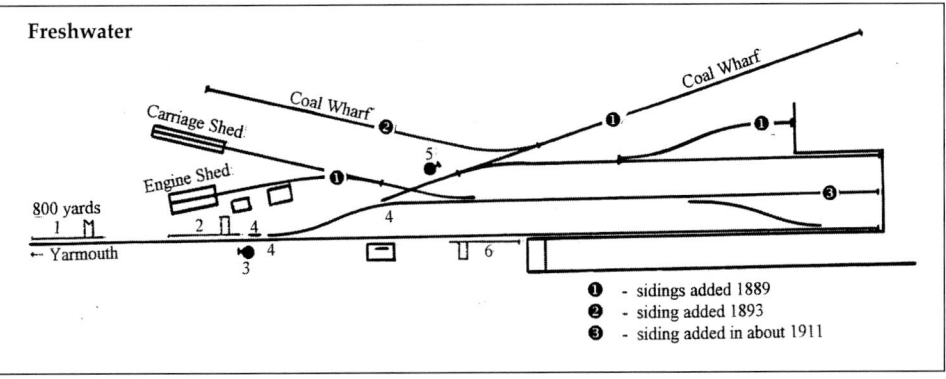

Appendix Four

Summaries of Locomotives and Rolling Stock

Locomotives

	Freshwater	No. 1	No. 2
Maker	Robert Stephenson & Co.	Manning, Wardle	LBSCR*
Built	May 1880	28th February, 1902	December 1876
Works No.	2383	1555	
Class		'Q'	'A', later 'A1'
Type	0-6-0T	0-6-0T	0-6-0T
Inside cylinders	16 in. x 20 in.	14 in. x 20 in.	13 in. x 20 in.
Diameter wheels	4 ft 6 in.	3 ft 6 in.	4 ft 0 in.
Wheelbase		12 ft	12 ft
Boiler diameter		3 ft 6 in.	3 ft 6 in.
Boiler length		8 ft 8 in.	7 ft 10 in.
Heating Surfaces - tubes		628.5 sq ft.	463.0 sq. ft
firebox		60 sq. ft	55.0 sq. ft
total		688.5 sq. ft	518.0 sq. ft
Working pressure (psi)		140 lb.	150 lb.
Grate area		8.5 sq. ft	10 sq. ft
Tank capacity		600 galls	500 galls
Bunker capacity		20 cwt	30 cwt
Tractive effort		10,700 lb.	8,970 lb.
Weight in working order	21 t.	27 t.	24 t. 7 cwt
Cost to FYN		£1,800	£1,800
To Isle of Wight	June 1887	1913	1913
SR name		*Medina*	*Freshwater*
To mainland	1891	23rd June, 1933	4th May, 1949
Withdrawn	*circa* 1937	9th July, 1932	November 1963

Rail motor car

The rail motor car supplied by the Drewry Car Company in 1913 was described as one of the firm's standard 20 hp models. The body was built in teak with a wooden roof, glass end screens and open sides with roll-down weather sheets. It was fitted with three reversible upholstered bench seats capable of accommodating 12 passengers, later quoted as 15 including the driver. The car could be driven from either end. The engine and gearbox were carried on an inner frame of steel angle such that the whole unit could be removed for maintenance. The water-cooled petrol engine had four cylinders measuring 90 mm by 130 mm with interchangeable valves all on one side - there were radiators at each end. The crankshaft ran in phosphor-bronze bearings lined with white metal. Lubrication was by a gear driven pump, ignition was by magneto and accumulator and coil. There was a fully reversible three-speed gear box, transmission being transmitted to the driving axle by chains. The 2 ft diameter cast steel wheels and forged steel axles were carried in railway type axleboxes fitted with phosphor-bronze bearings and wick lubrication. A pedal brake worked on a drum on the countershaft supplemented by a hand brake acting on the wheel tyres. Allocated the SR running number 2462, that of a third class carriage, the rail motor was withdrawn on 31st December, 1924. It then became an inspection vehicle 437s before being broken up for scrap at Newport in 1927.

* Preserved on the Isle of Wight Steam Railway as LBSCR No. 46 *Newington*.

APPENDIX

Passenger carriages

FYN No.	Type*	Origin	SR No.	Date renumbered	Dimensions length, width, height	Brake	Withdrawn
1	Brake composite	MSJ&A	6990	23.8.24	26'9" x 8' x 7'3"	V	14.2.31
2	Third	MSJ&A	2457	7.2.25	26'9" x 8' x 7'3"	D	14.2.31
3	Third	MSJ&A	2458	31.3.24	26'9" x 8' x 7'3"	V	14.2.31
4	Composite	MSJ&A	6358	10.24	26'9" x 8' x 7'3"	V	31.12.30
5	Third	MSJ&A	2459	6.9.24	26'9" x 8' x 7'3"	V	14.2.31
6	Composite	MSJ&A	6359	30.4.24	26'9" x 8' x 7'3"	V	31.12.30
7	Brake third	MSJ&A	4104	31.5.24	26'9" x 8' x 7'3"	D	16.9.33
8	Composite	LSWR	(6360)	not	24' x 8' x 6'9"	W	27.2.26
9	Brake third	CNR	(4105)	not	25'10" x 8'3" x 6'9"	W	27.2.26
10	Third	LSWR	(2460)	not	27'3" x 8'x 6'9"	W	27.2.26
11	Composite	LSWR	(6361)	not	24' x 8'x 6'9"	W	
			renumbered 2475 on 31.10.25				19.11.27
12	Third	LSWR	(2461)	not	27'3" x 8'x 6'9"	W	27.2.26

* as inherited by the SR in 1923. The SR running numbers shown in brackets were allocated but not carried.
W = Westinghouse air brake, V = Vacuum brake, D = dual fitted.

Originally, Nos. 1-7 carried the vacuum brake and Nos. 8-12 had the Westinghouse air brake. The carriages were purchased in 1912-1913 from the MSJ&A (Nos. 1-7) and IWC (Nos. 8-12).

Goods Stock

Type	Quantity	FYN Nos.	SR Nos.	Withdrawn
8 ton open wagons	20	18-22, 24-25, 130, 132, 133, 135, 137, 138, 178, 181, 183, 185, 187-190	28227-28246	1927-1932
10 ton open wagons	6	20,169,170,175,179,184	28247-28252	1927-1932
8 ton covered vans	4	14-17	47032-47035	1928-1930
Goods brake van	1	13	56038	20.3.26

All were purchased from the IWC in 1913. Nos. 14 to 22, 24 and 25 are believed to have been formerly IWC Nos. 131, 134, 136, 139, 171 to 174, 177, 180 and 186 but not necessarily in that order. The FYN converted Nos. 18 to 22 to cattle trucks but they were restored to open wagons by the SR in 1923. Nos. 130 onwards retained their old IWC numbers. The wagons came from a variety of suppliers, the vans were IWC rebuilds dating from 1911 and the goods brake was a Stroudley standard design of *circa* 1873.

Appendix Five

Vessels plying between Lymington and Yarmouth prior to 1923

Vessel	Type of hull propulsion	Builder	Owners	Entered service	Withdrawn
Glasgow	wooden hull paddle steamer	Stephen Wood, Gateshead	1, 2	1830	9.1849
Duke of Buccleugh	wooden hull paddle steamer	Joseph White, Cowes	5	1830	1841
Solent (I)	iron hull paddle steamer	Day Summers, Southampton	2	1841	1863
Red Lion	wooden hull paddle steamer	Thorburn & Alman, North Shields	2	1858	sold 1880
Solent (II)	wooden hull paddle steamer	Inman, Lymington	2, 3	1863	6.1901
Mayflower	iron hull paddle steamer	Marshall Bros, Newcastle	2, 3	1866	1910
Lymington	iron hull paddle steamer	Day Summers, Southampton	3, 4	9.5.1893	sold 3.1929
Solent (III)	steel hull paddle steamer	Morden Carney, Southampton	3, 4	3.1902	sold 1948
Carrier	tug and cargo		3, 4	6.2.1906	1931
Jumsey	tug		6	1910	1938

Key

Owner: 1 - Original owner not recorded
        2 - Solent Sea Company
        3 - LSWR
        4 - Southern Railway
        5 - Relief vessel owned by the Southampton company
        6 - Hired when required

Bibliography

General

Freshwater, Yarmouth and Newport Railway. A. Blackburn & J. Mackett, Forge Books 1966.
Centenary of the Freshwater Railway 1889-1989. N. Chandler, Centenary Trust 1989.
The Isle of Wight Central Railway, R.J. Maycock and R. Silsbury, The Oakwood Press 2001.
The Isle of Wight Railway, R.J. Maycock and R. Silsbury, The Oakwood Press 1999.
The London & South Western Railway (2 volumes). R.A. Williams, David & Charles 1968.
Rails in the Isle of Wight. P.C. Allen and A. B. MacLeod, George Allen & Unwin Ltd 1967.
Once Upon a Line (4 volumes). A. Britton, Oxford Publishing Co. 1983, 1984, 1990 and 1994.
The Signalling of the Isle of Wight Railways. Signalling Record Society 1993.
Wight Report and *Island Rail News,* magazines of the Isle of Wight Steam Railway.

Locomotives and rolling stock

A Locomotive History of Railways on the Isle of Wight. D.L. Bradley, Railway Correspondence & Travel Society, 1982.
The Island Terriers. M.J.E. Reed, Kingfisher Railway Publications, 1989.
Isle of Wight Steam Passenger Rolling Stock. R.J. Maycock & M.J.E. Reed, The Oakwood Press, 1997.
An Illustrated History of Southern Wagons, Volume Two. G. Bixley & others, Oxford Publishing Company, 1985.

Addendum

Since the publication of *The Freshwater Yarmouth & Newport Railway* in 2003 additional research has uncovered some new information and clarified facts in the original book. This new material is presented here as an addendum.

Chapter 3. Construction and opening

Robert Thomas Olivier Barbenson was appointed "contractor's engineer". Born 28th November 1845 in Alderney he articled to James May, resident engineer to works on Alderney. In 1862 he worked in the office of Walker and Burgess and then McClean and Stileman from 1863 to 1869 where he prepared drawings, made surveys and supervised contracts. He worked as resident engineer under Stileman at Portishead Docks and at Neath Docks before returning to Alderney where he died 1st June 1893. [Obituary in Journal of the Institute of Civil Engineers] Although calling himself a civil engineer, William Lidstone was never mentioned in the Journal of the Institute of Civil Engineers.

Chapter 4. A descent into bankruptcy

Lloyds Bonds were named after John Horatio Lloyd. They were sealed covenants issued by a company promising to pay the debt on a certain future date. The recipient would use it to get a loan from bankers but, although interest on debentures might be 5-6%, Lloyds Bonds were often charged at 10% or higher, depending on the risk. The ultimate security was the company's property. [*The London, Chatham & Dover Railway* by A. Gray]

Chapter 6. The Board of Trade step in

Sir Barrington Simeon tried to avoid any involvement with the FYN despite having other railway connections. He was a Director of the Waterloo & City Railway and the LSWR from 1893 to 1907. [*The Waterloo & City Railway* by J. C. Gilham. Oakwood Press]

Chapter 7. A change of owners

In an agreement dated 1st December 1899 with the landowner, Mr Manning, the FYN undertook to build the siding and pay an annual rent of 1/- until the siding was removed. Despite closure of the line payments continued until March 1955 when six months' notice was given that the agreement was being terminated. [IWSR archives]

In the FYN Minutes for 3rd May 1904 the Board asked for a guarantee of traffic from Dowty's siding of at least £100 a year for a minimum of seven years, Dowty paying the costs of its installation. A later entry on 1st November 1904 read "accept £50" but not to concede a limitation on costs of £75. The £50 appeared in the agreement. [FYN Minutes and *Island Rail News* issue 22]

Chapter 9. The break with the Central
The date of the hearing that resulted in the appointment of a Receiver was 4th June 1913, a month earlier than stated in the text. [*The Times*, 5 June 1913]

Chapter 10. An independent railway
After an offer letter was sent by the LSWR to the FYN there was a meeting at Waterloo on 9th March 1922 which included Sir Herbert Walker, Sam Fay and Mr Aman. Walker estimated the net earnings at approx. £2,000 per annum and this capitalised at 4% would be £50,000. Aman said the Solent tunnel if built would bring a lot of business to the Freshwater railway. He was certain that the tunnel would be built and thought its value to the FYN should be taken into account. Following the meeting Walker wrote "Offer them" £23,333.6.8 in 3% Debenture Stock, £20,000 in 3½% pre Debenture Stock producing £700 per annum and £35,000 in 4% Guaranteed Stock to meet the remainder of their stocks. This was rejected and at a second interview on 26th July 1922 it emerged that Aman wanted £80,000, the price he and Sir Blundell Maple had paid for the company. The LSWR made a final offer that was rejected:

FYN stock	LSWR Stock
£20,000 3½% Debenture Stock	£233,222.6.8 3% Consolidated Debenture Stock
Remainder	£50,000 4% Consolidated Guaranteed Stock

On 4th July 1923 the SR wrote saying that the Railway Amalgamation Tribunal met on 20th June and had imposed the settlement summarised on page 111. Fay replied on 20th August:

"I have received the ... absorbtion scheme of the Railway Amalgamation Tribunal under which the Freshwater, Yarmouth & Newport Railway became the property of your Company from the 11th inst. The scheme did not reach me until the 17th inst. with the result that monies have been paid out and received since the date of absorbtion. The wages for last week have been paid. I understand you have not taken over the administration of the railway and shall be glad if you will acknowledge receipt of this letter by bearer and let me know that you have taken over the line..."

On 23rd August 1923 a letter was sent by the SR stating it will take over the FYN on and from Monday 27th August. On 27th August a letter was sent to staff informing them that the SR took charge from midnight 26th August and Messrs Newcombe and Tahourdin were now their managers.

Passed to the SR was a copy of the bylaws and regulations. It seems to have been a standard RCH book with inappropriate paragraphs blocked out. It had been signed by S. Peck on 7th November 1905 and certified by the Board of Trade as acceptable. The legal documents were incomplete and seem to have been in no better state than those of the IWC and there were problems in tracing some stockholders to exchange FYN for SR stock. There were several internal memos asking about the whereabouts of missing conveyances and agreements for private sidings. [LSWR documents, National Archives, Kew ref. RAIL411/1129]

Chapter 11. The line described

The gradient diagram was prepared by the IWC, not the FYN. It is not clear what colour schemes were used on the FYN stations. As the FYN was responsible for their maintenance it is unlikely that they carried the same colours as the IWC. Possibly they were green like the locomotives.

The photograph of Wellow siding on page 128 is Dowty's siding following removal circa 1929. Wellow lasted until 1938 when the SR paid the owners £60 for permission to remove it. Gunville is unlikely to have seen any traffic after the brickworks closed in the 1940s but was in the working timetables until at least 1948; it was removed with the rest of the line in 1957. [SR Working Timetables in the National Archives, Kew]

Chapter 12. Locomotives and rolling stock

Appendix 4 suggests that the contractor's locomotive *Freshwater* was withdrawn in 1937. It was out of use a year later but the exact date of scrapping is not known. On 22nd February 1888 there was an auction sale of locomotives, wagons, etc. on behalf of the "Executors of the late Joseph Firbank Esq." The FYN wagons may have come from that sale. [*Brighton Circular*, magazine of the Brighton Circle, Winter 2004 issue page 208]

In the photograph on page 147 (upper) the last vehicle in the train was the IWC mail van. The photograph on page 157 shows the waiting room which was demolished with the remains of the station within weeks of the photograph being taken. The signal box was moved to Freshwater and the booking office to Calbourne. The photograph on page 158 shows engine w3 *Carisbrooke* and not w2. It was taken between 1930 and 1932. The GCR van body may have arrived with locomotive No. 1 and the MSJA carriages containing spares but was not worth returning to the mainland. The FYN had enough goods vehicles from the IWC so it became a grounded body. It was later took the place of an IWC van bodyat Freshwater.

No. 2 poses with the MSJ&A carriages at the company's new Newport station in July 1913. The run-round loop has yet to receive its layer of ballast.   *R. Silsbury Collection*

The sum total of the passenger facilities at Newport FYN station can be seen in this photograph taken facing Freshwater in 1920. The sharply curved running line complete with a check rail has evidently seen little maintenance of late but the buildings on the platform look in good order. The waiting shelter has gained a wood and glass extension and there is the usual clutter of advertising and furniture.   *R. Silsbury/IWSR Collection*

Index

Abandonment of extensions, 23, 24, 25, 28
Accidents and mishaps, 53, 55, 66, 67, 83
Act of Incorporation, 21
Amalgamation with SR, 109, 111
Aman, Frank G., 27, 71, 87, 88, 90, 92, 109, 159
Barbenson, R.J.C., 29, 30, 31
Booty & Bayliffe, 22, 24, 55, 63
Bouldnor Land Company, 13
Bouldnor, Yarmouth & Freshwater Railway & Pier Co., 13
Brading, Newport & Yarmouth Railway, 12
Bridges, 113
Calbourne station, 65, 123
Capital, 21, 23, 25, 27, 41, 43, 46, 65, 67, 69, 71, 87, 92, 102
Carisbrooke station, 50, 53, 57, 58, 59, 102, 119
Carriages - see rolling stock
Collins, Philip G., 71, 88
Colman, George F., 58, 60, 63, 65
Construction, 24, 29, 30, 31, 33, 36, 37
Cotterill, C.M.L. and William, 61, 65
Cowes & Newport Railway, 12, 17, 24
Crossing keeper's houses, 75, 77
Crowther, Clement and William A., 44, 46, 63
Debentures - see capital
Drower, George, 56, 67, 75, 89, 90
Excursions, 33, 36
Fares, 48, 73, 79, 99
Fay, Sir Sam, 71, 90, 91, 92, 93, 103, 109
Ferries, 9, 23, 161, 163
Financial problems, 41, 43, 46, 54, 55, 87
Fox, Edwin, 22, 36, 43
Freshwater station, 33, 50, 75, 81, 133
Freshwater, Yarmouth & Newport Railway (1873), 17, 19
Heytesbury, Lord and Lady, 15, 17, 77, 159, 161
Hogan, George H., 43, 61, 63
Inspections by the Board of Trade, 36, 53, 56, 57, 58, 66, 92, 93, 95
Isle of Wight Central Railway, 30, 38, 39, 50, 54, 66, 71, 90
Isle of Wight (Newport Junction) Railway, 17
Isle of Wight Railway, 11, 12
Jackson, Henry, 44, 45, 53, 54, 61
Jackson, William, 24, 29, 36, 43, 44, 45
Jones, Edwin JP, 61, 63
Lidstone, William, 25, 31, 33, 36, 44, 45, 54
Locomotive *Freshwater*, 29, 31, 33, 36, 139, 141
Locomotives, 99, 100, 141, 143, 151, 155, 157, 158
London, Brighton & South Coast Railway, 22, 65
London & South Western Railway, 9, 22, 66, 161
McPherson, George G.L., 22, 41

Middleton, Richard W.E., 71, 159
Newport, Chale, Freshwater & Yarmouth Railway, 19
Newport FYN station, 95, 100, 117
Newport IWC station, 50, 117
Ningwood, 33, 50, 127
Nixon, Christopher, 13, 15, 17
Norton, John, 22, 41
Norton, Walter P., 71
Omnibuses, 11, 73, 103, 105
Opening for goods traffic, 33
Opening for passenger traffic, 39
Peck, Samuel, 65, 67, 69, 71
Perks, George D., 58, 59, 60, 61, 63, 69
Permanent way, 113
Ponsonby, Hon. Ashley, 47, 58, 59
Private sidings, 53, 60, 65, 73, 83, 119
Properties Securities Co., 63
Railmotors, 77, 81, 87
Railway & Canal Commissioners, 81, 93, 94
Refreshment rooms, 71
Regulation of Railways Acts, 48, 56
Rolling stock, 141, 143, 151, 155, 157, 158
Ryde & Newport Railway, 24
Sale of railway, 66, 67, 69
Sawyer, George H., 61, 63, 66
Services, 48, 77, 79, 81, 95, 99, 100, 101, 103, 105, 111
Shanklin & Chale Railway, 20, 27
Signalling, 36, 113, 169
Smith, W.H. & Co., 75
Solent Sea Company, 9, 23
Solent Tunnel, 71, 77, 159, 161, 163
Staff, 111
Stocks and shares - see capital
Strikes, 103, 105
Tennyson, Alfred Lord, 11, 25
Tickets, 48, 73
Timetables - see services
Totland Bay branch, 23, 24, 25, 27, 29
Totland Bay Pier & Hotel Co., 24, 25, 27, 46
Traffic receipts, 49, 63, 69, 83, 91, 102, 109
Tramways at Newport, 20
Trial trips, 30, 31
Wagons - see rolling stock
Walker, Charles R., 67, 85, 90
Walker, Lt Col John, 22, 47
Ward, Edmund G., 41, 47, 159
Watchingwell station, 59, 60, 123
Waterhouse, William J., 75, 85, 89, 90
Williamson, John William, 13, 17
Working agreements, 37, 38, 39, 50, 58, 71, 79, 87, 88, 89, 90, 91, 92, 93, 94
Yarmouth station, 33, 50, 53, 57, 58, 59, 83, 129
Yarmouth & Ventnor Railway, Tramway & Pier Co., 15, 17
Yarmouth extensions, 25, 27